South of the Border

South of the Border:

WOMEN TRAVELERS TO LATIN AMERICA

Edited by Evelyn M. Cherpak

Charleston, SC
www.PalmettoPublishing.com

South of the Border

First Edition

Paperback ISBN: 978-1-64990-079-1

eBook ISBN: 978-1-64990-078-4

I have related what I have seen, what I have heard, and what I have learned by inquiry.

Herodotus

Acknowledgements

MANY LIBRARIANS, ARCHIVISTS, AND CURATORS have been helpful in obtaining sources for this work. I am grateful to the staff of the Bristol Historical and Preservation Society for access to the papers of Sarah Sabin Wilson. They include Dr.Catherine Zipf, the Director; Lisa DeCesare, the curator; Reinhard Battcher III; Clara Read; and Volunteer Claire Benson, who was a fount of knowledge regarding the Sabins, the DeWolfs and the history of Bristol, Rhode Island. Nancy Hackett at the Redwood Library in Newport, Rhode Island did yeoman work obtaining interlibrary loans for me. Dr. Daniel Snydacker, former Director of the Newport Historical Society in Newport, Rhode Island, gave me permission to read Mary Robinson Hunter's six diaries. The staff of the Sophia Smith Collection at Smith College in Northampton, Massachusetts, including Reading Room Supervisor Mary Biddle; Archivist Amy Hague; Director of Special Collections, Elizabeth Meyers; and archivist Nanci Young, were exceedingly helpful. Charles Miles graciously granted permission to publish excerpts from his mother's autobiography.

Contents

Introduction

During the nineteenth century, women travelers began to make their way to South America. Years before, European and North American men had preceded them as explorers, scientists, merchants, businessmen, missionaries, naval officers, and diplomats. But with improvements in transportation and communication and the more settled politics of the countries after achieving independence, adventurous women made their way to this lesser-known part of the world that was exotic, tropical, unvisited, and unknown to most of the population.

Several women in this book lived in South American countries for a long period of time, while others traveled and stayed for a shorter period of time. Why did they go? There are as many reasons to travel as there are people who travel. Married women followed their husbands to duty stations in Peru and Chile, as Sarah Madeleine Vinton Dahlgren did in the 1860s when her husband, Admiral John Dahlgren, was commanding officer of the USS *Powhatan* on the west coast of South America. She made the hazardous trek through Panama by railroad and mule with young children to get to the ship that took them to Peru. Another navy wife, Marguerite Dickins, sailed onboard her husband's ship, the USS *Tallapoosa*, on the east coast of South America for two and a half years, from 1887 to 1889, where she visited Brazil, Argentina, Uruguay, and Paraguay. Wilma Miles, an admiral's wife, visited every country in South America in the 1950s and lived at Fort Amador, a navy base in Panama

City, when her husband was commanding officer of the Fifteenth Naval District there from 1954 to 1956.

Diplomats were assigned to the newly independent South American republics once the United States granted recognition. Mary Robinson Hunter of Newport, Rhode Island, lived in Rio de Janeiro for fourteen years, from 1835 to 1848, when her husband was chargé d'affaires and later promoted to minister plenipotentiary. When he was recalled in 1844, Mary stayed on in Rio, as her two daughters and her grandchildren lived there. She briefly lived in Montevideo, Uruguay, during the political conflict between the liberals and conservatives, and in Buenos Aires, Argentina, during the rule of the dictator Juan Manuel de Rosas. United States diplomacy brought Loretta L.Wood Merwin to Valparaiso, Chile, in 1853, when her father was appointed American consul. He served in the post for several years, then her husband assumed the position of consul before the two families returned to the United States in 1856.

Economic reasons, the hope of a prosperous livelihood, led Sarah Sabin Wilson and her husband, Joseph Oliver Wilson, to immigrate to Camarioca, Matanzas, Cuba, in 1818. Joseph Wilson, captain of the brig *Yankee* during the War of 1812, had purchased a sugar and coffee plantation there. The couple hoped to turn a profit in five years and then return to their home in Bristol, Rhode Island. As time went on, they prospered and bought another plantation, thereby establishing themselves permanently in Cuba. Sarah learned Spanish, brought up her children there, and remained in Cuba for the rest of her life.

The lure of the natural environment and the scientific possibilities it held for the naturalist and ichthyologist Louis Agassiz inspired him to organize a yearlong expedition to Brazil in 1865. His wife, Elizabeth Cabot Cary Agassiz, a teacher and founder of a girls' school in Boston, went along as the scribe of the group. She copied his lectures and notes wherever they went, whether it was in Rio de Janeiro or the Amazon jungle. Fearless and intrepid, she was a major contributor to the expedition and coauthored the book describing their trip, which was published in 1868.

While Alice Rollins was not a scientist, she was a nature lover. In the 1880s, she traveled to Brazil with her husband, whose company had interests there, and she extolled the beauties of the natural world.

Single women made their way south of the border for professional and personal reasons. Nellie Bly, whose fame came from completing a round-the-world trip in record time in 1890, was a newspaper reporter for the *Pittsburgh Dispatch.* In 1885, tiring of her routine assignments, she and her mother traveled by railroad to Mexico, where she made observations and sent her reports back to the newspaper to be published. Nellie stayed in Mexico almost six months but was critical of lack of freedom of the press and had to leave or face jail, as the dictator Porfirio Díaz brooked no criticism. In 1855, Mary Lester, an Englishwoman and a teacher, sailed from Australia to Central America in hopes of landing a teaching position and the promise of a plantation in San Pedro Sula, Honduras. Mary traveled two hundred miles by mule across the mountains of Honduras, fording streams and dealing with unscrupulous mule drivers, only to have her hopes dashed as the school was not built, the colonists had fled, and the offer of employment was fraudulent. Virginia Heim George went alone to Rio de Janeiro, Brazil, in 1940 as an employee of the YWCA. She rented an apartment, traveled throughout the country, and served in Brazil for three years.

Women went to South America as adventurers, just as some of the men had done. Ida Pfeiffer, an Austrian, was a world traveler who arrived in Brazil in 1845 and then sailed through the Strait of Magellan to Chile. In 1851, she traveled to the Far East and then sailed up the west coast of South America and the United States; this time she visited

California, Mexico, Panama, Peru, and Ecuador. She traveled alone, made her own arrangements, endured hardships, foul weather, and a near-death experience in her efforts to satisfy her curiosity about the non-European world. Lady Florence Dixie, an aristocrat born in Scotland, was a reporter, suffragette, and writer of some repute. She and a party of four men spent several months in the wilds of Patagonia in 1878, solely because it was remote, inaccessible, and untraveled by Europeans or by women. A crack shot, she reveled in horseback riding and shooting ostriches and guanacos.

Julia Ward Howe, best known as the composer of the lyrics to "The Battle Hymn of the Republic" that was an inspiration to the troops of the Union Army during the Civil War, sailed with her husband and Reverend and Mrs. Theodore Parker to Cuba in 1859 for a vacation to escape the cold New England winter. While her purpose there was to rest and relax, she visited plantations, civic institutions, and commented on the differences between the Creoles and the Spanish, as well as the status of women, Cuban slave laws, and the condition of slaves.

Josephine Hoeppner Woods and her husband, a mining engineer, moved to Bolivia and Peru in the 1930s. Josephine lived in remote high-altitude mining camps where she oftentimes was the only Caucasian woman there. She eagerly explored her surroundings and the Indian markets, climbed mountains, traversed glaciers, and taught briefly in La Paz and Cochabamba.

The women who traveled and lived in South America were not professional authors, but several documented their experiences and encounters that they turned into books, as the public was eager to read travel literature of distant places that the average person could only dream about. Elizabeth Agassiz and her husband, Louis, collaborated on *A Journey in Brazil,* published in 1868, which documented their experiences and voyage up the Amazon River. Sarah Madeleine

Vinton Dahlgren used her letters home as a basis for *South Sea Sketches: A Narrative*, which described her travels through Panama and down the Pacific coast by ship to Peru and Chile. Marguerite Dickins wrote articles for a newspaper that eventually became a book entitled *Along Shore with a Man-of-War*, which included her impressions of Argentina, Uruguay, and Paraguay when she sailed aboard her husband's ship, the USS *Tallapoosa.* Nellie Bly, a professional journalist, wrote *Six Months in Mexico*, which she dedicated to the editor of the *Pittsburgh Post*, who gave her the opportunity to travel. She went to Mexico as a foreign correspondent and sent her stories home to be published. Loretta L.Wood Merwin entitled her contribution *Three Years in Chili*, which documented her life in Valparaiso, Chile, a city that was prone to earthquakes. Ida Pfeiffer, a world traveler, spent time in Mexico, Panama, Peru, and Ecuador in the 1850s, which was captured in *A Second Lady's Journey Round the World.* Mary Lester's travels across the mountains of Honduras appeared in print as *A Lady's Ride Across Spanish Honduras.* In 1878, Lady Florence Dixie's hunting and shooting adventures in Patagonia were published as *Across Patagonia.* The flora and fauna of Brazil in the late nineteenth century captured the imagination of Alice Rollins, who wrote *From Palm to Glacier, with an Interlude: Brazil, Bermuda, and Alaska.* In the twentieth century, Wilma Jerman Miles wrote her autobiography, *Billy, Navy Wife*, which contained large segments on her travels and life in South America. Josephine Hoeppner Woods's years in mining camps in the Andes in the 1930s resulted in the publication of *High Spots in the Andes: Peruvian Letters of a Mining Engineer's Wife.* The book was based on her letters to friends.

Other women documented their residence in South America by either keeping a diary or writing letters home. Mary Robinson Hunter lived in Brazil for fourteen years, with periods of time in Argentina and Uruguay during the 1830s and 1840s. She was a faithful diarist who wrote in her diary every day. Her six Brazilian diaries are located in the Newport (RI) Historical Society. Sarah Sabin Wilson's life in

Cuba comes to light in her letters to her former guardian and friend, John D'Wolf, in Bristol, Rhode Island, over a twenty-year period, from 1818 to 1838. Her letters are located in the John D'Wolf Papers in the Bristol (RI) Historical and Preservation Society. Virginia Heim George, a YWCA director in Rio de Janeiro, Brazil, from 1940 to 1943, wrote letters to family and friends that described her travels and life there. These letters reside in the Sophia Smith Collection at Smith College in Northampton, Massachusetts.

The women who lived and traveled in South America wrote about a wide variety of topics. Nature and the natural world of the Amazon were important to Elizabeth Agassiz, as that was the purpose of the Thayer Expedition. Alice Rollins was impressed by the flora and fauna of the Brazilian countryside that she extolled so rapturously. Nature wasn't always kind to the traveler. The natural world of mountains and rivers were impediments to travel in Honduras and Ecuador, as noted by single travelers Mary Lester and Ida Pfeiffer. Lady Florence Dixie lived one with nature and the animals during her travels camping out in Patagonia.

Slavery and the emancipation of slaves were subjects that interested four women. Sarah Sabin Wilson in Cuba and Mary Robinson Hunter in Brazil owned slaves yet feared slave insurrections as they occurred in nearby areas. Elizabeth Agassiz wrote that the emancipation of slaves was not the contentious topic in Brazil as it was in the United States. People of all classes supported emancipation and felt it would happen gradually. Julia Ward Howe commented on the treatment of slaves on sugar plantations in Cuba and lauded the fact that there were opportunities for slaves to purchase their freedom. The Cuban slave laws were more liberal than those in the United States, she wrote. Despite this, racial equality and miscegenation were not topics that merited support by either Agassiz or Howe.

Women travelers were interested in the status of women in the countries they visited. Julia Ward Howe wrote that women in Cuba suffered an almost Middle Eastern confinement, as they could not go out alone on the street without a male escort. Sarah Madeleine Vinton Dahlgren described the dress of Limean women on the street that contrasted to their untidiness at home. However, women could go out without a male escort in Lima, albeit with a servant. Elizabeth Agassiz decried the fact that upper-class Portuguese women were sequestered at home and uneducated, while Afro-Brazilian women and the Indian women of the Amazon had more freedom to go about unchaperoned in the public square. Loretta L.Wood Merwin thought that the women of Chile were intellectually superior to the men but lacked education and were limited to home and church. Nellie Bly commented on the ritual of courtship in Mexico that ended in marriage where the upper-class women were confined to home, family, and church, while the wives (*soldadas*) of Mexican soldiers followed the troops and cooked for them. In Ecuador, Ida Pfeiffer found that women participated in business and in politics as much as men.

Women whose husbands were renowned met highly placed government officials and ranking members of the diplomatic corps and the military. Mary Robinson Hunter met Emperor Dom Pedro II of Brazil and socialized with his sisters, the princesses Januária and Francesca. Elizabeth Agassiz also met Emperor Dom Pedro II and Empress Teresa Cristina while in Rio de Janeiro. Sarah Madeleine Vinton Dahlgren and Admiral Dahlgren were guests of President and Mrs. Mariano Ignacio Prado Ochoa at the president's palace in Lima. Marguerite Dickins met Dictator Francisco Solano López's son in Buenos Aires and mingled with the diplomatic corps at balls in Montevideo, Uruguay. Navy wife Wilma Miles entertained ambassadors and admirals in Panama, as well as a descendant of Christopher Columbus, Don Cristóbal Colón, the Duke of Veragua and Admiral of the Ocean Sea. Women who traveled alone, like Ida Pfeiffer and Mary Lester, had more opportunity to mix with the indigenous population, as they had to hire mule drivers and servants upon whom they depended. Oftentimes, they stayed in lodgings run by the local people.

Religion and, in particular, the Catholic Church, its religious services and holidays, and the Catholic priesthood, met with criticism from Mary Robinson Hunter, Ida Pfeiffer, and Loretta L.Wood Merwin. The priests were immoral, lived with concubines, and had illegitimate children. In Chile, they even sold indulgences. The pomp and ceremony of Catholic rituals and holidays, as well as the raucous pre-Lenten celebrations and carnivals, were foreign to these Protestant observers.

Sarah Sabin Wilson, Loretta L. Wood Merwin, and Mary Robinson Hunter had to keep house in a foreign land and deal with servants. Sarah had difficulty obtaining articles of clothing and the food that she was accustomed to—hence her letters to John D'Wolf, her former guardian and lifelong friend in Bristol, Rhode Island, asking for seeds and food. Mary Robinson Hunter complained about the food in Brazil and pined for Newport pork and ketchup. She never was adventurous enough to try the Brazilian staples of *vatapá* or *feijoada*. She was troubled when slaves were whipped and helped those in need, but she was frustrated dealing with her own servants. Loretta L Wood Merwin was not impressed by the grocery stores in Valparaiso. She also had difficulty adjusting to servants who did not conform to North American standards and, at times, bolted.

The urban landscape was of interest to women travelers. Most of them arrived in a major city or port and visited other cities, where they described the layout of the town, government buildings, churches, and urban dwellings. Mary Robinson Hunter took walks in Rio de Janeiro, visited the emperor's palace, the public gardens, and the churches. Loretta L Wood Merwin praised Santiago, the Chilean capital, as did Sarah Madeleine Vinton Dahlgren, while Ida Pfeiffer found only the churches of Quito, Ecuador, worth seeing. Marguerite Dickins described her visits to Montevideo, Uruguay, and Asunción, Paraguay. Elizabeth Agassiz visited the major civic institutions of Rio de Janeiro, including schools, hospitals, and asylums that she found well run. Alice Rollins was impressed by the cities of Pará, Maranham, Pernambuco, and Bahia. And Wilma Miles found Cayenne, the capital of French Guiana, primitive and undeveloped.

The travelers commented on customs of the Hispanic countries that were so unlike North American or European ones. The concept of *mañana* was the order of the day wherever they went. Time was of no importance, and patience was required before anything got done. The fact that women smoked was commonplace in Peru and Chile yet surprising to women travelers and deserved mention. A passion for gambling was reported by Nellie Bly in Mexico and also in Chile by Loretta L Wood Merwin. Bly remarked that Mexican soldiers smoked a weed called marijuana and passed the cigarette along one to another. The Paraguayans drank numerous glasses of maté, a bitter tea, every day, wrote Marguerite Dickins. One very admirable quality of South Americans was their courtesy and charm that Loretta L.Wood Merwin felt should be copied by North Americans. And Josephine Hoeppner Woods was not allowed to go into a mine in Bolivia, as the Indian miners thought it was bad luck if a woman entered. She had to bow to their ancient superstitions.

The governments of South American countries came under the critical eye of women travelers. Both Loretta L Wood Merwin and Sarah Madeleine Vinton Dahlgren stated that Chile and Peru were republics in name only. Elizabeth Agassiz acknowledged that, although there was a liberal constitution under Emperor Dom Pedro II in Brazil, little was done for the people. Julia Ward Howe said that Spanish rule in Cuba equated with bad and corrupt government, and that no improvements in roads or education were made to benefit the people. Ida Pfeiffer leveled the same criticism about the government in Ecuador. Marguerite

Dickins, in Uruguay, averred that the country was not an ideal republic. These women lived in a liberal democracy and could not help but note the great differences between the governments of South American countries and the United States.

How these women reacted to their travels and observations in South America was influenced by their gender, race, class, nationality, religion, values, and morals. The prejudices and the politics of the times in which they lived colored their observations; hence, the opinions that these women expressed tell us as much about them and the times in which they lived as they do about what they observed.

The selections in this book are arranged chronologically, beginning with the second decade of the nineteenth century and ending in the mid-twentieth century. Each selection gives the traveler's insight into the topics that interested and impressed her the most. The countries that are covered range from Cuba in the Caribbean to Chile, Peru, Ecuador, Bolivia, Mexico, and Panama on the west coast of South America and Brazil, Argentina, Uruguay, Paraguay, and French Guiana on the east coast, as well Nicaragua and Honduras in Central America.

Sarah Sabin Wilson

Mistress of a Cuban Plantation

SARAH SABIN WILSON (1799–1847) WAS a native of Bristol, Rhode Island, a seafaring town on the shores of Mount Hope Bay, whose privateers played a part in capturing British vessels in the War of 1812. Sarah was an orphan, as her father, John Sabin, captain of a slave ship belonging to wealthy and politically minded James D'Wolf, died in 1808, and her mother, Lucretia Wardwell Sabin, died in 1811. During her youth, John D'Wolf, the brother of James D'Wolf, was appointed her guardian. He took his responsibilities seriously and was a friend and trusted advisor to her for over thirty years. On June 1, 1814, Sarah, at the tender age of fifteen, married twenty-six-year-old Joseph Oliver Wilson (1788–1838), the former captain of the brig *Yankee* that brought in the largest amount of booty during the War of 1812, in Bristol's Congregational Church. Wilson, who was from Windsor, Connecticut, was well known and considered a catch, although there is no information on how or when the couple met. Wilson used his profits from his seafaring career to buy a plantation in Camarioca, Matanzas, Cuba, together with his partner, Captain John Smith, and in 1818 the couple and their three-year-old son John moved to Cuba. The Wilsons intended to make a profit from raising sugar and coffee and return to the United States within five years, but they spent the rest of their lives in Cuba.

The Cuba that Sarah Sabin Wilson encountered in 1818 was still a Spanish possession. From 1492, when Columbus landed on Cuban shores, to 1792, the island was a backwater, with no Indians to exploit or gold to discover. In the colonial period, Cuba was the jumping-off point for the invasion of Mexico by Hernando Cortés in 1519 and later served as a stopover for the galleons with their cargo of gold and silver on their way to Spain. By 1762, when the British occupied Havana, trade with the English opened up the country to new products. But the 1790s were transformative for the island, as the Haitian planters immigrated to Cuba after the slave revolt in Haiti destroyed their plantations and crops. They reestablished themselves, and the production of sugar went into full swing, as the growing population of the United States demanded the product. And the need for workers to cut the cane resulted in Cuba becoming an importer of slaves. Over time, about six hundred thousand slaves were brought to the island. Cuba suddenly became Spain's most prosperous colony and attracted settlers like the Wilsons and other North Americans who hoped to make a fortune cultivating sugar and coffee before returning home.

During her twenty-eight years in Cuba, Sarah wrote faithfully to her former guardian John D'Wolf in Bristol, and it is from these letters that the contours of Sarah's life in Cuba emerge. She confessed to him that life on a plantation was isolating, and she confided that she missed the company of other women, as her nearest female neighbor was twelve miles away. In a depressed mood, she saw "no prospect of getting clear of a plantation life altogether." But she wrote to D'Wolf that she wanted him to dispel rumors that she wanted to return home. She averred that she had too much to do to be homesick, and she set about her household duties with energy and determination.

Sarah raised six children over a fifteen-year period—five boys and one girl, Susan, whom she named after D'Wolf's wife—and she devoted herself to seeing that they were well educated and trained. She wanted the children to learn Spanish, and she herself was determined to learn the language as fast as she could—and she did. Sarah resolved to read books only in Spanish and became proficient in the language. In an attempt to assimilate, Joseph began to call himself José and was addressed as Don José. As time went on, the Wilsons became, for all intents and purposes, Cuban, although they never forgot their roots, and sent their children to school in the United States.

Besides raising her children, Sarah took on new responsibilities on the plantation. She took care of poultry and hogs; planted a kitchen garden; superintended the house slaves had a hospital built on the grounds, where she nursed the sick; and tutored her own children. She reported to D'Wolf on the status of the coffee and sugar crops that were being raised and marketed, so she was acquainted with the crops produced and the prices that they brought. She took an active interest in the produce that the plantation yielded, as that was their livelihood. Her letters to D'Wolf contained requests for items that they were not able to get in Cuba, including shoes, cloth, bonnets, ribbons, tea, seeds, potatoes, books, and vinegar. In turn, the Wilsons sent D'Wolf molasses, sugar, coffee, and fruit. Sarah also begged the D'Wolfs to visit, as the climate would be agreeable in the winter months.

The Wilsons had to face a number of life-threatening events in Cuba. A cholera epidemic was rampant by 1833. A number of their slaves died of the disease, including their cook. Sarah also came down with cholera but fortunately, recovered. Pirates were another threat that plantation owners had to face. The pirates of the Caribbean preyed on ships carrying cargo of sugar, molasses, and coffee leaving Matanzas harbor. To stem the losses, the United States government sent United States Navy ships to protect commerce. In 1823, Sarah's fourth of July party had to be postponed because her neighbors refused to leave their homes, as pirates were in the vicinity. Sarah was carrying on a hometown tradition, as Bristol, Rhode Island, held the first Independence

Day parade in the country. Finally, slave uprisings threatened the lives and property of the white plantation owners. A slave insurrection occurred in Cuba in 1825, some six leagues from the Wilson plantation. The Wilsons were not harmed, but their neighbors were. Eighteen people were killed, their homes destroyed, and goods stolen. Eventually, the insurrection was put down, but the ringleader was never caught. Joseph Oliver Wilson was a member of the militia that kept order, and he suggested ways to deal with the crisis, including closer supervision of slaves.

Although the Wilsons were in debt to creditors, in 1833 they were able to buy another plantation that they named Esperanza in Saguinillas, some nine miles from San Juan. Sarah and her son John lived there and managed the plantation that "succeeded beyond her expectations." Besides managing the estate and marketing sugar, she refurbished the house, had homes built for slaves, and extended the cane fields.

By 1834, the Wilsons' marriage had deteriorated, and they no longer lived together. Joseph was abusive and an alcoholic who resented his wife's independence and management abilities, remarking that she should exchange her skirts for pantaloons. In April 1835, Sarah petitioned the archbishop of Havana for a divorce, but since divorce was not condoned in Catholic Cuba, she was granted a separation and given custody of the children; henceforth, the couple lived apart. In 1837, when Sarah visited San Juan, Joseph struck her, shot her horse from under her, and chased her into the cane fields, threatening to kill her; however, she managed to escape. One year later, he died and was buried in Camarioca. Sarah never expressed any sorrow about his passing in her letters.

Sarah continued living at Esperanza until she departed for Spain in 1846 with her daughter Susan Fortún, who had married a Spanish officer stationed in Cuba. She became ill in Seville, where she died on

January 8, 1847, and was buried in San Sebastian Cemetery there. Her son Charles married a Cuban woman and her other children most likely remained in Cuba, where they continued to work the estates that she so carefully protected to ensure their patrimony.

The following letters written to John D'Wolf in Bristol, Rhode Island, beginning in 1818 and continuing in the 1820s and 1830s, give a picture of her life in Cuba and the events that impacted both her and her family: a slave insurrection, a cholera epidemic, pirates, marital problems, and the difficulties of adjusting to life in a foreign country and a different culture while trying to maintain contact with her home country and friends there. Sarah's letters are honest and, although her first impressions of Cuba were unfavorable, she adjusted to living there and went on to manage two plantations, market crops, settle her husband's debts, execute contracts, and leave an estate for her children. She never returned to live in Bristol, Rhode Island.

Sarah Sabin Wilson's letters published here are courtesy of the Bristol Historical and Preservation Society in Bristol, Rhode Island.

Plaza la Libertad, Matanzas, Cuba, Library of Congress

JULY 11, 1818, CAMARIOCA, ST. JUAN PLANTATION

HON J D'WOLF

Dear Sir,

Proud to obey your request. I improve the first opportunity to write you of our situation, and to send my respects to yourself and Lady. Doubtless you have received Oliver's letter from Matanzas dated June 15, informing you of our voyage, health, etc.

On the 17th we left the detestable town of Matanzas in a launch at dark and arrived on the shore of Camarioca at sunrise, where the Mosquitoes, Sandflies and Landcrabs were ready to receive us. Having to send for horses to carry us five miles further, we lay down on the sand with our new companions to rest, the boat being so loaded we had not room to lie our heads.

We arrived at the St. Juans by noon, I found as I expected a pleasant country, and to me a great many new and interesting objects. I think I shall like to stay five years, but I am sure I will stay no longer if God preserves my life to return to America.

I am sorry to inform you of the ill state of our little boy who has had to undergo a very severed seasoning, but I flatter myself he is at present mending, but he has grown very poor and weak, his sickness was a dysentery; that has been great trouble for me, being unacquainted with my few neighbors, distant from friends, inexperienced in sickness and fatigued by watch, almost made me curse my fortune, but I hope I shall not again have so severe a trial of my fortitude and patience (which by the bye) you know I never possessed a very large stock.

We have plenty of fruit so bad I cannot eat it and little good, but I hope next year to have more, and not be dependent either, for anything that land will produce. The estate has been very much neglected and abused several years, but is now rapidly improving. We find the stream or river at the foot of a very steep hill in front of our house very convenient, and pleasant, too, for bathing and it supplies us with plenty of nice fish and eels. I like our situation better than any I have seen. Our thatched hut is very inferior but we are expecting Carpenter to repair and make tight from the rain, when we shall be comfortable & look at least as well as our neighbor.

I depend much on seeing you or your son next winter, pray encourage him to come. I am sure he would spend the winter more pleasant here than at home. Oliver is very anxious to see him. It is very healthy in the country, but the small pox rages yet in Matanzas. We had a letter from Mr. Fales dated June 24th stating their baby was sick, the expected with that disorder & I am anxious to hear the result.

I find no time to be homesick, a woman was much needed to regulate the house and we have always had negros sick until now. We have buried three children but they had long been weakly.

I wish Mrs. D'Wolf would as near as she can send me a receipt for making butter and cheese, and if without trouble you could procure some garden seeds for our second planting in September it would much oblige us, as we are troubled to find any. When we begin to make sugar I shall send your wife some sweetmeats having plenty of limes.

Please present my love to your good Lady, and family, and Yourself accept the highest respect and Gratitude of

S.S.Wilson

P.S. Dear Sir, if you see my Grandfather be kind enough to show him this and he will instruct Mr. Church to direct his letters to the care of Zacharia Atkins, esq., Matanzas.

CAMARIOCA, ST. JUANS PLANTATION, FEBRUARY 10, 1819

CAPT. JOHN D'WOLF

Dear Sir,

By Capt. Smith I acknowledge the receipt of your letter to Oliver, and also of the many presents you by Capt. Batt sent us and we are inexpressibly grateful for the kind recollection manifested in the trouble you must have taken to select and forward articles, every one of which was great raraties for us. We received safely every article and had not the apples been detained in Matanzas a fortnight I think would have reached us sound, and as it was, we had our feast of them. The Potatoes all nice and sound; the butter I think as nice as when first put up, and I must tell you is all we have had since we came from Bristol except a keg last summer that we could not eat and which we never unheaded but drew like oil. We milk but one cow and that is little for our family consisting of ten workmen five in our house & we must allow little negros also some. We shall have more by and by but we must take care of the most needful first.

I feared by an intimation in your letter to Oliver by Capt. Munroe that you thought me discontented and I must advise you of the contrary ; but tell you why I content myself, and on what grounds I am dissatisfied. First, Dear Sir, you know the only thing that induced me to leave a country so beautiful as the U.S. (particularly so on account of the protection ever{y} man enjoys in just laws) and come to one as unsettled as this was. I judged it would in the end prove advantageous to my family. This same idea still governs me in wishing to stay a few years and in fact I am so interested I would not (if left to me) on any account leave this place while prospects are so fair of making us able to live where we please as the expiration of the proposed time, but think not that interest shall keep me here longer. Why I am dissatisfied. First, I dislike the Spaniards, and have no female society (except Mrs. Smith) nearer than twelve miles, in case of sickness. This I have found very unhappy, and no Physician in any case. I will recite to you the adventures lately passed and judge yourself if any woman of ever so firm resolution would not fear to have her friends exposed to like accidents although they are seldom.

Last week an Irishman (named Barry) who lives three miles from us got a little tipsy and attempted to kill his negros in the night because he said they did not work enough; he severely wounded by dull sword six of them before assistance reached the poor wretches. The Sunday eve following a man by the name of Doogen (also Irish) an honest obliging neighbor (who frequently dined and supped with us) was returning from the next Plantation to his own about fifty yards from a friends house where he had just bid good night, was murdered. Oliver was the third person who saw him lying across the road upon his face apparently killed with the blow of a sword which had broken his skull. It was not thought that he had the least difference with any person, but was supposed to have been murdered by some runaway Negroes he might have met who were afraid of being retaken. The Tuesday after a Spaniard who lived a mile from us had sold his little farm and was returning from Town with One thousand dollars, when three robbers stepped from the woods and demanded his cash which he refused, saying it was the only dependence of a large family, that he had worked hard for that $, when one of them fired a blunderbuss at him, broke his arm, injured his breast and eyes, took his money then ran. The man is yet in danger of his life and without medical aid. Villians have little to fear from justice, a few ounces will be very likely to settle all differences and it is little consolation to have law in any case.

We did not come here expecting an easy life but although there are many disagreeables there are more advantages at our command than we could elsewhere enjoy. I have given my report fully and candidly because I heard it was reported in Bristol that I was in fact distracted to return which if you hear any person (if their

opinion is of value) speak of it I will thank you from me to contradict it.

Feb 14th Last week Oliver with me rode on horseback fifteen miles to visit Mrs Beth but was disappointed in her being absent from home, but we had a pleasant ride and spent our spare time at Mrs Wm Bowens coffee estate. Yesterday I rode (with company) to Point Jacko bay (as sailors call it) and took breakfast in an old Fisherman's hut. It is seven miles from our house.

I heartily thank John for his present of those fine fowls, and ask him not to forget the promise I had in your letter of a line from him, I wish to see how he improves. I shall send him by the first safe opportunity some oranges and I am wishing the young limes to be fit that I may have the pleasure of sending Mrs. D'Wolf some preserved. They will be plenty I think in three weeks.

I have stretched my letter to an unpardonable length, I fear you will not have the patience to read half. I will break off immediately and leave other things for O. who will write very soon. Please present my affectionate regards to Mrs. D' Wolf, Mr. D'Wolf and his son. Oliver joins me in respects to yourself and family and Dear Sir, pray indulge with another letter.

Your ever Grateful

S.S. Wilson

P.S. In my letter to Mr. D'Wolf of Jan 3rd (which I think doubtful if received) I requested to purchase (If he had

leisure) some books for me and likewise requested you would furnish him with 30 dollars. I do not like to risqué too much at a time upon the ocean. I would like some poems, a few plays or in fact any thing that will amuse me. If he finds *The tragedy of Bertram or castle of St Alderbrand* ask him to send it {to} me but *Exchernes Journey* if he has not already purchased, I have since seen and did not like it, if he has bought it very well, it will assist in making a small library which I intend. I wish for the *Shipwreck* if he happens to see it. I am really ashamed of so many wants I fear you will think the more favours I receive the more I take liberty to ask but we purchase very little here as we can seldom obtain what we wish. Adieu again, Dear Sir.

CAMARIOCA, JUNE 26, 1825

HON. J D'WOLF

Dear Sir,

The present is a moment of peculiar interest to us. I presume you have heard of the partial insurrection of the Negros in the District of St. Jose in the neighborhood of Sumidero and Limonade which is about nine leagues S.E. from Matanzas and six of us. Believing you will feel anxious to hear the particulars I embrace the first opportunity of informing you of the affair as much of it as the unsettled manner of information will allow. Upon the 15th off the present month at 3 o clock in the morning the negros upon a very small French estate revolted and killed their owner. They then proceeded to the second estate where the negros joined them and killed the owner of that estate, his wife and two oldest sons, their youngest son five years of age was protected by a Mulato slave, although she was forced to follow the gang with the child in her arms, but made her escape as soon as possible. Upon the third estate the negros joined, and the owner and son was killed, the wife and children were protected by their own slaves, for in the revolt some negros remained faithful to their masters, but upon five estates nearly all joined the insurgents and upon others only a few. The rebels then proceeded to the fourth estate (owned by a Spaniard) where they killed the master, upon the fifth (also Spanish) burned the buildings, but the white people escaped. They then came to a tavern where they murdered two Spaniards and proceeded to Mr. Webster's coffee estate (situated on the great road to Principe) where they murdered one white man, and wounded another, the other whites retreated after killing a number of Negros. They kept on the easterly road, came to another tavern where there was four or five men who made great resistance and killed a number of negros, then went on the next estate owned by a W Taylor of Baltimore here, the negros fought in defence of their master drove off the insurgents and killed a number. They then attacked the estate of Gasper Hernandez where the negros remained neutral. By this time, 8 o clock the whites were assembled under arms in considerable force and attacked the Negros amounting then to 200 making terrible slaughter and sparing none whom they could reach. The negros broke and ran for the woods and were pursued in every direction. About noon a company of Dragoons arrived from the Matanzas and it is estimated that 400 armed men were in pursuit of the fugitives with dogs, killing as they overtook them. There was 6 white people assassinated by the blacks. Upon the 16th a company of Dragoons arrived from Havana and continued the work of extirpation upon the ruthless savages who had murdered and fled from their masters. Government had ordered a strict inquiry to be made on all the estates in that neighborhood for disaffected negros, a number has been discovered upon several estates, and immediately executed. It seems the slaves were incited to perpetrate these horrible deeds by some free negros living in the neighborhood, one of whom had lately received his freedom from his master who he murdered. Several free negros have been shot, as being principals in this affair. We received information by 10 o clock upon the day it occurred, but did not much credit it, at 12 o clock Mr. Wilson received an official order to prepare his arms and be upon the alert, also to advise his neighbors to do the same. All the white men in the neighborhood were immediately under arms. Orders were enforced to cut off all communication with the disaffected district, and all stray negros arrested. A detachment of men were sent to assist in quelling the insurrection. Guards are still patrolling the country, and frequently come into our house at night for refreshment. The insurrection at first alarming is now considered to be internely suppressed. They are still pursuing the few that have not been killed or taken prisoner. It must have been a terrible scene of consternation. The planters first object was to secure their wives and children whom they sent to Matanzas for protection. No occurrence has taken place in our neighborhood to give the least suspicion of disaffection among the slaves. The second estate named was owned by an American by the name of Armitrage and were the most intimate neighbors of Mr. Stephen Fales' family. In a letter of this days date from Mr. Fales addressed to his daughter now with us and who at our house at the time of the disturbance in the following manner "I was greatly relied on account of your absence from us upon the terrible 15th. You poor mother who is hourly expecting her confinement bore the fatigue wonderfully walking two leagues, and remained concealed in the woods without any nourishment in the middle of the day." He further observes "The Mulato woman, her own child and the child of Mr. Armitrage and another servant of their family are now at our house." One of the negros had on Mrs A shawl for a scarf, mounted on horseback and encouraging the rebels. Some had pillage ciths of their Masters, and one had on the uniform of a Spaniard he had murdered. The silver was left in Mrs. Armitrage's house, but knives, forks, and every such article missing, and everything in the house destroyed. Three days since a negro was brought to our house who had been taken up by a Spaniard, and Miss Fales recognized him to be the slave of Armitrage—he had when taken his masters sword and a handkerchief was found with him marked with Mrs. A's name, He was taken to the captain of the district three or four days and he confessed he was concerned murdering farther of his fate I have not heard.

I beg you will excuse the incorrectness of my writing, as I retired late after being fatigued by company, and I cannot now see a letter that I write but being anxious to dispatch by this opportunity prevents my copying or being more particular.

Mr.Wilson wrote you upon the 15th but dispatched his letter previously to his receiving official information of the disturbance. Mr. W joins me in kind wishes for your health and that of your family. Please present my love to your good wife, daughter and family. Be so kind as to remember us both affectionately to our dear child.

Am Dear Sir

Yours respectfully,

S.S.Wilson

CAMARIOCA APRIL 3, 1826

Mrs. Susan De Wolf,

I dare not think of going to America, I see nothing but opposition to such as idea. Mr.W sometimes is going next year with his family to pass the summer; but I am sure he will not except he is obliged to do so on account of his health. You undoubtedly recollect the sever fit of illness he had two years ago which terminated in an inflamation upon his seat that superrate and I think for want of proper Surgical attendance, was never properly healed; it has the last season threatened to be troublesome, but he does not complain at present, and I hope will never seriously suffer from it, but I know he must take better care of himself, than in years heretofore. I am confident it was first occasioned by frequent and fatiguing journies upon horseback. The road between Camarioca and Matanzas has just been completed, so as to render it practicable to go upon it in the Vehicle we here call a "Volante" which is kind of an awkward looking Chaise.

I shall write again in a few days when I also write to my little John, and tell him all about his little brothers and sister. Susan talks a great deal about him, and Charles too often speaks of John. I feel your kindness to my child as one of the greatest blessings of my life, and I am grateful to each member of your family for the kind interest they take in his welfare. The indisposition of John that you mentioned a short time since is the same I expect with which he so long and much suffered in this country, but had at one time the Dysentery for nine months and for many days together passed only blood.

I apply myself every leisure moment to studying Spanish, as I see great necessity that one of the family should understand it so as to write it with ease, and Oliver is interested that I should do so. I made a promise when the year commenced not to read a volume except it was in Spanish, and I have so far kept it, and have reread all I can find in the neighborhood, but I assure you books in this country are scarcely to be found. I have read Don Quixote, Gil Blas, and a number of novels with as much pleasure as I read English. I beg you to procure for me (through the assistance of your son) a few volumes in Spanish, which will amuse me now, and be useful to John by and by as he must learn the Spanish Language, as soon as he can read and write English. I wish for amusing works, tales, moral novels, or in fact such as can be obtained as there may be no choice.

We have been very unfortunate with the little negroes of late, ten have died within the last month, and eight of them within the last week. I assure you it is very painful to see the little things that have been raised under my own eyes suffer as they have done, it has been a complication of diseases, the Whooping Cough, Thrush and Dysentery. Every one of my children has had the Whooping Cough. And has given me a great deal of anxiety, they are not yet entirely well but have passed the worst of it. There is one little negro being dead, one I do not think can live, but we have no new cases , and I hope we shall lose no more, some of them died in twelve hours after they were taken sick.

Our brother Charles is better than he has been, but not perfectly sound. I feel some fatigue & know it is not prudent to exercise myself longer although I feel a disposition.

Please present my regards to your good husband, my compliments to your son, & his Lady, my love to all the children. Please accept yourself the affection of your obliged friend.

Sarah S. Wilson

MAY 10, 1833, CAMARIOCA, SAN JUAN PLANTATION

Hon John D Wolf,

Your affectionate letter dated was gratefully received, and I impose the present moment to write you a few hasty lines and will begin by starting that at present my family is in good health. In every moment of unusual anxiety my first wish is to communicate to you my situation although I am frequently so situated as to render it nearly impossible to give either you or myself much satisfaction by a cirucumstancial detail of affairs or events. It is a critical moment in regard to my private concerns but I must wait events and hope for the best. Documents of the deepest importance to me are all prepared and only require certain signatures for the conclusion of arrangements that I sometime since made.

The cholera has paralised every kind of business, not a lawyer is to be found in his office and no person of any distinction will leave his family, and generally speaking there is no communication between one estate and another. Our agent promised to come this week to attend to the business I have suggested to you, but would not leave his family until a physician for whom he had sent should arrive upon his estate to take charge of his family in his absence but circumstances have taken place with us which will again delay the business. This morning at 6 oclk I was called from my bed into the hospital, and although I had never before seen a cholera patient it was impossible to mistake the features of that disease. Alexander and myself took our stand by the patient, and used all the possible remedies, viz, frictions, mustard poultices, cupping and etc, but at 10 A.M. the negro was a corpse. At 9 oclk A.M. a little negro girl 5 years old was taken with the same symptons and died at 11. The two were buried in the same grave: we at this time have no cases and hope for the best. I have sent every one of my children off of the place, but although I said I should leave the estate if any case of cholera occurred upon it, I do not expect to do so as I feel no apprehension for myself. I am much less likely to suffer by the disease. I do not suppose that Alexander will leave the estate and I shall remain here as long as he does. Mr Wilson was from home when the deaths occurred, but arrived here just as they were being taken to the burying ground. As soon as I saw the cholera patient sent the 8 negroes belonging to us to the pasture lands near the sea and was just starting off 30 of the best negroes from the estate when Mr. W arrived and he did not approve the move and so they all remain on the estate. I hope he will not have reason to repent it. Before the disease was officially announced upon the estate we could have made some recovery, but now all intercourse with abroad will be strictly prohibited. In Matanzas and in the Havana the disease is extinct, but is doing its work of destruction in the country & upon the plantations. In several instances every single negro has died upon estates. 144 died on an estate near Matanzas, most of them in the field, where carts were found half loaded with cane, the cattle dead at the neap, the negroes by their side. Do you recollect a gentleman by the name of Lobio—every white person abandoned his estate and the negroes were left to die and rot unburied : the government took charge of the estate at last :this estate joins Mrs. Jencks and is not distant from Madriega. John DW no doubt will recollect the first sugar estate after crossing the ferry belonging to a French gentleman by the name of Belshaz as I remember pointing out to him the enclosure where his wife was buried, and the marble monument—39 have died upon that estate and a daughter of the partner M Dalcour—she was an interesting and accomplished young female. Before any opportunity affords of forwarding this letter I hope to be able to give more flattering accounts, but I was unwilling to delay writing for fear some accident might deprive me altogether of doing so; no one at this season feels secure from one hour to another. I am going to lie down to sleep if I can for I have been severely exercised this morning, but shall write again tomorrow. Alexander is now asleep & so is M Wilson but I thought I should sleep better after having written you a few lines—Unfortunately D Taplin left us only a week ago, after staying with us five weeks waiting for the cholera. William Jencks has lost two of his children by cholera, both boys. Martha Fales had the disease but lightly.

I have just seen John Sabin & Susan R start for Matanzas. John is to enter a counting house & Susan a French boarding school. I wrote you on the forgoing pages that I had sent all the children off the estate but as we were upon the 11th without any case of cholera I hoped we should escape further loss and not liking to inconvenience my neighbors I sent for them home again. Last evening we had 2 cases but both are convalescent: this morning 3 are down & I have very little hopes of either. Hipolita the cook is one and Ellen the washerwoman is another. You know their being house servants must disarrange my domestic concerns entirely. I am now alone upon duty as Alexander was taken to his bed yesterday, but I do not consider him in any danger: at present he is convalescent. I have just written to Mr. Spalding & expect something comfortable by return of long—prescriptions from a Dr. or perhaps a physician. So John might continue to receive 300 annually from the estate it may be thought a wrong step to send him where for several months he may not receive anything but my reasons for sending were that he would not improve his mind or manners among the low Spaniards he must associate with upon the estate, and the house he goes to is of the highest reputation and if he wants it he will be taken notice of.

I have just received a letter informing me of the death of my very particular friend Mrs. Crabb- Dr Crabbs widow of Limonal—the cholera made its appearance among her negroes about the same time that it broke out upon this place—she died without a female friend near her—she had a physician, her slaves attended her & Mr. Mccomb closed her eyes & was the only white friend who saw her land into her silent grave—she has left two beautiful boys—Mr. C was speechless from the first moment. I was going to her house the day our negro died and was only detained by the sickness at home. I cannot devote another instant to writing. God preserve you my very dear friend. I will not delay more than one day writing to you again. Remember me affectionately to every individual of your beloved family. I have a letter began to your grandson JJ DWolf but must deter finishing it for the present. To your good wife my heartfelt love.

Your affectionate

Sally

HON. JOHN DEWOLF, MATANZAS, 25, APRIL 1835 (PETITION FOR DIVORCE)

My dear Sir

I can only promise by this opportunity to write you fully in the course of a few days. I have entered upon the most distressing tedious and difficult undertaking known in a Catholic country, but nothing could prevent any prosecuting the business to the last extremity not even the dangers of an Inquisition nor my present circumstances. I have lately returned from Havana where I made my petition to the "Illustrious Archbishop" for a divorce from Mr. W. The full control of my children has been given to me, and a reparation from Mr. W granted during the investigation of circumstances relating to our disagreement. I have no doubt this business will be speedily concluded. Mr. W is here & we met this morning respecting future family arrangements: tomorrow I expect to go through the last exercises & before then cannot attend to any thing whatever. I do not believe Mr. W will stand a trial before the tribunal.

Have only time to present my love to all your family & subscribe myself your truly

Affectionate friend,

Sally S Wilson

P.S. John is attentive to business received $34 a month salary & promises fairly for the future. Susan R is with me. The new estate is flourishing. Will write you again immediately.

MATANZAS 21 JAN 1837

HON. J D'WOLF

My dear Sir,

Capt. John Smith has cleared today, and weather permitting will sail tomorrow. Alexander has just gone down to the wharf to send the articles I have purchased for my friends on board of Capt S's vessel and I meantime acknowledge the several letters, presents, you have been so kind to send me. I wish you to charge to me all the expenses upon the articles by Capt Smith, and if you will take charge of and send to my children their share I shall be very grateful for the attention.

I ordered six dozen boxes of guava jelly packed for me to be divided equally among Hon John D'Wolf, Dr. John D'Wolf, Mrs. Horton, Mrs. Valentine and my two children. I send you a barrel of oranges and a jar of lemons for Joseph & Edward, and a barrel of oranges for yourself. I have given the Capt a barrel of oranges and a jar of lemons to secure his attention to the remainder.

Your remarks about the old house are neither unexpected nor surprising. I hoped Mr. Wilson would have sold it, and have spent the money for his own amusement, and not have drawn more money from here since he left me under a weight of obligations by notes he gave for amounts he will never again have possession of and which I must struggle with. The only calculations I made for him or the house were these –if he repaired it, he would be occupied, and do less damage there than here and it would be better for his estate if he would go and pull down the same and rebuild it again. If nothing but business and hard work trouble me I would in a short time pay his debts and settle honorably but I have struggled long and hard and am about making a retreat.

An estate I have made (which if not thrown away) will amply provide for Wilson, his children and I shall now place the same in the best situation I can and leave

Mr. W to manage for himself. Truths are too disagreeable to afford my fiends pleasure, and the troubles of another are always unwelcome to the ear. Misery has made me more alone in the world than an orphan and were it not for your repeated letters & favors you would never hear from me.

I am here with all my children (except John) to settle up the last years accounts. I am also in negotiation with Gaumand for the sole control of my interest in Esperanza (to sell sugar myself) and expect to make a favorable arrangement with him.

I have given my full power of attorney to Mr. Daniel Jencks in case of any absence, but must act for myself as long as I remain here, and it was with difficulty that I persuaded Wilson to allow me this reprieve, as I told him it was impossible for me to get along without assistance.

Alexander has just been in a moment, and I have given him an order for a hundred dollars which he has gone out to collect and I expect will send it to you by this opportunity or certainly by the next. Perhaps Mrs. Val is ignorant of the season for croping here. I told her I would send her some sugar as soon as made it, and have already given Mr. Griswold an order upon the state for sugar for you, for her & others, which he will forward in due season by the most suitable opportunity.

I am any moment expecting my partner Smith & Mr. Jencks from the country to conclude our joint arrangement & sign contracts. When all is concluded I will inform you. It is a task, a hardship to write at all, and only my obligations to you induce me to touch a pen.

I shall leave here in the spring but have not determined which way to travel.

I remain dear Sir

Yours affectionately,

S.S. Wilson

Mary Robinson Hunter, Newport Historical Society

Mary Robinson Hunter

A Diplomat's Lady in Brazil, 1835–1848

MARY ROBINSON HUNTER (1787–1863) ARRIVED in Rio de Janeiro on January 2, 1835. She and her husband William, the newly appointed chargé d'affaires to Brazil, and five of their six children left Newport, Rhode Island, for what was then a distant and exotic land. Mary had never traveled outside of the United States before and was unprepared for life in a tropical environment. Unbeknownst to her, she would remain in South America for the next fourteen years.

Mary Hunter settled in Rio de Janeiro amid political turmoil. In 1831, Dom Pedro I, who had pronounced Brazilian independence in 1822, abdicated the throne and returned to Portugal. His son, Dom Pedro II, was still a child; hence, a three-man regency was appointed to govern for him, later to be replaced by a single regent, Diogo Antônio Feijó. The regent had to deal with a number of revolts over political, economic, local, and regional issues, as well as slave revolts. The most serious threat to the stability of the central government was the revolt in the southern province of Rio Grande do Sul in 1835. Republican sentiment was strong in the province, as well as regionalism, and there was resentment over taxes and unpopular provincial governors. In 1836, Rio Grande do Sul seceded and remained an independent state for the next ten years.

This was the state of politics in Brazil when Mary arrived. She was not a flexible person and had difficulty adjusting to life in a Luso-Brazilian Catholic culture, so different from her New York and New England upbringing. For the first three years in Rio de Janeiro, she was homesick and eagerly awaited letters from friends and family. She spent a great deal of her time writing letters and keeping a diary to record her daily activities, impressions, and thoughts. One constant complaint was the lack of decent food in Brazil. She never had the courage to or interest in trying *vatapá* or *feijoada*, which were staples of the Brazilian diet, and she complained of being thin, wrinkled, and forlorn as a result of her dietary deprivation.

Mary wrote that her life in Brazil was dull and boring, although her diary indicated that she was busy calling on friends and neighbors, socializing with members of the diplomatic corps, and visiting with United States and Royal Navy officers. She never attempted to learn Portuguese; hence, her social contacts were limited to the English-speaking exile community and the few Brazilians who spoke English. The Hunters had the opportunity to attend court events and socialize with Dom Pedro II, who was crowned emperor in July 1841, and his sisters, the princesses Januária and Francesca, as well. These encounters were duly noted in her diary, as she was impressed by connections with royalty and looked forward to these events. But as time went on, she retreated more and more from what she considered the decadent social life of gamblers and partygoers in Rio, preferring a quiet home life.

When she had time, Mary eagerly explored the city of Rio de Janeiro. The lush and beautiful scenery captivated her, and she eagerly set out with her devoted slave, Roberto, to explore her surroundings.

She climbed Corcovado Mountain, picnicked on an island in Guanabara Bay, visited the royal palace of São Christóvão, the national museum, and walked in the public gardens or on Flamingo Beach. During the hot summer months, she retreated to a cottage in the Tijuca Mountains, far from the dust and heat of Rio.

Mary's diary is full of references to planned but unsuccessful slave revolts and the harsh treatment of slaves by their masters. She was especially fearful of the prospect of a slave revolt, as the numbers in Rio de Janeiro favored the Blacks. She felt sympathy toward the enslaved, as she chastised owners who whipped their charges. But at times she was frustrated dealing with her own servants, and resorted to whipping and slapping her slaves. For the most part, she tried to practice Christian charity toward her fellow men.

Catholic religious customs and celebrations, and the scandalous behavior of the Roman Catholic clergy, were causes for criticism. Mary was a devout Episcopalian and attended church regularly. Despite her disapproval of Roman religious practice, she noted Catholic saints' days in her diary and witnessed the Corpus Dei procession. However, she refused to participate in the riotous pre-Lenten festivities called the *Entrudo,* when the population assaulted passersby with wax bottles full of water. She kept her door locked to avoid the noisy celebrants.

In 1844, William Hunter returned to Newport, Rhode Island, when his appointment as minister plenipotentiary was over. Mary elected to stay in Rio, as her two daughters, Elizabeth Birckhead and Kate Greenway, were there. For the next four years, she moved back and forth between Rio, Montevideo, Uruguay, and Buenos Aires, Argentina, where her daughter Kate lived. Mary experienced a civil war between the *Blancos* and *Colorados* for control of the government in Uruguay, with interference by the Argentine dictator Juan Manuel de Rosas. Her diary contained descriptions of wartime conditions and deprivations in Montevideo and Buenos Aires.

After her daughter Kate died in childbirth in 1846, Mary remained in Montevideo to take care of her grandson Charles. Two years later, in 1848, she returned to Newport, Rhode Island, to take her daughter's body home, although she admitted that she would miss "dear sweet Rio." Mary continued to keep a diary once she was home, but she never again mentioned her life in Brazil. She lived in Newport until her death on March 14, 1863, at age seventy-six, and was buried in Trinity Churchyard's cemetery, next to her husband and her beloved daughter Kate.

The selections here are from the Brazilian diaries of Mary Robinson Hunter, located in the Newport Historical Society in Newport, Rhode Island.

EXPLORING RIO DE JANEIRO, MONDAY SEPTEMBER 7, 1835

Mr. H and self took a walk to see the new Church on the Larangeres built for the reception of an Image, Nossa Senhora de Gloria, which is to be carried by a grand procession from the venerable Church on Gloria hill where it has been worshipped by Royalty for ages. This is the last Church frequented by the first wife of Don Pedro 1st. Every Saturday morning she drove from the Palace to mass here, followed by crowds. As she ascended the long flight of steps, to whom she distributed coins and gracious smiles to them. She was adored by her subjects. After the birth of her children, she was seen here the first time. She went out propitiating this Saint, who is the Patron Saint of ladies in child birth. She was the Mother of the present Emperor and the Queen of Portugal.

SEPTEMBER 20, 1835

Walked to church with my son Thomas. Excellent sermon. After church walked in the Passeo publico for the first time, delightfully situated on the shore of the bay, kept in fine order, but very little frequented by the Brazillians. They are too indolent, too lethargic to enjoy the advantages that their fine climate affords them of exercise in the open air.

VISIT TO THE PALACE OF SÃO CHRISTÓVÃO, NOVEMBER 15, 1836

Received a note from Mr. Keemlie to say that Mr. Clapp had obtained leave for us to visit the Palace of St. Christóvão, the Royal family being at Santa Cruz but were expected to return in a day or two. As the day was unpleasant I thought at first it was best to decline, but at last wrote that we would be at his house at half past three. Mrs. Keemlie went with us and a Mr. Potts, etc. It became quite pleasant before we got out and were much gratified inspecting the residence of Royalty. The most interesting rooms were the usual sitting room of these interesting orphans where we saw a splendid painting of Donna Maria, present Queen of Portugal, and one there of the last Empress, a beautiful woman, if the likeness is correct. Here were the children's drawings and playthings, piano and different toys. In a small basket on the table, I found some little paper boats which the little Emperor had made. Eliza and I each took one as a relic of the scene, just such as my boys used to make. I wanted to purloin one of the childish specimens of his drawings of ships and horses but could not effect it, tho I believe some of our party who were more daring did so. … Upstairs, we were shown a theatre, prettily fitted up for their amusement, and another very large one where an extensive and wonderful collection of specimens of mineralogy and shells were neatly placed and labelled in glass cases, out of which another large room contained the library which our time would not allow of our examining as we felt inclined to do. One of the most interesting rooms was the very large chamber exactly in the way it was when the Emperor abdicated and went on board ship to embark for Portugal. It has never since been used but kept locked and shown to visitors only, superbly furnished with chairs covered with blue embroidered silk, French tables and mirrors, French bedstead with white silk curtains. Eliza tore a part of the bed covering of figured muslin where there was previously a rent made in it. She layed herself on the bed and gave way to some enthusiasm. I wished that she and I together could have passed a whole day there, looking and indulging the various thoughts such a scene gave rise to, but night approached and we hurried to our carriage.

VISIT TO THE MUSEUM, NOVEMBER 17, 1836

After breakfast Thomas asked me to go in to the Museum which is near our residence and open to the public gratis every thursday. The Museum is in a fine spacious building and every thing neatly arranged, though with out any catalogue or book of reference. The collection of Indian dresses, ornaments, and weapons is very large and beautiful. There are several Egyptian Coffins and Mummies and other antiquities, a great and truly wonderful variety of the feathered tribe. The plumage and formation of some are truly exquisite, so that I think this place is well worth visiting more than once and especially with some intelligent person who understands the Portuguese language.

FOOD, MARCH 14, 1836

Miserable dinner today-- nothing I could eat. This is certainly the greatest objection to the Country. I am almost starved. Neither am I difficult in this respect. I have never required delicate or costly viands and try to be grateful for what I receive, but everything presented here is revolting to the sight as well as taste. Money cannot purchase anything like what the poorest person can procure at home in our highly favored land. I have always felt the sin of complaint and discontent and at home was easily satisfied. If I could get a piece of sweet bread and butter or marmelade I was content, but here you have none of the substitutes: the beef tastes like tainted liver; mutton, black and tough; the poultry stringy and tasteless; the fish good when fresh but before you can get them on your table they are hawked about in the sun or the heads of negroes and the process they go through with a negroe cook makes them utterly disgusting. The only thing I have eaten with any pleasure was salt beef sent from NYork; this I know had not died from disease before it was salted. And when I think I have so much longer to starve before I can be released from this wretched place. I can scarcely control my patience.

TREATMENT OF SLAVES, FEBRUARY 5, 1836

While at breakfast heard our neighbor, Mrs. A., scolding very violently at one of her black women and directly the lash was heard. I got upon the wall in the yard to witness for once such a scene. This lady was looking out her back window directing the blows which were administered by a white servant man. The wash woman crouched up in one corner and was whipped for about 15 minutes over her face, neck and arms with four or five leather thongs, not uttering a sound, but now and then catching at the whip. How I longed to give vent to my indignation. I could eat no breakfast.

OCTOBER 29, 1839

Among 6 or 7 blacks belonging to our landlord who pass here twice a day from their labour is one old man with a heavy chain from his shoulder to his ancle. The next visit Barutto made I asked him why he was punished? He broke out with great vehemence , *muito mal, muito mal, Señora.* Why? What were his offences? He killed, he stole, he ran away, he hid himself in a hole 3 weeks, living on bananas, green oranges. When he was found, he looked more like a *bichu* than a negroe. He has had 10 different owners, had severe punishment from all. The former French Minister, St Prise, intruded to have his irons taken off, but he resumed his bad habits. Barutto says he cannot sell him for no one will buy him. He makes a low obeisance every time he passes. Before I knew these particulars, he came to the kitchen after a week's hard rain. Said he had been in the woods 5 days without food and begged me to give him a paper to his Master not to have him punished. I was anxious to do so, but I could not write a word of Portuguese. I got the Dictionary and tried to make Barutto understand what I meant, which I found afterwards he did, and the man was not whipped. He ate voraciously what I told the Cook to give him.

AUGUST 30, 1845

I was awakened this morning by the sound of the lash upon one of the poor blacks near the house. I got up, went to the window, saw the *Feitor* screaming and another black doing the whipping upon his miserable fellow labourer. I called out "*basta & diablo*" when they went off out of sight but not of hearing. The screams at last of the victim to bad passions were horrible, my heart beat, and feeling I could do no good turned from the window. After asking one of our blacks what was his offence, *Nada Signora;* he pulled up the wrong cabbage.

SLAVE REVOLTS, DECEMBER 23, 1835

The negroes of some Brazillian family had been bribed to admit others into the house at night which was to be a watchword for a general massacre and extermination of the whites. These reports alarm me very much. It seems to be the beginning of a retributive justice mercifully delayed, the distant but certain precursor of the thunder which must break on this benighted land.

A few days ago there was another insurrection in preparation up the bay at the foot of the Organ Mountains. On Christmas day they were to march down to the City, secure both Arsenals and murder all the Whites. People here feel perfect security from the circumstances of the slaves coming from various parts of Africa and are not as in Bahia, Para, and Rio Grande all of one or two tribes. They speak different languages and are in a state of hostility towards each other at Home. The Whites believe they would not cooperate against them, but I think this is false security. The blacks of different tribes and interests when at home have been here long enough to feel deeply the oppression and cruelty of the whites towards all of that colour. They will one day join heart in hand to avenge it. It will be black against White and the difference is fearfully in their favour as to numbers. The computation is 20 black to one white and daily increasing the same ratio as ship loads of these poor wretches are constantly landed on the coast near Rio and marched down to the market and to other parts of the Country. The circumstance that more than half the time we have none of our ships of War in this part increases my fears and my sleep is often disturbed by them. I lay watching for daylight to dispel the gloom and fears of night.

SLAVES' CRIMES AGAINST OWNERS, OCTOBER 29, 1841

I walked with Roberto round the beach. Stopped at Julia's window who told me a female slave of theirs had mingled some poisonous root (which is known only to the blacks) in some chamomile tea her master had ordered her to make for him. Finding something bitter in the taste, he did not drink it and thought some soot had fallen into the water. They found it afterwards in a *marengo* of water from which he was in the habit of drinking, without pouring into a glass. He then went to the City, brought out thumb screws to make her confess. A Physician pronounced it poison. They confessed that three of their own blacks had assisted and two belonging to some other person. They were all severely whipped for three days in succession and they are now about selling the girl.

JULY 13, 1843

On the 4th of the month, a Brazillian merchant living where the Nortons did was murdered by his Cook on his return from the Theatre with his wife & two sons. It made me shudder to look towards the house. He was one of the most respectable, useful, influential men on Change where Mr. B met him every day. He very imprudently bought his black, knowing him to be a bad one, because he was a good Cook, for his Counting House in town. He was angry with his Master, it is said, for making him go out on Sundays and holidays when he was not wanted in town to work on the place S*enor* Phillipe had lately bought and confesses he had been long been waiting an opportunity of revenge. The night was dark & rainy. He had sent the footman up to the house for an umbrella for the *Señora* to walk up the hill. While she sat in the carriage, the black came out of the stable, passed the two sons and ran a knife into his Master who just said:" He has murdered me" and fell dead.

JANUARY 14, 1844

Gregory Molke rode over to make a call. Told us the particulars of the murder of the *Feitor* by some of their young blacks. He left home very early for town to pass the day with his brother, 4 of them overtook him on the road and killed him with clubs. They have confessed the act, but no reason given can be assigned for their conduct. They had received no punishment and say they did it for a frolic. He had 100 *milreis* , his watch, etc., which they did not touch. One of the boy was only 14, born on the estate.

RELIGIOUS CUSTOMS, LENT OR THE ENTRUDO, SUNDAY, FEBRUARY 14, 1836

The Carnival on Shrovetide, called here *O Entrudo* (this lasts three days), when every body is at liberty to throw water on all they meet which makes much merriment among the Brazillians and negroes. A barbarous custom. The most civilized throw balls of coloured wax filled with Cologne and other perfumes. I have just given orders to keep the front door fastened as last year our house was invaded by these privileged intruders and no displeasure will check their approach. *Au Contraire,* it seems to give a zest to their mirth to see it excites displeasure, as it often does in those who are unacquainted with the customs of the Country.

RELIGION, JANUARY 17, 1842

The Pope's Internuncio is a fine looking man, an intelligent countenance, looks like some Italian pictures, about 40 years of age I should judge. Talks a great deal, but in French. He is much shocked to find Religion in this Country in so low a state. He (the Papal Nuncio) says there is none that he can discern, even among the clergy. Their houses are filled with children of every colour. Not only no Religion, but no morality. There is no Parochial teaching, no Confession. He speaks freely even with the Protestants on this subject and gave several instances which have come to his own knowledge. He says his servant, a white man, whom he brought with him asked permission to go to Confession. When he got out persons his own grade ridiculed the idea "Why should you go to Confession, you are not ill".

RESIDENCE IN THE TIJUCA MOUNTAINS, FEBRUARY 24, 1840

Morning fog but soon cleared away. High wind and quite cold. I sewed all the morning. ...the Country is now in the height of its vegetable beauty...large flowering trees of the richest purple and yellows, the plant of which hedges are made with its fuzzy white blossoms, and the various shades of green that fill the mountains and vallies delight and refresh the eye and other senses. And earthly sensual and degraded must be the mind which is not raised in awe and gratitude to Him who maketh "The Wilderness blossom as the rose." Truly, this is a glorious

Country, a favoured Country in the spot we dwell in so quietly. Nothing is wanting to complete the landscape when below and around us from a long drought, water is scarce. Here a fresh torrent & soft is constantly pouring at our feet, delicious for quenching thirst and cooling our bodies in its delicious, natural baths. I never felt the advantages of a residence in Brazil so entirely as since my location at Tijuca. My health and that of my family is perfect and uninterrupted.

SOCIETY IN RIO, SEPTEMBER 8, 1840

I feel so miserable in health that it is irksome to continue this Journal, especially as my life is so monotonous even in the midst of gaiety. But it is gaiety that at my time of life is rather more agreeable to avoid. Mr. H and myself were much less lonely in the midst of the wilderness of Tijuca. The most desirable society of Rio is composed of those who dance; those who gamble for these intellectual and laudable objects. A certain set meet every night, if possible, that is, if they can find any housekeeper fool enough to hire music, buy *doces,* and set 8 or 10 card tables for their accommodation. The dancers are first, Mrs. O & Mrs. Young; The gamblers, the whole Diplomatic corps with 2 or 3 exceptions, among whom are Mr. O and the Belgian. These tables are crowded by young men who either cannot or will not get partners or an opposite couple and who bet largely on those who play. Thousands are thus lost & won every night! When we lived here before, there were a few rational people, who visited us in a social, friendly way, but now Mr. H and

I sit every night entirely alone, almost devoured by mosquitos till the longed for hour of ten gives us an apology to go to bed, where if we cannot sleep we are at least secured by the curtains from these pests. I have never since I lived in Brazil led so forlorn, so solitary, so comfortless a life as now, and Mr. H is of the same opinion.

POLITENESS OF BRAZILIANS, MARCH 16, 1836

I have often had occasion to observe the civility of this oppressed class of human beings since I have been in this Country, many instances showing they have the milk of human kindness circulating as freely if under a white skin. Indeed, the Brazillians themselves are very civil and obliging to strangers. I have frequently been out till quite dark, without a gentlemen or servant, in the street called Catete, much frequented by the lower orders, as well as gentlemen returning to their homes from the City, and have never received even a look of insult or disrespect, even when so dark as to make it doubtful whether I was old or young, which no female of any age could do in our Cities in the US without being alarmed by impertinence.

EMPEROR DOM PEDRO'S BIRTHDAY, DECEMBER 21, 1837

The Emperor's birth day, 12 years old. Waked by the firing of the Cannon at day light. Went in to see Eliza after breakfast as Mr. B tells me she is not well. Returned to dress to go with Mr. & Mrs. Gardner to the Palace to see the splendid, new carriages. Called for the Keemlies. I ordered dinner early as the Royal party were to leave the Palace at 3 o'clock to hold a Court in the City. The troops were drawn up in front of the Palace and shouted, joined by the assembled pedestrians," viva Don Pedro segundo, viva the constitution, viva the Brazillian nation or people," at which the little Emperor and his sister appeared at the open window of the veranda. We drew up close to the steps to see them come down and get into the carriages used for the first time. I stood so near them that I ventured to put my hand on the shoulder of the youngest. Into the first carriage the Emperor and 2 or 3 old Marquises and his Tutor entered first, having the girls or Princesses on the steps wait for theirs to draw up so that we had a good chance to examine them. They are fair, light haired girls, fat and rather well formed, dresses in blond lace over satin, diamonds and pearl necklaces and other ornaments. Three elderly ladies got into the carriage with them, each carriage drawn by 8 horses. Then one with 6 horses drew up into which 4 maids of honour were seated, the greatest frights as to person and dress I ever beheld. The most common women in the UStates would have excelled them in good looks and grace of motion and appearance. We then got leave to go through the Palace and were much amused and interested. I saw more of it than my first visit.

EMPEROR DON PEDRO II'S MARRIAGE TO PRINCESS TERESA CHRISTINA OF NAPLES, JULY 31, 1842

News arrived a few days ago of the marriage of our boy Emperor with a Neapolitan Princess by proxy. It is said he is quite delighted at the new proof of his consequence. Her portrait has been received by the Palace which is handsome. She is 20 years of age, three years his senior. Poor girl, I pity her destiny to live among these stupid Brazillians.

LIFE IN MONTEVIDEO DURING A CIVIL WAR, NOVEMBER 20, 1842

Clear but cold again. Two large flags are waving from the President's mansion near us. Guns are firing and every countenance has a smile of triumph over the tyrant Rosas defeat. The last news from B Ayres was that a Man and his wife walking in the day time were both murdered as Savage Unitarians, that the cry thro the streets now is...death to the English, death to the mediators (French & English)...after dinner Mr. G walked with us to the English burial ground, a very pretty place. The first trees & shrubbery I have seen here. The walks are covered with burnt bones as ours are with gravel... there were seats under trees where we sat to rest. Outside the gate is a rude amphitheater where the bull fights are held. It was crowded with the lower order of the populace and their shouting was a most unpleasant interruption to the feelings that might be excited by the place we are reposing in.

THE WOMEN OF MONTEVIDEO, DECEMBER 9, 1842

As this [is] warm weather all the female population exhibit themselves there in ball costume in all the brilliantly lighted shops, in crowding the sidewalks, while men who go to gaze and make assignations stand in groups at the doors or follow on behind----old women with arms and necks exposed with a troop of daughters, nieces, and cousins, little girls of all ages, infants screaming and sleepy in their nurses' arms. To me, it is a disgustful and painful sight, and no wonder the women in these countries are uneducated & vicious, they are never attended by husbands, Fathers, or brothers those natural guardians to female character. They are round the gaming table while their wives, daughters & sisters are thus exhibiting themselves to the courted gaze of every vulgar libertine. In all this crowd I did not meet one who in the UStates would be thought even pretty, tho this was my object in going out, having heard such eulogies of the exquisite beauty & grace of the Spanish women of the River Plata.

CONDITIONS IN MONTEVIDEO DURING THE CIVIL WAR BETWEEN THE WHITES AND REDS, SEPTEMBER 26, 1844

It is distressing to see what suffering there is among the poor. Our door is beset with starved beggars constantly. Took a walk after dinner to the lines and a little beyond. Mr. Blair, Greenway, and we three women were implored by many to give something to buy bread with. Even the soldiers on duty here have no animal food, nothing but rice & farina. As we passed through the market, we heard a man at one of the stalls crying cats for sale, and it is said the number of dogs that used to fill the streets are diminished by being used for food. There are continual skirmishes with the outside party, and we saw soldiers carrying a wounded man on a cot to the hospital, which is a scene of dreadful suffering from hunger as well as wounds.

JUAN MANUEL DE ROSAS
TUESDAY, OCTOBER 11, 1842

Mr. Greenway says that by the last packet from B Ayres Rosas, the Governor's portrait was again put up in one of the churches for adoration. This seems more horrid to me than even the butcheries he has caused. The watchman when they give the hour of the night there add " death to the savage Unitarians" and all the old Spaniards and men of character and education and all who oppose the course Rosas has pursued of murder, confiscation, and extermination, all who are even suspected by not acting with him in his cruelties are under this class.

THURSDAY, MARCH 30, 1848

This is Rosas' birth day; a salute has been fired at the Cerrito and there is to be a ball there this evening. I hear the US Brig *Perry* goes to the *Busco*,that the officers are to attend it, so Moss told G, which I was sorry to hear. The birth day of such a Monster should be kept with great humiliation that such a scourge to humanity has been allowed to prosper for even a time. About walking time, G went into Mosses' to see a letter Moss got today from our Minister, Mr. Harris, at BAyres which say he has seen all the correspondence between the Mediators & Rosas and there will be no peace; that Rosas will not listen to anyone of their propositions; and a paper of Rosas of the 28th asserts that unless the English and French Govt agree to give up the Falkland Islands and 20 million pounds sterling as an indemnity for this war, which they have protracted by their interference, he will not treat with them.

ARRIVAL IN THE UNITED STATES, DECEMBER 28, 1848

But what a relief to feel that, as I must come, the long dreaded sea voyage is accomplished, but how I do regret the climate and the health of beautiful Rio. I could shed a deluge of tears when I think of its varied beauties, its familiar scenes, and to think I shall never, never see & enjoy them again. I dream I am there walking about with Roberto behind me as of yore. I awake with a pang when I think where I am and what is yet in store for me! I have in prospect a cold, inhospitable clime, cholera, steam & railroad disasters, and if G leaves me to take my precious

Kate to her resting place in his native soil, I shall indeed feel forlorn.

Ida Pfeiffer, Library of Congress

Ida Pfeiffer

A World Traveler in Mexico, Peru, and Ecuador

IDA L. PFEIFFER, WHOSE VOYAGES around the world resulted in two books that were popular with nineteenth-century readers, was born in Vienna, Austria, in 1797. Growing up, she engaged in outdoor activities that strengthened her, unbeknownst to her at that time, for her subsequent life of travel all over the world. At age twenty-two, she married Mark A. Pfeiffer, a prominent lawyer some years her senior. The couple had two sons, but the marriage was not a happy one, and in 1835 the couple separated. Ida came into a small inheritance when her mother died in 1831, and once she was free of family obligations, her two sons settled, and after her husband's death in 1838, she set off to see the world, oftentimes traveling alone, which was not considered proper for a woman, or safe.

Ida first traveled to the Holy Land, Egypt, and Italy and published a book, *Visit to the Holy Land, Egypt, and Italy*, about her travels in 1846. She next went to Iceland, Sweden, and Norway that resulted in another published work, *Journey to Iceland, and Travels in Sweden and Norway*. Determined to go around the world, she left Germany with

Count Berchtold, bound for Rio de Janeiro, Brazil, in June 1846—the first of many countries she planned to visit. Ida arrived in Brazil after a voyage of two and a half months. She explored Rio de Janeiro and visited the Corcovado Mountain; the emperor's palaces; and Petropolis, the summer vacation destination of royalty. Determined to see the Puri Indians, she traveled by mule deep into the interior with a native guide, staying in lonely houses and occasionally in a *fazenda*.

After five months in Brazil, she left Rio for Valparaiso, Chile, sailing around Cape Horn and through the Straits of Magellan in December 1846. Her time in Valparaiso was brief, as she departed for China after two weeks in the city, but while there, she explored the city. Ida was a keen observer of people, institutions, customs, and the natural world, and commented both favorably and unfavorably on what she saw. She held strong opinions, and these are reflected in her writings.

China, India, the Middle East, and Russia beckoned next. Her travels there resulted in a best seller, *A Lady's Voyage Round the World.* Published in 1848, the book made her famous, and she was offered free transportation from railroad and steamship companies. In 1851, she started out for Singapore, Borneo, and the Dutch East Indies. On her way home, she stopped in South America, where she visited California, Mexico, Panama, Peru, and Ecuador. She stopped at Acapulco, Panama City, Lima, Guayaquil, and then made a hazardous trip across the Andes to Quito, Ecuador. She commented on the Spanish, Indians, and slaves, their dwellings and dress, the scenery, her accommodations, religious practices, the climate, and the problems she faced as a woman traveling alone. She returned home after an absence of four years to write her second book, *A Lady's Second Journey Around the World*, in 1855, which soon became another best seller. Her last trip was to Madagascar, where she contracted a tropical disease that lead to her death in 1858 in Vienna.

Ida's travels brought home to her readers the lives and customs of peoples and the topography of faraway places that they never would see. An intrepid traveler in an age when women did not venture out alone, she dared to defy convention and pursued her journeys. Honors came her way when she was elected to the geographical societies of Berlin and Paris, but not that of England because she was a woman.

The selections here are from the four countries that she visited on her second journey to South America.

ACAPULCO, MEXICO

December 23rd. I have set foot for the first, and probably also for the last time, on Mexican soil.

The small town of Acapulco lies on hilly ground, in a corner of the bay, so hidden, that it is hardly to be seen at all; and the fort is enthroned on a majestic promontory, that throws itself far into the sea. The town contains only 1500 inhabitants, and has a very poor appearance; the houses are of unburnt brick, wood, or clay; only one story high, and with windows strongly barred. The interior is pleasanter than one might expect, as the rooms are lofty and airy, and furnished towards the court with verandahs, where the people take their meals, and pass the greater part of the day.

Near the square, which serves as a market-place, and which is disfigured by many little booths, is a handsome Catholic Church, built of unburnt brick; a rather favorite material seemingly with the Spaniards, as all their buildings in California are constructed with it.

The whole place has a ruinous look, for in the last year, on the 4th of December, an earthquake took place by which most of the buildings were more or less damaged, and some of them thrown quite down. Fortunately it happened at nine o'clock in the evening, when everybody was up and ready for immediate flight.

Acapulco is celebrated for the pearls which are found on some islands lying twenty or thirty miles off. The fishery is carried on in a very simple manner, by men who dive seventy or eighty feet deep into the sea, taking with them knives to loosen the pearl-oysters from the rock, and baskets to put them in, and after remaining below one or two minutes, they come to the surface again, with or without booty. The chief danger of the pearl-fishers is from sharks, which swam round the coast, but which the fishers are very dexterous in escaping from. They always take with them a long rounded piece of wood, which, when they cannot get away by swimming or diving, they stick into the open jaws of the monster as he comes toward them; and they have plenty of time to escape before he can recover from this peculiar kind of locked-jaw.

The inhabitants of Acapulco are of very mixed origin, proceeding from the ancient race mingled with the Negro and Spanish, by which the country was conquered three hundred years ago; and according to the predominance of the blood of one or the other people is the variation of every shade of black, brown, and white.

PANAMA

December 28th. Panama is the chief town and largest harbor of the district of the same name in the republic of New Granada, which contains more than two million inhabitants, and has its capital, Bogota, in the interior. The country round is very beautiful; rocks and islands, amongst which are Taboga and Taboquilla, rise out of the water, and a chain of hills, of not more than 500 feet high, runs down to the sea-shore. The great mountain chain of Mexico and New Granada, which is seen at a distance, has here sunk considerably.

The town with the suburbs, and the immediate environs, contain nearly 10,000 persons. It has important fortifications, furnished on the sea side with half a dozen guns and some mortars. It has three squares, the largest of which is spacious and very clean; a cathedral with a handsome façade; and a most agreeable impression was made on me, by not seeing old clothes, shirts, hats and shoes, dead dogs, cats and rats, etc. lying about the streets.

Of churches and chapels there is no lack, for this small towns has more than a dozen in use, besides many other lying in ruins. If religion and virtue went on increasing in the same ratio as churches and priests, the people of Panama would certainly be exemplary; but unluckily it sometimes seems as if one must calculate them rather in the inverse proportion.

The population of Panama is of the same mixed race—Indian, old Spanish, and Negro—as the inhabitants of Acapulco; but among these mongrels are some very handsome people, with remarkably fine eyes, hair, and teeth. Their hands and feet are also admired for their smallness; but, as among the Malays, the rounded form is wanting, the fingers are too long, and the bones too much.

Since there has been so great a concourse of passengers across the Isthmus these people need want for nothing, if they were only ever so little industrious; but many of them much prefer poverty and filth to work. They live chiefly on rice and fruit, though they like beef and pork when they can get it without earning it. A great deal of dried beef is brought from Buenos Ayres in long narrow strips, and sold by the ell.

Among the short excursions round Panama I found a walk to the mountain Aneon best worth the trouble. You can get to its summit with perfect convenience in an hour and a half; and, when there, you find a prospect that you might sit and gaze at for hours without tiring. You look over the whole town, a part of which juts out far into the sea. Behind this extends a large, richly luxuriant valley, watered by a river; but still, alas! mostly covered by forest. On one side lies the wide ocean, with its numerous islands and inlets; and on the other rise ranges of hills and mountains, and enclose the beautiful picture like its frame. Unfortunately, Panama is not healthy; the climate is very hot, and strangers are continually attacked by the malignant fever of the country, which, in many instances, proves fatal. The cause of this unhealthiness is said to be in the uncultivated state of the land; and that beautiful and richly luxuriant valley is principally a morass.

WOMEN OF LIMA, PERU

I never in my life saw women of the lower classes so richly and extravagantly dressed as here. You meet milk and fruit women riding their asses to market, and with their goods before them, in silk dresses, Chinese shawls, silk stocking, and embroidered shoes, all of staring colours; but most of the finery more or less ragged, and hanging half off. I did not think it at all became their yellow or dark brown faces; and they often reminded me of Sancho Panza's remark concerning his lady, who, as queen of the "undiscovered islands," he says, will look like " a pig with a gold necklace."

THE LLAMA

The llama is much better used. It is made to work, indeed, as a beast of burden, but it is gently and tenderly treated; and one might almost say that the Peruvians have a respect for this animal. It is of the camel species, by its long neck; and from the foot to the top of the head is about five feet high. Four species of llamas are known: the *llama proper*, the *alpaco,* the *vicuna,* and the *guanaco*; but the llamas only are used as beasts of burden, as they are far more serviceable in the bad roads of the Cordilleras than asses or mules, and are employed to bring down the ore from the mountains. A llama will go from three to four leagues in a day, and carry a hundred pounds; but if anything more is put upon him, he will lie down, and not stir till the extra weight is taken off.

These beautiful gentle animals are not often seen in the city of Lima; for they cannot well bear the heat; but while I was there there chanced to come a troop of forty or fifty of them, to fetch salt to carry to the mountains. I grieve to state, that these pretty creatures, when they are angry, have a nasty trick of spitting about them; and the saliva is so sharp and acrid, that it causes a burning pain when it falls on the skin.

ROBBERY IN LIMA

One very unpleasant thing in Lima is the great insecurity, and the frequency of robbery. After six o'clock in the afternoon, when it is scarcely dark, it is thought imprudent to venture outside the gates, or on the Alameda or any other little frequented spot alone; even if you are on horseback you will be very likely to be attacked. In burglaries the thieves do not merely let themselves in at doors and windows, but climb up to the terraced roof, which is mostly of very slight materials, make an opening in it, and let themselves down into the room.

A few years ago these affairs were carried on on a still grander scale; and bands of thirty or forty men, frequently on horseback, would come in the evening to a house that did not happen to be in the most busy part of town, and, leaving the half of their number outside to keep watch, burst in, fasten the door, and politely request the inhabitants not to disturb themselves, but merely to give them their keys, and they would find what they wanted for themselves. Before the guards outside had attracted the attention of the neighbours or passers by, and a sufficiently strong armed force could be brought against them, the birds were flown with their booty.

THE JOURNEY IN ECUADOR BEGINS

I arrived at Guayaquil, unluckily, during the rainy season, which begins in December, and lasts till May, and is of course the most unfavorable for travelling into the interior. I was told that the roads were so bad, that all communication, except for the post, was interrupted, and that even the bearers of the mail had the greatest difficulty to get along, and were frequently obliged to climb up in trees, and scramble from bough to bough, in order to pass places where the morass was unfathomable. I thought it probable, however, that there was a good deal of exaggeration in this, and believing that I had as much strength and perseverance as the letter-carriers, and that if they could get through so could I, I set about my preparations for the journey. Three weeks, nevertheless, I was compelled to delay setting out, for I had another attack of Sumatra fever.

During my stay the anniversary of the declaration of independence, the 6th of March, arrived, and was celebrated in the morning by high mass in the churches, and in the evening by an illumination of the town. A most deplorable attempt at an illumination it was though; nothing more than here and there a few candles glimmering in a window; but the same childish proceeding was repeated, nevertheless, on the next evening. From this celebration slavery was to be abolished; although, according to the arrangement made at the declaration of independence, it should have lasted ten years longer.

ON TO QUITO

On the 22nd of March I and the letter-carrier set off together in a small boat for the little town of Botegas. People had tried to persuade me to take a servant with me, especially as I was not acquainted with the Spanish language; telling me that during this rainy season, when all intercourse between different places was interrupted, the tambos (little mountain inns) were uninhabited, as their occupants went down for the time into the plains; and that I should not be able to get so much as fuel or a draught of water. In spite of my objection to people of this sort, I allowed myself to be persuaded, and the result showed that I had been quite wrong not to remain firm in my first resolution.

In Botegas one person to whom I had a letter defrauded me, as I have said, in the matter of the saddle; the other, in whose house I stayed, gave me only a mat to sleep on, though everybody else in the house had a bed under a mosquito-net; and then allowed me to depart in the morning, though it was nine o'clock, without offering me anything to eat.

March 26th. Torje, six leagues. This day we got a more correct idea of the roads of this country during the rainy season, and were not at all surprised that people are unwilling to travel at this time—indeed never do, unless summoned by the most important business. We had to go much up hill, and the ground was so slippery and sticky that the cattle slipped all sorts of ways, from hole to hole, and from puddle to puddle; and it was well when they could find the bottom at all, and struggle out again, for very frequently they went in so deep it was necessary to dismount, take off their loads, and pull them out. Precisely at the very worst place we had to go on foot. I could scarcely get on at all, but slipped and fell almost at every step; I called to my servant for help, but I was only a woman, and unfortunately his mule was already paid for; so he quietly went on his way, and left me to my fate. Fortunately, one of the arrieros, an Indian, took compassion on me, dragged me out of the pool, and helped me on; but to every league we took two full hours.

Many deep rushing torrents crossed our path, though in summer there is scarcely water enough to cover the bed of the river. The country was very fine, and we had splendid glimpses of valleys traversed by hills and embosomed in mountains, the first range of the Cordilleras.

CROSSING THE ANDES

The 30th of March was one of the most remarkable days of my life, for on this day I crossed the grand Cordillera of the Andes, and that at one of its most interesting points, the Chimborazo. When I was young this was supposed to be the highest mountain in the world; but the discovery since then of some points in the Himalaya, which far exceed its height of 21,000 feet, has thrown it into the second class.

We set off at a very early hour in the morning, for we had eleven leagues, mostly over dreadful roads, and on a constant steep ascent, before us. For this distance there was no kind of shelter in which to pass the night.

At first it was really terrible. I was compelled as before to dismount at the worst places; and the sharp mountain air had begun to affect my chest severely. I was oppressed by a feeling of terror and anxiety, my breath failed me, my limbs trembled, and I dreaded every moment that I should sink down utterly exhausted; but the word was still "forwards," and forwards I went, dragging myself painfully over rocks, through torrents and morasses, and into and out of holes filled with mire. Had I been at the top of the Chimborazo, I should have ascribed the painful sensations I experienced to the great rarefaction of the air, since it frequently produces symptoms of the kind; indeed the feeling is so common as to have had a name given to it. It is called "veta," and lasts with some people only a few days, but with others, if they remain in the high regions, as many weeks.

After the first two leagues the way became more rocky and stony, and I could at least keep my seat on my mule. We had continual torrents of rain, and now and then a fall of snow, which mostly melted, however, as soon as it touched the ground, though it remained lying in some few places, so that I may say I travelled over the snow; but the clouds and mists never parted for a single moment, and I got no sight of the top of Chimbarazo,--a thing that I grieved at much more than at my bodily sufferings.

QUITO, ECUADOR

Quito lies in an elevated plain, fine and extensive certainly, but by no means equal to that Latacunga nor surrounded by such giant mountains. You do not see the towns till you come within two leagues of it, and then the sight has nothing in it at all imposing. The houses are low, and covered with sloping tiled roofs, and neither domes nor towers break their uniform monotony.

The immediate environs of the city certainly show fields and meadows, but neither gardens nor fruit trees; the houses in the suburbs are small, half-decayed, and beyond all description dirty; the streets are full of puddles and filth, and grievously offensive to one's olfactory organs; the people clothed, if you may call it so, in the most disgusting rags.

They not only stared, but laughed and pointed with their fingers at me as I came along, and sometimes ran after me, for strangers are rare in this forgotten country; and, if they were not dressed exactly like the natives, as I was not (for, although I had the poncho, I had not the little straw hat), they become objects of mockery to the populace. Nearer to the Plaza the houses improve a little in appearance; they are of one story, and instead of windows have glass doors into the balconies. The square itself has some handsome buildings; amongst which are the Cathedral and the palaces of the bishop and the President; both of which have their facade adorned with rows of columns. Unfortunately the President's palace is half in ruins, especially the flights of steps in the front; but at least it is not disfigured, like that in Lima, by having little shabby booths stuck against it. The square is ornamented with a fountain, though unluckily the fountain has the trifling defect of having no water.

In the city of Quito, which is said to contain 50,000 inhabitants, there is not a single inn; and, though I had several letters of introduction, I had only one ready at hand, as the others were locked up in my trunk, and that again packed in waxed cloth.

THE WOMEN OF QUITO

The ladies appear amiable, but very ignorant; which may be in some measure attributable to the out-of-the-way situation of their city; for it is very seldom indeed that a good teacher can be procured there, or that a stray artist or man of learning comes wandering that way. The good people scarcely hear of such a thing as art, science, or literature; and I do not suppose a Quito lady ever by any chance takes up any book but a devotional one. In native talent and capacity they are said, like the ladies of Peru, greatly to excel their masculine companions. They take part in all kinds of business, and especially in politics, in which they seem far more interested than the men; and it is to be observed, that the women and girls are punished for political offenses just as much as men, and often imprisoned for months or even years in convents. I became acquainted here with a young and interesting woman, the daughter-in-law of General Algierro, who was sentenced to a year's imprisonment, but managed to keep herself concealed till the matter was pretty well forgotten, and so escaped.

THE CHURCHES OF QUITO

The churches are the only things worth seeing in Quito, and amongst these that of the Jesuits, the Franciscans, the Dominicans, and the Cathedral are the most distinguished. They are in the same style as St Augustin's Church at Lima, richly decorated and gilt from the roof to the floor, with beautiful wood carvings, the statues only excepted, which are real caricatures, although I have heard frequent mention of the fine sculptures to be found in Quito. The high altars and pillars round the tabernacle are covered with plates of silver; and there are other churches which, though smaller, are no less costly in their adornments.

THE INDIANS

In Ecuador, the lot of the Indians, of those who are really the legitimate possessors of the soil, is peculiarly melancholy. It might be supposed that this State was in advance of others, since, as I have already mentioned, during my stay in Guayaquil, slavery was entirely abolished; and the phrase "perfect freedom" doubtless sounds very well, but to the Indians there it is a mere empty word. Their situation is worse than slavery; for they have not one, but many masters, and yet no one of whom is bound to feed and clothe them, and the only advantage they obtain from what is called their emancipation is, that they must provide for their own wants. Every male Indian also must pay a poll-tax of three dollars a year, beginning when he is seventeen years old, and continuing till he is fifty; a tax from which the old Spaniards, whether peasant or not, are entirely free. A money-tax even of this amount is extremely oppressive on those who have no property at all, and in a country whose position, surrounded as it is by high mountains, and with roads all but impassable, renders it excessively difficult to earn any in the way of trade.

The Ecuadorians maintain indeed that, with the exception of this tax, the Indians possess the same rights as the rest of the community, as they are capable of holding land, that is to say, if they can get it; but why should they desire to have land that they have no means of cultivating, and when they cannot maintain themselves to the next harvest? Their usual plan is to hire themselves out as labourers to the owners of the haciendas, who give them a small piece of ground, as well as what is needful for its culture, and then pay their tax—keeping of course a strict account—in returns for their services. The Indians generally get also provisions, clothing, and brandy from their master, frequently in advance, so that they are never out of his debt, and cannot leave him, otherwise there is nothing to prevent their doing so; but it must be added that, if they die, their debt dies with them, as the master has no claim on the family.

The Indians are exempt from military service; but they are obliged when troops are on the march to carry provisions and baggage on their backs without receiving any compensation but abuse and blows. If one of these free Indians chances to pass by a barrack in which the service of some labourer is at the moment required, a soldier will rush out, and snatch his straw hat from his head, as a sign that he is wanted. If he does not obey willingly, he is soon compelled to do so by violence; a brutal outrage so common, that I myself witnessed it several times during my short stay in Quito. They are despised not only by the old Spaniards, but by the mere mongrel races; and even the negroes consider the Indians as far beneath themselves, and treat them accordingly; yet they are actually the best and most upright of the inhabitants of the country.

THE ROAD BACK: A NEAR DEATH EXPERIENCE

The road from Guaranda to Savonetto was still more dangerous than when I had come, as we had now to make a rapid descent. The animals slipped and stumbled at almost every step, and continually fell into holes, of which the road was full. Just as I was on a very steep declivity, down went my mule into one of these; and my saddle-girth breaking at the same moment, I was flung, saddle and all, right over his head. My amiable companion the arriero burst out laughing, and appeared to enjoy it amazingly, and fortunately I suffered no serious damage.

My greatest peril, however, was on the river Guaya. From Savonetto to Guayaquil, a three days' journey, I had to go in a small boat; and during the voyage, happening to step incautiously on the side, I slipped and fell into the river, which, by the way, is full of caymans.

I was not excessively terrified, as, though I cannot swim, I thought it likely the boatmen could, and did not doubt they would save me. This was my instantaneous thought;

and after this I was conscious of rising twice to the surface, so that they must have seen me. The caymans I had forgotten. When I rose the first time, I looked vainly around for help. I could see the boat, and also that no one in it stirred, and then I sank again. Now, indeed, I felt terror, but, luckily, did not lose my senses; and remembering to have heard that in such case you ought to put out your hands before you and use them as oars, I did so as far as my strength permitted. I was beyond all human help; but behold! When I rose for the second time, I found myself quite close to the boat, and had only to cling to it. The boatmen contemplated me, indeed, with the most perfect tranquility, and no one put out so much as a hand or even an oar to help me; but, fortunately, one of the fellow-passengers, an Indian, took compassion on me, and assisted me into the boat; and I was saved.

Julia Ward Howe, Library of Congress

Julia Ward Howe

A Social Reformer in Cuba

Julia Ward Howe was born on May 17, 1819, in New York City to Samuel Ward, a wealthy banker, and Julia Rush Ward. Julia had a privileged childhood, with exposure to the arts and culture. She was privately educated by governesses and, as a result, was well read and became proficient in French, German, and Greek. Her mother died when she was five, and at age nine she attended school. In 1841, she met Samuel Gridley Howe, MD, a graduate of Brown University and Harvard Medical School, who was founder and head of the Perkins Institute for the Blind in Boston, and an ardent social reformer and abolitionist. Howe was some eighteen years her senior. The couple married in 1843 and honeymooned in England and Italy for a year, where Julia had her first child of six, a daughter, Julia. The couple returned to Boston, where they lived in the Perkins Institute. Julia was unhappy living with the inmates, and she thought Boston society was unfriendly. The marriage was not a happy one, as Howe wanted a submissive and dependent wife who he could dominate, and he was opposed to Julia pursuing her literary interests and reform work. Her home and family—not literary ambitions—he determined should be her main interests. Howe was a workaholic and did not give Julia the sympathy and affection she craved. They both contemplated divorce at times, but instead, in 1850 she took the children to Rome for a year, where she had the freedom to write poetry, travel sketches, and plays. In 1853, she published a book of poems entitled *Passion Flowers.*

In March 1859, the Howes went to Cuba with their friends, the abolitionist and Unitarian minister Theodore Parker and his wife, Lydia, on a winter vacation that resulted in her book entitled *A Trip to Cuba,* published in 1860. Cuba, just ninety miles off the Florida coast, was a Spanish colony, known as the pearl of the Antilles. Sugar was the main agricultural export crop on the island, and slaves provided the labor force that harvested it. Slaves, however, were restive over harsh working conditions, and revolts occurred during the first half of the nineteenth century. The Creole elite resented Spanish policy that hampered economic and political development, and were open to ending Spanish rule. By 1860, discontent was simmering below the surface, which resulted in the unsuccessful War of 1868 for Cuban independence.

Julia was open to exploring all aspects of Cuban life, and she described what she saw in a carefree and amusing vein. She commented on slavery in Cuba, as she was an abolitionist; the cities and towns that she visited; Cuban customs and entertainments; civic institutions; education; religion; carnivals; Cuban women; the Cuban Creoles; the Spaniards; visits to a coffee and sugar plantation; and the climate. While she supported the abolition of slavery in Cuba—albeit gradually—she did not champion racial equality, and her portrayal of Cuban Blacks was mixed and, at times, negative. A woman of her time, her views on gradual emancipation resulted in criticism from William Lloyd Garrison, founder of the antislavery newspaper *The Liberator* in Boston.

In 1861, Julia and her husband traveled to Washington, DC, where Howe, as a member of the Sanitary Commission, delivered supplies to Massachusetts troops stationed there. Julia visited the military camp, and while staying at the Willard Hotel she was inspired to write the words to "The Battle Hymn of the Republic" that was sung to the tune of "John Brown's Body." The song became the rallying cry of the Union forces. As a result of the publication of the lyrics in *The Atlantic Monthly* in 1862, Julia became famous and emerged from under the control of her husband.

In 1868, as a result of her fame, Julia asserted her independence and pursued her reform work and her writing. She became a prominent national figure in the suffragette and peace movements. She devoted the rest of her life to these causes and to improving educational and employment opportunities for women. Julia founded the *Woman's Journal*, a suffragette magazine, and the General Federation of Women's Clubs. She was president of the Massachusetts Woman Suffrage Association, the New England Woman Suffrage Association, and the Association for the Advancement of Women. With Lucy Stone, she was a leader in the National Suffrage Association and cofounder of the American Woman Suffrage Association. She traveled the country championing these causes, gave speeches, delivered sermons, and wrote articles to support her views. She was also involved in the peace movement and served as president of the American affiliate of the Women's International Peace Association. Her association with likeminded women over the years gave her the support she did not have in her home life and energized her. In 1876, Samuel Gridley Howe died.

Julia continued her literary interests while she pursued her reform activities. She is best known for her biography of Margaret Fuller, a collection of essays entitled *Modern Society, Women's Work in America, Reminiscences, From the Oak to the Olive, Is Polite Society Polite?*, and *The Hermaphrodite*, as well as five books of poems. She was the first woman elected to the American Academy of Arts and Letters, and received three honorary degrees. She died on October 17, 1910, at Oak Glen, her summer retreat in Portsmouth, Rhode Island, and was buried in Mount

Auburn Cemetery in Cambridge, Massachusetts. Her children wrote and published her biography in 1916, which won the Pulitzer Prize for biography that year.

The excerpts published here are from *A Trip to Cuba.*

VISIT TO A SUGAR PLANTATION

We take the Sunday to visit the nearest Sugar-plantation, belonging to Don Jacinto Gonzales. Sun, not shade, being the desideratum in sugar-planting, there are few trees or shrubs bordering the sugar-fields, which resemble at a distance our own fields of Indian corn, the green of the leaves being lighter, and a pale blue blossom appearing here and there. The points of interest here are the machinery, the negroes and the work. Entering the sugar-house, we find the *Maquinista* (engineer) superintending some repairs in the machinery, aided by another white man, a Cooly, and an imp of a black boy, who begged of all the party, and revenged himself with clever impertinence on whose who refused him. The *Maquinista* was a fine looking man from the Pyrenees, very kind and obliging. He told us that Don Jacinto was very old, and came rarely to the plantation. We asked how the extreme heat of his occupation suited him, and for an answer he opened the bosom of his shirt, and showed us the streaks of innumerable leeches. The machinery is not very complicated. It consists of a wheel and band, to throw the canes under the powerful rollers which crush them, and these rollers, three in number, all moved the steam-engine. The juice flows into copper cauldrons, where it is boiled and skimmed. As they were not at work, we did not see the actual process.

Leaving the sugar-house, we went in pursuit of the *Mayoral,* or Overseer, who seemed to inhabit comfortable quarters, in a long, low house, shielded from the sun by a thick screen of matting. We found him a powerful, thick-set man, of surly and uncivil manners, girded with a sword, and further armed with a pistol, a dagger, and a stout whip. He was much too important a person to waste his words upon us, but signified that the mayor-domo would wait on us, which he presently did. We now entered the Negro quarter, a solid range of low buildings, formed around a hollow square, whose strong entrance is closed at nightfall, and its inmates kept in strict confinement till the morning hour of work comes round. Just within the doorway we encountered the trader, who visits the plantation every Sunday, to tempt the stray cash of the negroes by various commodities, of which the chief seemed to be white bread, calicoes, muslins, and bright cotton handkerchiefs. He told us that their usual weekly expenditure amounted to about twenty-five dollars. Bargaining with him stood the Negro-Driver, a tattooed African, armed with a whip. All within the court swarmed the black bees of the hive, the men with little clothing, the small children naked, the women decent. All had their little charcoal fires, with pots boiling over them; the rooms within looked dismally dark, close, and dirty; there are no windows, no air and light save through the ever-open door. The beds are sometimes partitioned off by a screen of dried palm-leaf, but I saw no better sleeping-privilege than a board with a blanket or coverlet. From this we turned to the Nursery, where all the children incapable of work are kept. The babies are quite naked, and sometimes very handsome in their way, black and shining, with bright eyes and well-formed limbs. No greater provision is made for their amusement, but the little girls nurse them tenderly enough, and now and then the elders fling them a bit of orange or *chaimito,* for which they scramble like so many monkeys. Appeals are constantly made to the pockets of visitors, by open hands stretched out in all direction. To these "*Nada*" "Nothing" is the safe reply; for if you give to one, the others close about you with frantic gesticulation, and you have to break your way through them with some violence, which hurts your own feelings more than it does theirs. On strict plantations this is not allowed; but Don Jacinto, like Lord Ashburton at the time of the Maine treaty, is an old man, a very old man; and where discipline cannot be maintained, peace must be secured on any terms.

We visit next the Sugar-house, where we find the desired condiment in various stages of color and refinement. It is whitened with clay in large funnel-shaped vessels, open at the bottom to allow the molasses to run off. Above are hogsheads of coarse dark sugar; below is a huge pit of fermenting molasses, in which rats and small negroes occasionally commit involuntary suicide, and from which rum is made. N.B. rum is not a wicked word in Cuba; in Boston everybody is shocked when it is named, and in Cuba nobody is shocked when it is drunk.

And here ended the description of our visit to the sugar-plantation of Don Jacinto, and in good time, too-- for by this it has grown so hot, that we made a feeble rush for the *volante,* and lay back in it panting of breath.

Encountering a negress with a load of oranges on her head, we bought and ate the fruit with eagerness, though the oranges were bitter.

MATANZAS ON SUNDAY

The second thing to be done in Matanzas, if you arrive on Saturday, is to attend military mass at the Cathedral on Sunday morning. This commences at eight o'clock; but the hour previous may be advantageously employed in watching the arrival and arrangement of the female aristocracy of Matanzas. These enter in groups of twos and threes, carrying their prayer-books, and followed by slaves of either sex, who bear the prayer-carpet of their mistresses. The ladies are wonderfully got up, considering the early hour; and their toilettes suggest that they may not have undressed since the ball the night before. All that hoops, powder, and puffery can do for them has been done; they walk in silk attire, and their hair is what is technically termed dressed. Some of them bring their children, bedizened like dolls, mimicking mamma's gestures and genuflection in a manner more provoking to sadness than to satire. If the dressing is elaborate, the crossing is also. It does not consist of one simple cross, "*in nomine Patris,*" etc; they seem to make three or four crosses from forehead to chin, and conclude by kissing the thumb-nail, in honor of what or whom we could not imagine. Entering the middle aisle, which is divided from the rest by a row of seats on either side, they choose their position, and motion to the dark attendant to spread the carpet. Some of them evince considerable strategic skill in the selection of their ground. All being now in readiness, they drop on their knees, spread their flounces, cross themselves, open their books, and look about them. Their attendants retire a little, spread a handkerchief on the ground, and modestly kneel behind them, obviously expecting to be saved with the family. These are neatly, sometimes handsomely dressed. In this *status* things remain until the music of the regiment is heard. With a martial sound of trumpets it enters the church, and fills the aisles, the officers taking place within the chancel, and a guard of honor of eight soldiers ranging on either side of the officiating priest. And now our devotions begin in good earnest, for, simultaneously with the regiment, the *jeunesse doree* of Matanzas has made its appearance, and has ranged itself along the two long lines of demarcation which separate the fair penitents from the rest of the congregation. The ladies now spread their flounces again, and their eyes find other occupation than the dreary Latin of their missals. There is, so to speak, a lively and refreshing time between the youths of both sexes, while the band plays its utmost, and *Evangel, Kyrie,* and *Oredo* are recited to the music of Trovatore and Traviata. ...The moment comes to elevate the Host, thump goes the drum, the guard presents arms, and the soldiers, instead of kneeling, bend forward, in a most uncomfortable manner. Another thump, and all is over; the swords are returned to their sheaths and soon, the loud music coming to an end, the regiment marches out of church, very much as it marched in its devotional experience being know to Heaven alone. Ladies and lovers look their last, the flounces rise in pyramids, the prayer-carpets are rolled up, and with a silken sweep and rush, Youth, Beauty, and Fashion forsake the church, where Piety has hardly been, and go home to breakfast.

THE EMANCIPATION OF SLAVES

The enfranchisement of a race, where it is lasting, is always accomplished by the slow and solid progress of the race itself. The stronger people rarely gives Freedom to the weaker as a boon, when they are able, they rise up and take it with their own hands. It is an earning, not a gift, nor can the attributes which make liberty virtual and valuable be commanded, save under certain moral conditions. A man is not noble because he is free, but noble men constituting a nation become free. Let the wounds of Africa first be stopped, let her lifeblood stay to enrich her own veins. The enslaved population of Cuba and our own South, must, under ordinary circumstances, attain in time a condition in which Slavery shall be impossible.

BLACK AND WHITE COEXIST

The black and white races are, by all accounts, more mingled in Cuba, than in any part of our own country. People who have long been resident there assure us that some of the wealthiest and most important families are of mixed blood. Animadvert upon this as you will, it is nevertheless certain that it weaves close bonds of affinity between them, and ties of Nature which, though ignored, cannot be unfelt. I have not seen in Cuba anything that corresponds to our ideal separation of the two sets of human beings, living in distinctness one from the other, hating and wronging each other with the fierceness of enemies in the death grapple. The Negro cannot be so hated, so despised, it is not in the nature of things. His *bonhomie,* his gentle and attachable nature do not allow it. Nor can he, in return, so hate.

TREATMENT OF SLAVES

The increase of the slaves, is, of course, an important test of their treatment, it is small throughout the Island, and amounts to little save on the best plantations. There is now a slow improvement in this respect. The repression of the slave trade has caused such a rise in the price of negroes that it is become better economy to preserve and transmit their lives than to work them off in eight or ten years, leaving no posterity to supply their place. Vile as these motives seen, they are too near akin to the general springs of human action for us to contemn them. Is it otherwise with operatives in England, or with laborers in Ireland? Emigration lessens their numbers, and raises their value, it becomes important to society that they shall be fed and sustained. One wrong does not excuse another, but where a class of wrongs is universal, it show a want of moral power in the race, at which the individual cannot justly carp.

HUMANE SLAVE LAWS

The slave laws of Cuba are far more humane than our own. It is only to be doubted whether the magistrates in general are trustworthy in carrying them out. Still, it is the policy of the Government to favor the Negroes, and allow them definite existence as a third class, which would be likely to range with the Government in case of civil war. It is affirmed and believed by the Cubans that the colonial President has in his hands orders to loose the slaves throughout the Island, at the first symptoms of rebellion, that they may turn all their old rancors against their late masters. The humane clauses of which we speak are the following;--

In the first place, every slave is allowed by law to purchase his own freedom, when he has amassed a sum sufficient for the purchase. He can moreover compel his master to receive a small sum in part payment, and then, hiring himself out, can pay the residue from his wages. The law intervenes also, if desired, to fix the price of the slave, which it will reduce to the minimum value. Every slave has the right to purchase his child before birth for the sum of thirty dollars, a fortnight after, for fifty, and so on, the value of course rising rapidly with the age of the child. Again, a slave who complains of ill treatment on the part of his master may demand to be sold to another, and a limited space of time is allowed, during which he can exert himself to find a purchaser. These statutes do not seem to contemplate the perpetuity of slavery as do our own institutions. What a thrill of joy would run through our Southern and South-western states, if every slave father and mother had the power to purchase their own offspring for a sum not all together beyond their reach. How would they toil and starve to accumulate that sum, and how many charitable friends would invest the price of a dress or shawl in such black jewels, which would be the glory of so many black mothers. On the other hand, it is to be feared that the ignorance and poverty of the slaves may, in many places, make the benevolent intention of these statutes null and void. Official corruption, too, may impede their operation. In many parts of our own South, superior enlightenment and a more humane state of public feeling may do something to counterbalance the inferiority of legislation. Still, Americans should feel a pang in acknowledging that even in the dark article of slave laws they are surpassed by a nation which they contemn. Slaves are not sold by public auction, in Cuba, but by private sale. Nor are they subject to such rudeness and insult as they often receive from the lower whites of our own Southern cities. The question now rises, whether in case of a possible future possession of the Island by Americans, the condition of the blacks would be improved. There is little reason to think so, in any case, as our own unmitigated despotism would be enforced;....

CREOLES AND SPANIARDS

Not in such familiarity live the Creoles and Spaniards. Here, the attitudes are sharply defined. Oppression on the one hand and endurance on the other hand appear in a tangible form, and the oppression is conscious, and the endurance compulsory. The Spanish race is in the saddle, and rides the Creole, its derivative, with hands reeking with plunder. Not content with taxes, customs, and prohibitions, all of which pass the bounds of robbery, the Home Government loosed on the Colony a set of Officials, who ae expected to live by peculation, their salaries being almost nominal, their perquisites, whatever they can get. All State-offices are filled by Spaniards, and Judgeships and Professorates ae generally reserved to them. A man receives an appointment of which the salary may be a thousand dollars per annum. He hires at once an expensive house, sets up a *volante*, dresses his wife and daughters without economy, lives in short at ten times that sum, and retires after some years, with a handsome competency. What is the secret of all his? Plunder,--twofold plunder, of the inhabitants, and of the Home Government. And this, from the lowest to the highest, is the universal rule.

TREATMENT OF THE CHINESE

Even the race of Coolies, hired at small wages for eight years and exploited at that time with murderous severity, have found a suicidal remedy that nearly touches their selfish masters. So many of them have emancipated themselves from hard service by voluntary death, that it became matter of necessity to lighten the weight about their necks, and to leave them that minimum of well being which is necessary to keep up the love of life. The instinct itself is shown to be feeble in the race, whereas the Negro clings to life under whatever pains and torment.

FEW CIVIC IMPROVEMENTS

Of the great sums of money received by the Government through direct and indirect taxation, little or nothing revisits the people in the shape of improvements. The

Government does not make roads nor establish schools, nor reform criminals, nor stretch out its strong arm to prevent the offenses of ignorant and depraved youth. The roads, consequently, are few and dangerous, a great part of the Island being traversable only on horseback. There is little or no instruction provided for the children of the poorer classes, and the prisons are abominable with filth, nakedness, and disorder of every kind. There is the same espionage, the same power of arbitrary imprisonment as in Austria, Rome, and Naples, only they have America near them, and in that neighborhood is fear to some, and hope to others. The administration of justice would seem to be one of the worst of all the social plagues that abide in the Island. Nowhere in the world have people a more wholesome terror of going to law. The Government pays for no forms of legal procedure, and a man once engaged in a civil or criminal suit, is at the mercy of Judges and Lawyers who plunder him at will, and without redress. If a man is robbed, the Police come to him at once with offers of assistance and detection. It is often the case that he denies and persists in denying the robbery, rather than be involved in the torment of a suit. Much of what we narrate was common to all the civilized world, a hundred years ago, but the Cubans do not deserve to be held under the weight of these ancient abuses. They are not an effete people, but have something of the spring of the present time in them, and would gladly march to the measure of the nineteenth century, were it not for the decrepit Government whose hand has stiffened with their chains in it.

CUBANS AND SPANIARDS

The Cubans, considered in comparison with the Spaniards, form quite as distinct a people as the American, compared with the English. Climate and the habits of insular life have partly brought about this difference, but it has also a moral cause, a separate interest makes a separate people. The mother-countries that would keep their colonies unweaned must be good nurses. The intermingling of the black element in the Creole race is, as I have said, strongly insisted upon by competent judges, it is evidently not purely Caucasian, and there seems to be little reason for supposing that it perpetuates any aboriginal descent. The complexion, and in some degree the tastes of these people give some color to the hypothesis of their indebtedness to the African race. The prevailing color of the Creole is not the clear olive of the Spaniard, nor the white of the Saxon, it is an indescribable, clouded hue, neither fair nor brown. We have seen children at school who were decidedly dark, and would have been taken for mulattoes in the North, they had straight hair, vivacious eyes, and coffee-colored skins, those whom we interrogated called them "*Criollos*," as if the word had a distinct meaning. We could not ascertain that they considered to be of black descent though the fact seemed patent.

The taste of the Cubans, if judged by the European standard, is bad taste. They love noisy music,their architecture consults only the exigencies of the climate, and does not deserve the name of an art. Of painting they must have little knowledge, if one may judge by the vile daubs which deface their walls, and which would hardly pass current in the poorest New England village. As to dress; although I have whispered for your good, my lady friends, that the most beautiful summer dresses in the world may be bought in Havana, yet the Creole ladies themselves have in general but glaring and barbaric ideas of adornment, and their *volante-toilette* would give a Parisienne the ague.

THE SECLUSION OF WOMEN IN CUBA

Let me here say that a few days in Havana made clear to me the seclusion of the women in the East, and its causes. Wherever the animal vigor of men is so large in proportion to their moral power as in those countries, women must be glad to forego their liberties for the protection of the strong arm. One master is better for them than many. Whatever tyranny may grow out of such barbarous manners, the institution springs from a veritable necessity and an original good intention. The Christian religion should change this, which is justifiable only in a Mohammedan country. But where that religion is so loosely administered as in Cuba, where its teachers themselves frequent the cockpit and the gaming table, one must not look for too much of its power in the manners and morals of men.

They of the lovely sex meanwhile undergo, with what patience they may, an Oriental imprisonment. In the public street they must no account set foot. The Creole and Spanish women ae born and bred to this, and the hardiest American or English woman will scarcely venture out a second time without the severe escort of husband or brother. These relatives are, accordingly, in great demand. In Havana, ... the American woman suddenly becomes very fond of her husband; "he must not leave her at home alone; where does he go? she will go with him; when will he come back? Remember, now she will expect him." The secret of all this is that she cannot go out without him.

Sarah Madeleine Vinton Dahlgren

An Admiral's Wife in Peru

Sarah Madeleine Vinton Dahlgren was an author, an anti-suffragette, and a religious Catholic. She was born in Gallipolis, Ohio, in 1825, the daughter of US Congressman Samuel Finley Vinton. Sarah spent much of her life in Washington, D.C., where she attended the Georgetown Visitation Academy and served as her father's hostess after her mother's death. In 1846, at age twenty-one, she married Daniel Convers Goddard, a lawyer from Ohio and first assistant secretary of the Department of the Interior. The couple had two children, a daughter, Romaine, and a son, Vinton Augustus. Upon Goddard's death in 1851, she turned to writing to help support herself and their children.

Sarah was an educated woman who was proficient in foreign languages, especially Spanish, French, and Italian, and was well educated for her time. At first, her writing consisted of translations of religious tracts, but later she began to write short stories and poems under the pseudonym Corinne and later Cornelia. Her early writings were published under the title "Idealities." In the 1880s, she began to write novels, and then moved on to anti-suffragette works, and a book entitled *The Etiquette of Social Life in Washington* that went through several editions.

She was a prominent society hostess and arbiter of social behavior in the nation's capital.

In 1865, she married Rear Admiral John A. Dahlgren, inventor of the Dahlgren gun and founder of the navy's Ordnance Department. Dahlgren spent fifteen years at the Washington Navy Yard where he developed, tested, researched, and improved naval gunnery. The Dahlgren gun was mounted on Union navy ships and Confederate ships during the Civil War and never misfired. He was appointed commanding officer of the Washington Navy Yard in 1861 and chief of the Bureau of Ordnance in 1863. Dahlgren was a widower with three sons, Ulric, Paul, and Charles. Soon after he married Sarah, he was appointed commanding officer of the South Pacific Squadron on the west coast of South America. The couple had three children together: Ulrica Mary Madeleine, Eric, and John Vinton. When Sarah left for South America in 1867, she brought two of their young children with her.

It was not unusual for naval officers in the United States Navy and Royal Navy to take their wives with them to foreign postings. According to navy regulations, Sarah and her children could not live on her husband's ship. She always had a residence in the port city that the admiral would visit when not on duty. Admiral Dahlgren's flagship, the *Powhatan*, left for the west coast of South America ahead of Sarah. On June 1, 1867, she sailed from New York City on the steamer *Ocean Queen* to Aspinwall, Panama. She was unable to make connections with the steamer on the Pacific coast, as it had left by the time her ship arrived, so she was forced to stay in Panama where yellow fever raged. After a brief time, which she dramatically described, she made her way by railroad to the west coast and boarded USS *Ossipee* for Callao, Peru, where Dahlgren's ship was stationed.

By the time Sarah Dahlgren arrived in Peru, the country had been independent for forty-three years. The Army of the Andes, led by

José de San Martín, with troops from Chile and Argentina, and Simón Bolívar's army of Colombians and Venezuelans, had secured the independence of Peru from the Spanish army in 1824. The Peruvians played no part in the independence struggle. Both San Martín and Bolívar attempted to institute liberal reforms in Peru but to no avail. Bolívar decreed the dissolution of the Indian communal lands that were soon absorbed by the hacendados and put an end to the Indian tribute, only to have it reinstituted when he left in 1826. In the ensuing decades, Peru was ruled by military caudillos, who played an important role in politics, and the nation was rent by civil wars between rival leaders. During the 1850s, the economy recovered and coastal agriculture was modernized. Although the guano trade and the cotton and sugar production allowed the British and French investors to profit and the Peruvian elite to live in comfort, the Peruvian state was in debt due to wartime borrowing. To stabilize the situation and provide for development, the French Dreyfus Company was granted a monopoly of the guano trade in return for servicing the foreign debt and loans. This was the situation in Peru when Sarah Dahlgren arrived in Lima.

The Dahlgrens lived in Peru in 1867. Sarah settled into an apartment in a Lima hotel, where she was keen to learn about the city and visit the major tourist sites. She was an astute observer of the people, the politics, religion, women, and local customs—and she was knowledgeable about the country's history. Because of her husband's rank, she was able to meet and socialize with Mariano Ignacio Prado Ochoa, the president of Peru, and she was delighted to be admitted to the ranks of Lima's high society, which was usually closed to foreigners. She recorded her impressions of Peru in letters to her children in the United States. When she returned home, her letters were published as *South Sea Sketches* in 1881.

The Dahlgren family returned to Washington, D.C., in 1868, where the admiral resumed his position as commanding officer of the

Washington Navy Yard and head of the Bureau of Ordnance. Admiral Dahlgren died on July 12, 1870. Sarah continued her writing once she returned home. In the 1880s and 1890s, she published several novels, including *Washington Winter*, a sketch of Washington society and her best-known work. Sarah also wrote a lengthy biography of Admiral Dahlgren. She founded the Washington Literary society, served as its vice president, and was president of the Ladies Catholic Missionary Society. As a passionate anti-suffragette, she corresponded with leaders of the suffragette movement and protested the proposed Sixteenth Amendment to the Constitution, which would grant women the right to vote; the amendment did not pass.

Sarah Madeleine Vinton Dahlgren lived in Washington, D.C., during the winter and spent summers at her home in South Mountain, Maryland. She led an active life until her death on May 28, 1889, and was buried in the family crypt of the chapel built for her at South Mountain.

The following selections from *South Sea Sketches* focus on the races of Peru, upper-class women, the country's politics, a social occasion with Peru's president Mariano Ignacio Prado Ochoa and his wife Madeleine, the cityscape, and the devotion to Saint Rose of Lima by the Peruvians.

Torre Tagle House, Lima, Peru, Library of Congress

A MORNING STROLL IN LIMA

At times we stroll through the markets in the morning. They are very interesting, for there we get an animated glimpse of country life. Want of cleanliness, however, mars all.

We visit the Plaza, or public square called Independencia, which is adorned by a very fine bronze statue of Bolivar, of noble proportions. The statue is placed on the spot where the victims of the Inquisition were burned. Let those who say that Catholics have erected this fine statue, really dedicated to liberty in the person of Bolivar; and that they have given its present name of Independence to the very spot. The fact is, that in the history of nations crimes are constantly committed alike under the sacred names of Religion and Liberty; but this does not make the one or the other responsible for these acts. The old Inquisition building is now used as a prison. We visit it, and are allowed to enter the rooms where some political prisoners are confined. They have considerable range and appear to be kindly treated, except that they are in durance.

Placed on the Plaza Independencia is the Camara de Diputados, where we find some seventy members seated in a very suitable hall; and the proceedings are orderly and quite as respectable as those of our own Congress. If not more so.

Lima has very well conducted journals. The *Comercio, National, Mercurio,* and *Progresso* are the principal ones. The *Progresso* is at this moment the official organ. The leading articles are written with creditable ability.

SAINT ROSE'S DAY

President Prado seems to gain. The Deputies amidst the most factious opposition, have at last proclaimed him Provisional President, and decreed *La Fiesta de Santa Rosa,* the feast day of Saint Rose, August 31, as Inauguration day. On August 30 we have a grand procession carrying the image of St. Rose, who is the patron saint of Lima, through the city. On this day we have again a *temblor,* but only a slight shaking; on the next day we experience a repetition and a much heavier shock. Notwithstanding, the festivities go on after the momentary panic is over, inasmuch as no accidents have been reported. The society of Lima celebrate St. Rose's day very much as we do New Year's day. The ladies receive the visits of their gentlemen friends who call and offer flowers, and are in turn treated to *dulces.* These confections are made in great perfection and variety, although too sweet to our taste.

The religious ceremonial on this day precedes the political. The Plaza is filled with military. Five brass bands and perhaps more, make a terrible *tintamarre.* St. Rose is again escorted by the clergy, the troops, and the people, through the principal streets. She stops some five minutes under our balcony, and we have a good opportunity of inspecting the image. It is wooden and not artistic; life size, cheeks painted rosy red, wears a gilded crown, which is spread over its head to represent a halo, we suppose, and which is very suggestive of the Inca emblem, for it looks like a big, gilded sun. The image wears a velvet dress stretched over a hoop; the skirt covered with rich embroidery. Around the neck is an enormous gold chain and in one hand it carries an immense bouquet of artificial roses. It stands on a velvet-covered platform, which is supported from underneath by a number of men who carry the structure.

As they stop for a little rest, the heavy, smothering draper, which falls low, is lifted for air and with woman's curiosity we lean forward from our balcony to see what the mechanical motive-power is. We get a glimpse of a number of shabby-looking peasants, and we are satisfied if not gratified. Negro women, draped in flimsiest gauze ball dresses, and tricked out with pink roses stuck in their wool, burn incense with a swaying motion. All this helps to give a fuller idea of the barbaric taste of the masses, to which the clergy seem to defer on such occasions. The sentiment of the day we know is beautiful and elevating. It is the public homage to the saintly and lowly maiden who was born, lived, and died in their very midst. Her wondrous, her mystic life, was known to all. That which makes the gross materialism of the spectacle is purely the outcropping of the rude taste of a semi-civilized people. Yet the *idea* which stirs them is divine, is spiritual; and we join in the common aspiration.

After the religious ceremonial succeed the political and military parade, and the two occupy the entire day. On the evenings of August 30, 31 and September 1, we have brilliant fireworks, when very nearly the same scenes are re-enacted as on the Independence days of July 28 and 29, which we have already described. And now again, after so short an interval of time, this entire people stop work, close their shops of all kinds and give themselves up to the supreme felicity of *far niente.*

In the evening the Plaza is filled with booths, around and within which the people amuse themselves. The native dance *zamceceuca,* pronounced "Zam the quaker" probably not unlike the old Moorish dance called "*Zambra,*" is freely indulged in and must be very popular, as everywhere we hear the tinkling of guitars and merry shouts of the populace. We have never seen this dance, but we are told that it is neither graceful nor modest. There is a polite modification of it, occasionally performed to certain music especially adapted to its evolutions, in good circles, which of course differs from the wild abandon of the original.

The President gives a grand banquet of one hundred and fifty covers, to celebrate his installation. Diplomats, cabinet officers, justices of the courts, the French and American admirals and deputies of the Congress, sit down at four and rise at seven. At this entertainment there is much speech-making, and all is pleasant; and to the common eye at least, there is no foreshadowing of a revolutionary storm.

SLAVERY

In the streets here, as in Lima, we occasionally meet dogs of ferocious aspect, of a breed we are told, formerly used to hunt refractory slaves. Slavery presents, the world over, the same hideous features. We have beheld its workings in our own South, as well as in Cuba, and now we find the horrid vestiges here.

Slavery was abolished in Peru as late as 1857, by the patriot Castillas, who himself belonged to the Indian or enslaved race.

VISIT WITH THE PRESIDENT AND FIRST LADY OF PERU

A week after our arrival the wife of the President sent us her card by an officer of the rank of colonel, who is of the President's military family. A presentation for us is arranged. The *Palacio,* or President's house, has a very dilapidated exterior. The *bajo* is occupied by mean shops, but the interior is much finer than our presidential mansion. It was the old vice-regal palace, and presents a curious medley of monarchical and republican customs. Not far distant, in the background of the palace, looms the beautiful mountain, a cross planted on its summit. We often love to ascend its base.

The President of Peru, at the time we write of, is Colonel Prado. He has risen to power through a well planned revolution, and assumed the title of Dictator; and has reigned over the Republic for nearly two years. He has recently been elected constitutional President, and it is hoped will have a felicitous administration under the constitutional restraints which he has accepted.

Accompanied by the American Minister and Admiral, we arrive at the *Palacio* at the designated hour. As this is simply a presentation for the wife of the Admiral, of course the gentleman of our party dispense, as far as possible, with official dress. We ascend to the *alto*, and are conducted through several apartments. The President receives us in an outer salon. He is of middling height, has a well built, compact frame, an executive head, and a good face. He is perhaps forty years old, may be older,--has dark hair, heavy moustache, and beard full black. His countenance has the Spanish gravity, but the expression is pleasant. He shakes hands affably on meeting us. On state occasions he wears the bi-colored ribbon, the insignia of the Dictator, and also, we believe, of his present rank as President, and the uniform of colonel. He leads the way, after our introduction, offering us his arm, and passing through several spacious rooms, we reach an inner apartment, where Madame Prado receives us.

La Presidenta is a handsome woman of Limenian type; and our feminine appreciation pronounces her costume of green brocade, black lace, and black velvet entirely *comme il faut.* In fact, it has a refreshing air of *Worth.* As no language is understood by Madame than the stately Castilian, the conversation at first is somewhat embarrassed, until the motherly thought rises uppermost in our heart to ask to see the baby. The *chiquito* Maximiliano is at once brought in, superbly attired, held by a *Cholo* nurse, and squeezing tight in his little arms a very vicious and vivacious looking monkey. The entrance of the baby literally makes all language alike. The *mono* chatters and so do we. The President, the Minister, and the Admiral looked amused, laugh a little, and end by being as much pleased as we; and we part with exceeding demonstrations of friendliness.

FEMALE FASHION IN LIMA

Luxury of dress is a predominant passion in Lima. A system of free-trade, established in 1783, permitted unlimited intercourse between Spain and certain ports of Peru, Callao and Arica being of the number designated. The result was from the first highly favorable, and a flourishing commerce, principally with England, has grown up. Many merchant ships, still double Cape Horn, and bring the finest silks, velvets, linens, cutlery, glass-ware, superfine cloths, etc. It is extremely mortifying to a patriotic American that we have, so to speak, no commerce; and if we had we never could compete with this free-trade from Europe. Were it not for our navy we fear the *Peruanos* and, indeed, all South America would be blissfully unaware of our existence as a nation, for the English rule on this coast as to trade.

At this time, great amplitude of skirts are worn here, and the ladies trail their silks and fine satins through the filthy streets in a remorseless way that would even surprise our women of fashion at home. We ventured one day to offer a gentle expostulation on the subject, when we were instantly answered: "Of course our dresses cannot be worn but once or twice, nor do we desire to appear in them more often, no matter how costly or elaborate they may be!" The votaries of fashion are quite the same all the world over, and the *modiste* of Lima is just as giddy, reckless, and unreasonable as her sister *artiste* in New York.

FREEDOM OF WOMEN AND THEIR DRESS IN LIMA

The ladies of Lima are permitted great liberty in some things. For instance, if one wishes to attend an opera, unescorted by a gentleman, one can do so. Wrapped in the black *manta,* which quite conceals the features, and accompanied by a maid servant, one is quite protected. But in this *incognita* you are expected to take your seat in the parquet, which we are told is entirely respectable to do. In fact, ladies promenade the streets of Lima with freedom and safety at all hours, and quite unattended except by a *criada,* or maid.

A Limenian señorita, enveloped in *manta,* the bright eyes alone to be seem, the jeweled hand clasping the folds of the mantle drawn around her, is always to us attractive and interesting.

The old national dress of the women, called *saya y manta,* has disappeared. We have only seen it once since being in Lima, and cannot even find it photographed in any of the numerous galleries. This change is not to be regretted, as nothing, to our eye, can be more ungraceful than the species of straight jacket called *saya.* The *manta* is also fast giving way, and must soon be displaced by the modern bonnet. It is only worn at church, and used for négligé. The coquettish mantilla is much affected, and almost every señorita who calls upon us is so draped. The Spanish veil is very pretty, and extremely becoming to nearly every face, but for street promenade it is too public; at lest it seems to us to give slight protection when we attempt its use, hoping to escape the terrible stare our bonnet inflicts upon us.

LIMENIAN WOMEN ARE INDOLENT

The Limenian women as a class, are indolent. They rise early and go to mass; then they shop, and somewhat later visit their friends or receive calls; and all this time the hair is unkempt and the toilet is neglected. But the evening finds the Cinderella of the morning superbly attired.

Soon after our arrival some ladies in magnificent costumes call to see us one evening. We are somewhat dazzled, and return the visit about four of the afternoon a few days later. We find their residence an immense house, of which this family occupy the *alto.* At the top of the wide stairway of entrance we are arrested by a closed gate, and as we pause for a moment, a young girl crossing the patio advances at once, without hesitation, and admits us. She wear a draggled dress and has dishevelled hair, and we suppose her to be a domestic of the establishment and hand her our card, asking for the señoritas. At the same time, with laughing grace, and not in the least embarrassed, she replies: "But we have met." We blush at our mistake for it is our princess in disguise. We should here observe that even at the finest mansions you often knock at the glass door, which is opened by the mistress of the house if she happens to be in the *salons.* We attribute much of this habit of carelessness to the constant use of the *manta.* This is a long, black cashmere shawl, sometimes coarse in texture and plain, and again richly embroidered, trimmed with lace, and very elegant. Covering the head, and wrapped in loose folds around the person, it hides all sins of omission of the toilet.

PRESIDENT PRADO'S GOVERNMENT

Colonel Prado has never been acceptable to the best families of Peru, who really make their rulers. He is essentially a soldier, and came from Arequipa. He vaulted into power by a successful *coup de main,* and at once boldly proclaimed himself Dictator. He vigorously set about making those changes which he deemed needed reforms. It is a singular fact that so long as he governed with an absolute and usurped authority he was potent; but the moment he relaxed and sought to be considered the constitutional President, in other words, to re-establish the law which he had himself suspended, from that moment he seems to have failed. The legislative branch have become antagonistic, the clergy denounce his so-called reforms, and it is said his downfall must come.

He has been particularly unwise in attempting to restrict and abolish many time-honored privileges of the clergy. The sentiment of the people at large does not sustain him in making these changes. But Prado is in some senses a patriot. In money matters every one concedes that he is impeachable; and if he is ever compelled to fly Peru, he will still remain, after wielding almost unlimited power, a poor man. He found an impoverished treasury, and now there is a full exchequer. This is a pure record. In fact one cause of the present dissatisfaction is that he has greatly retrenched many expenditures of the government, cut down fat salaries, and particularly has modified some pension laws which diminish some large incomes. His task is at least an ungracious one; the aristocrats are displeased, and the masses do not know enough to care. He greatly relies on the army, we are told.

THE STREETS OF LIMA

The streets of Lima are narrow, paved with the roughest, jagged stones; and the open gutters, called *ezequias* run through their middle. The sidewalks are so narrow that it is more comfortable to trudge on, single file, *à l'Indienne.* The sharp stones make driving simply intolerable; which, we suppose, is the reason why it is quite the *costumbre del pais* (custom of the country) to walk.

Flocks of ungainly turkey-buzzards brood over these dirty gutters, where all garbage is thrown. These birds, act, in great part, as scavengers for the city, and are really picturesque in their ugliness. They sit motionless, often for hours, as if mourning over some past woe, and they frequently choose the most remarkable sites for lodgment; so much so, that at first we mistook them for architectural points of adornment to public buildings, as we viewed them, perched aloft on cloud-capped towers and glistening pinnacles. If ubiquity, utility, and endearing vitality can entitle them to such a preeminence, they may fairly be called the national bird.

THE RACES IN PERU

The races of Peru are very mixed. The pure Spaniard, or *sangre-azul,* may , I suppose, be found but he is seldom met. The Mestizoes are the off-spring of the Spaniard and Indian; while the Quarteroons, or the Children of Mestizoes and Spaniards have quite the Castilian look. But the *Cholos,* who are the descendants of the Mestizos and Indians, have the full Indian cast. There are also the negroes and the coolies, who were principally plantation slaves before the emancipation. The fatal mistake in the Inca rule was the undue development of a PEACE POLICY. They were intelligent and more than semi-civilized, well governed, and law abiding; but they were unwarlike, and thus emasculated by long continued peace, they fell an easy, and irremediable prey to conquest.

It is not pleasant to say it, but in the grand summing up they became wretched, depressed, and subdued, just in proportion as they had been peaceful.

THE UPPER CLASSES

The social element of the upper classes of Lima is highly cultured, and consists principally of the few families who really own and govern the country. These people are refined and high-bred, and of courteous and agreeable manners. Many of them, both ladies and gentlemen, have had long experience of Parisian life, where their immense wealth enables them to command every luxury and avail themselves of every educational advantage. But the country itself, as represented by the masses of people, seems to us as scarcely more than semi-civilized, the barbaric taste and ideas predominating.

Loretta L. Wood Merwin

A Consul's Wife in Chile

Loretta L. Wood Merwin was the daughter of Reuben Wood, who was a lawyer, state senator, judge of the Supreme Court of Ohio, and governor from 1850 to 1852. Financial difficulties caused him to resign from the governorship in 1853. Active in Democratic politics, he was given the post of American consul in Valparaiso, Chile. Wood, his wife, daughter Loretta, her husband George Buckingham Merwin, and their two sons left the United States for a three-year stay in Chile. They hoped to become financially solvent in this new position, as the California gold rush brought eager prospectors around the horn and up the Chilean coast to Valparaiso for provisioning. But by the time the two families arrived, the mad dash to California was over. Nevertheless, the Merwins and Woods remained in Chile for three years. At some point, Wood resigned his post, and his son-in-law assumed the position of consul. The cost of living was high, and the two families found it difficult to meet their household expenses. In September 1856, George Merwin resigned his post due to health problems, and the family returned to the United States.

The two families settled in Chile during the presidency of conservative leader Manuel Montt Torres. Montt was a lawyer and a scholar who supported public education, immigration, and the economic development of Chile. He eliminated tithing, which angered the church fathers, and abolished entail, with the goal of breaking up the large estates, but that did not happen. Chile was relatively peaceful during the three years the Woods and Merwins lived in Chile.

Loretta began her narrative of the trip to Chile that included a stop in Kingston, Jamaica, followed by the hazardous trip through Panama by railroad and mule to the Pacific coast. Once settled in Chile, she learned Spanish and was eager to explore Valparaiso and the capital, Santiago. She was a keen observer of the Chilean people, the different social classes, their holidays, religion, customs, manners, and dress. Her writing was rather light hearted, and she was not overly critical of the differences that she encountered. She documented her experiences and impressions of Chile in a book entitled *Three Years in Chili*, published in 1861.

Loretta L. Wood Merwin died in Brunswick, Georgia, on January 26, 1890, and was buried in Woodland Cemetery in Cleveland, Ohio.

The selections published here are from *Three Years in Chili.*

VALPARAISO, CHILE

This city is adorned with magnificent stores, constantly importing from Europe, and furnishing every article of use or luxury that can be required. The shop windows dazzle the eye with their rich display of laces, silks, and diamonds. There are silks made expressly for the South American market, and I have never seen such splendid fabrics anywhere else. An old resident who removed to

New York a few months since, sent back to Valparaiso to buy dresses for his daughter.

In the Almendral there is a fine public garden, filled with rare flowering plants, with broad walks sheltered by trellises of grape-vines—which is open to all times to visitors. Twice a week, during the summer season (Sunday and Wednesday evenings), the promenaders are enlivened by music. The garden is then a great resort for the elite of Valparaiso.

The streets are full of strange sights to us. Here in the Plaza Municipalidad are groups of women selling shoes—a piece of cloth or old carpet thrown upon the ground near the curb-stone, and the vendor sitting on a low stool, with her stock of trade arranged in the interior of a large, shallow basket before her. She has for sale men's and boy's coarse leather shoes, and women's gaiters of all colors. She sits here the whole day long, shifting her stool to keep out of the sun, and now and then resigning it to the purchaser, who wishes to try on a shoe.

Clattering along through the street comes the water-carrier—a little donkey with a wooden frame on either side, sustaining a keg which holds about eight gallons of water. The donkey has no bridle, but a man or boy follows him. He stops at your door, and if you live upstairs, the man ascends with one keg at a time, and pours it into your water-barrel. If you live on the first floor, the donkey is driven into the *patio.* After the water is delivered and the kegs replaced, the man mounts so far back upon the donkey's hind quarters that it is hard to tell which animal the tail belongs to—and away they go on a hard trot for a new supply, the kegs banging in their frames, and the rider belaboring the donkey over either ear, according as he wants him to turn to the right or left.

THE FIRST EARTHQUAKE

As this is the land of earthquakes, we began life in it, with daily expectations of the *temblor*—fearfully curious about our sensations. Our first experience was somewhat ludicrous. We had dined out, and about nine o'clock in the evening, while the gentleman were still at table, we in the parlor were discussing the subject of earthquakes, and our hostess remarked, "I always run into the street," and then sprang suddenly from the sofa, exclaiming "There is one now! Ladies, there is the door," and flew to the nursery to secure her little ones—leaving us standing transfixed with terror, staring at each other, utterly ignorant (for it was the first time we had been in the house) which door opened into the street. I only remember groping my way through a dimly lighted hall, and lifting my feet as if I were walking the deck of a rolling ship. This was so slight a shock that we should never have noticed it ourselves.

LIFE IN VALPARAISO

It was now the close of winter, and very cool, so that until nine in the morning, and after four in the afternoon, we suffered excessively even with thick shawls on. There were no fires in the house, and we ordered a *brasero* a brass pan on three legs, and filled with charcoal, which lighted and placed in the open air until well burned, when it is bought into the room. We always had a headache from it.

I went to market soon after our arrival in Valparaiso. The market-house – consists of two or three large rooms crowded with all sorts of things in season, piled up in baskets or on the floor, and the place swarming with dirty people. Every thing was so fearfully dirty, that I almost concluded to fast during my residence in Chili. There were in the market, green peas, beans, lettuce, radishes, squashes, turnips and potatoes, all of good quality; and turkeys, chickens, partridges, very good beef, poor mutton and veal, and various kinds of scale and shell-fish.

After much earnest search for a house, we finally decided to rent the house and purchase the furniture of an American engineer who had been in the employment of the Chilian government three or four years, and was now going home. In Valparaiso we found a small, but pleasant society of Americans, our nation being numerously represented there than either the English, Germans or French. There are two Protestant places of worship in the city—that of the Congregationalists, and that of the Church of England under the patronage of the British Consul.

With the natives, Sunday, so sacred with us, is a grand gala-day, and every Sabbath morning the streets are gay with military and music, pleasure parties starting to the country, and people hurrying from mass—the fine lady to finish the day at the opera, and the peasant to crown her devotions to the fandango.

A DAILY WALK

We walk daily. All but the principal streets are narrow, filthy, and crowded with men, women, children, donkeys and dogs, while the dust swarms with fleas. As you pass along through the poorer quarters, you notice in the doorways, picturesque family groups of people, making those interesting examinations of each others' heads, which, among the infested of some other lands, are usually conducted in private.

Places of resort with us are the Catholic and Protestant cemeteries, which are situated on the summit of one of the hills, and are both surrounded by *abode* walls, tastefully ornamented with plants and trees. These cemeteries are separated by a narrow lane. That of the Catholics is on the crest of the hill overlooking the Bay; that of the Protestants is in the rear of the other. Each has a chapel, to which it is the custom to bring the dead at midnight, and lock them up performing the funeral services at the appointed hour the next day.

In the Catholic grounds are some fine monuments, of which the most beautiful was erected by the Municipality of Valparaiso, to the memory of Portales, perhaps the most brilliant statesman Chili has produced. It is a shaft of pure white marble, with a pointed cap, which has been half turned round by earthquakes. The monument, which contains the heart of the deceased patriot is appropriately inscribed.

There are vaults and tombs to be used permanently by those who can pay for them, but other graves are rented for one year, at the expiration of which time the bodies are dug up, the bones thrown in a deep pit, and the coffins burned. For the wretched poor, those who have no money at all, excavations of fifteen or twenty feet square, and ten or twelve deep, are made, into which the bodies, wrapped in cloth, are thrown, layer upon layer, with earth over each, until the whole square is filled. It is then smoothed over, and another pit is prepared.

We are not satisfied with the location of our house, from which nothing is to be seen but filthy people, donkeys, dogs and sailors' boarding-houses.

A HOUSE ON CAPE HORN HILL

December. We are comfortably settled in our new house on Cape Horn Hill, which is a great improvement on the old locality. We are two hundred feet above the sea, and look (twenty feet from our front door) down an abrupt hill bristling with cactuses, upon the house-tops of the streets below. On either hand, the whole city lies in view; across a deep ravine are the *Pantheons* or burial grounds, while before stretches the bay with its shipping—and we see every vessel that goes out or comes in.

The mornings here are glorious, and the sunsets gorgeous. As most persons breakfast late, it is the custom to walk in the early morning before the wind rises. The hill-promenades are then thronged with people inhaling the healthful breeze. Nowhere in the world, I think, can it be more charming than here upon these hills in the summer mornings, far above the vileness, dust and tumult of the city.

THE OPERA

There is a very good Italian Opera Troupe now in Valparaiso, and we went the other evening to hear *Ernani.* The theatre is very handsome, and inside is not architecturally different from our own. Between the acts of the play or the opera, the gentlemen go out into the vestibule, or upon the side, to indulge in the universal cigar, and a bell is rung to recall them before the curtain rises. The house is so filled with smoke for a few minutes after each act that you can scarcely see across it. At the close of the performance all the gentlemen who have no ladies in charge, hurry into the vestibule, and take up their positions in a row, leaving a line through which the ladies must pass and stare at them with great earnestness, commenting upon their beauty. So far from considering this an impertinence, the Valparaiso fair think it very complimentary.

FEBRUARY, ANOTHER EARTHQUAKE

On the morning of the 4th of this month, we were aroused from sleep by a loud roar, and a jarring of the earth. In an instant we were on our feet, when there came another shock, yet more severe, rattling every door and window. The sensations produced by earthquakes are indescribable. In all other dangers, by sea and land, one has an instinctive feeling, that if it were possible to touch another earth, one would be safe, but when the earth herself quivers under our feet, the last refuge seems gone; all our preconceived notions of stability are shaken—we feel our utter helplessness; and to me the first idea was always of some crushing, overwhelming calamity—with a terror such as one might reasonably be expected to feel at the approach of the Day of Judgement.

A VERY SEVERE EARTHQUAKE

On the evening of the 28th of September, we experienced the severest shock of earthquake that occurred during our residence in Chili. It came upon us without a premonitory noise or tremor—a tremendous shock, that brought us all to our feet in consternation, and rocked the house till every door, window and dish rattled again. With a common impulse we sprang to the door and out upon the hill. It was dark, but in the streets below us we could hear the hum of voices, as the people rushed out of their houses, praying to heaven, and calling upon each other; while the dogs added terror to the scene by their doleful howls.

We knew our house to be perfectly safe; an earthquake that could demolish that, would destroy the city. Nevertheless, on the slightest tremor of the earth, an irresistible impulse of flight always possessed us.

No buildings were thrown down by this shock, but the walls of many were cracked, and immense damage was done in the fracture of window-glass and crockery. The motion of the earthquake seemed to be a perpendicular vibration, like great heavings from beneath; it was felt on the ships in the bay, and produced a heavy swell. During the next twelve days we had nine more, and we seemed in a fair way to be shaken out of our belief that the earth was *terra firme.* At another time, we had six earthquakes in one week; and in the three years we lived in Chili, we felt fifty-eight shocks.

Santiago, Chile, Library of Congress

SANTIAGO, CHILE

Santiago is immensely rich—richer perhaps, according to its population of 130,000, than any other city on this continent. The Chileno has few inducements to travel in his own country, and little ambition to go abroad. The great object of life is to accumulate wealth, and remove to the capital, to lavish it in costly furniture, equipage, and splendid living.

As Santiago is more elevated than Valparaiso, it is subject to greater extremes of heat and cold; and during the hot months of December, January and February, the rich retire to their *quintas,* or to Valparaiso for the sea bathing.

Manuel Montt, the President of the Republic during our stay in Chili, was then nearly sixty years of age. He was the first civilian who had filled the presidential chair, and was a gentleman of fine ability and liberal views.

THE CLERGY IN SANTIAGO

Intolerance and superstition, although bad enough in Valparaiso, are unchecked at Santiago. The character of the clergy is low, but they tell their people, "you must live what we preach, not what we practice." They are vowed to celibacy, yet many of them are known to have large families of children; and pretty country cousins are frequent guests at their households. A friend of mine told me that he once attended mass at a town in the interior, where the congregation, impatient at the absence of the priest, sent for his reverence. Their messenger found him at a cock-fight, which he refused to leave until the existing combat was ended. Recently a Chileno died leaving a thousand dollars in the hands of an executor, to be expended in masses for his soul; the native priests would only consent to perform five hundred masses for the money. According to the executor, who had an eye to business, wrote to Spain, and procured a thousand masses for six hundred dollars. The church of Chili then sued him for defrauding it out of its legitimate business.

At the door of every church in Santiago, printed indulgences are for sale on fast days. The usual tenor of the indulgence is, that whoever will observe faithfully certain ceremonies, shall have permission to commit minor sins for a specified length of time. The applicant kneels, a lighted candle is placed in his hand, a badge is thrown over his neck, and a priest mutters a prayer. At the close of the ceremony, the applicant rises, pays a dollar, and receives a printed indulgence, with his name written in the blank space, certifying, "In the name of God," that he, is permitted (for instance) "to eat meat one month during Lent."

THE MINES IN THE NORTH

In the northern provinces of Chili, there is almost unlimited wealth in silver and copper, but owning to the scarcity of water and fuel in many places, and the great difficulty of transporting the product, many of the mines have been abandoned, while others yield but a small profit. Nevertheless, speculation in mining sometimes almost amounts to mania; in many cases owners become discouraged—think they do not acquire wealth rapidly enough and sell out at a low figure, and the purchaser perhaps strikes a rich lode, and doubles his investment. There are proprietors of mines living at Santiago, whose income is so enormous, that they are ignorant of the exact amount.

Smelting, where there is fuel, is sometimes done at the mines, but usually at the port, and much metal is shipped in a crude state. Trains of mules laden with silver and copper ore in bags, or smelted bars, under military escort, and headed, each train, by an old mare, called the *madrina,* to whose neck as bell is hung—wend their way through the mountains and over the rugged country, bearing their precious cargo to the ports.

THE CHILEAN PEOPLE

The people here are divided into two classes: the gentry, and the *peones* or peasants. Of the former class, the men are rather below the minimum size. They invariably have black hair and eyes—with a sallow complexion which is sometimes very dark. Many of them are well educated in the Chileno schools and colleges, and a few have traveled in Europe or the United States; but they are indolent and effeminate, never doing to-day what can be done to-morrow—fond of gambling and dress-inveterate smokers, and loose in their notions of morality.

The beauty of the women has been greatly overrated. When they wore the graceful black veil, which harmonized so well with their jet-black hair and eyes, they had attractions which they do not possess now, when dressed in colors. As they approach middle life, they incline to flesh. They are indolent and slovenly.

Servants are abundant, and if one does not please, a better may be had; so that the ladies here are relieved entirely of one of the most harassing responsibilities of northern housekeepers. A young girl never leaves the house of her parents unless accompanied by some member of the family or a female servant. If she pays a visit, the *duenna* waits for her at the front door, or gossips with the other servants. Interviews between young ladies and gentlemen never take place except in the presence of others. Of course, marriages of convenience are frequent. There are also many instances of matrimony within the forbidden degrees of consanguinity—even to the union of uncles with nieces, and step-fathers with step-daughters.

THE WOMEN OF CHILE

The intellect of the females I think superior to that of the male sex, but in Chili there is little to excite their ambition. There are no lectures, no literary societies, but few cultivated minds to come in contact with. There is no opportunity of traveling in their own country, except up and down the coast to a few miserable ports, and back and forth from Valparaiso to Santiago. Both sexes confess to apathy. Personal labor is considered degrading. Want of occupation encouraged by the climate soon confirms a habit of indolence, where there is no mental energy to shake it off, and in a brief while the youth, who might have become a man of ability and enterprise, falls irreclaimably into idleness and listlessness. Thus life is one monotonous round—to the female, of going to mass in the morning, attending to a few domestic duties during the day, and the opera or *tertulia* in the evening.

THE POOR PEOPLE

As to the second and poorer class of the Chilenos—the *peones* are hideously ugly –with thick heads of hair hanging straight from the crown, high cheek- bones, wide mouths, and copper-colored complexions. Small hands and feet are property in the beautiful, common to all Chilenos. Some of the women of the *peones* are quite pretty, but there is a great want of chastity among them. Unions without marriage are frequent, and are excused on the grounds that the blessing of the church is too great an expense to be incurred. Born as inferiors and dependents, the highest ambition of the *peones* is to serve masters or mistresses of wealth and consequence, addressing them as Patron, and Patrona. Their necessities are few, and may be summed up in a mud, or abode hut, a hide in one corner on which to sleep, an iron pot and mate cup, bread and beans for substantial food, with garlic, or onions and fruits for relishes. In the cool rains of winter they shiver uncomplainingly, and when the sun shines, crouch into every sheltered nook and corner to enjoy its grateful warmth. Like all ignorant people they are superstitious, believing in charms and amulets as powerful to drive away diseases; and it is common to see them with little round plasters upon their temples as antidotes for headache. On Sundays they visit the barber, who is one of their own class, and whose shop is the shady side of a bit of cloth stretched upon poles; and there perform their toilet for the week to come. The wages of a year's labor is often spent upon a poncho to wear at the *diez y ocho* . Mechanics and shopkeepers are a degree removed from these, but there is a want of cleanliness in all; and a passion for display and finery that, to gratify in public, they will suffer any deprivation at home.

TITHES

Although all tithes are abolished, many of the old families would be proud to retain them, and still keep up the retinue and state of nobility. The Countess de Toro, whom I saw at Santiago, pays the government a yearly sum for the privilege of being called countess—an empty gratification for which she can well afford to pay for her wealth is fabulous. At a ball given during the festivities of the *diez y ocho,* besides being richly dressed, she wore diamonds estimated to be worth forty thousand dollars. She sports a Parisian coach and four, with four outriders and a postilion. Her house is a large, two-story brick mansion, painted a brilliant red, with white doors and window casings. He husband ordered in his will that the color should remain unchanged, and the slightest deviation would forfeit the property.

SMOKING

No place except the church is sacred from the fumes of the cigar. Gentlemen, whether riding or walking, with or without, ladies are always smoking. The priest in the Pantheon takes a whiff between prayers; and even the firemen while running with their engines, must pause to light the cigarrito, let the urgency be ever so great. The Senoritas have the name of being addicted to this habit, and I was told that formerly the greatest compliment a lady could pay a gentleman was to light the cigarrito and pass it to him from her own lips; but I never saw any thing of this.

CHILEAN COURTESY

We profess to be a cultivated people and stiffen our necks with Yankee independence, but in some things we might learn courtesy from the Chilenos. They never enter or leave a public vehicle without a bow to its occupants, and we never make one unless to an acquaintance. At the table d'hote at the hotel in Santiago, no lady or gentleman ever sat down, or rose from table without a graceful inclination of the head to all who were present. So in shopping, they bow to the merchant or his clerks on entering and leaving the store. These simple acts of politeness always impressed me pleasantly, and as so much better than our own don't-care-for-any-body sort of way. In the street, however, the Chilenos might learn from us. If a group of gentleman are conversing on the narrow sidewalk, and a lady approaches, they often will not notice her, or will perhaps step back, leaving her the curb-stone. Sometimes she is obliged to step in the gutter to pass around them.

Elizabeth Cabot Cary Agassiz

An Educator in Brazil

Elizabeth Cabot Cary Agassiz was born on December 5, 1822, to a prominent Boston family. Her father was Thomas Graves Cary and her mother Mary Ann Cushing Perkins. Growing up, she was tutored at home and developed into an educated, sensitive woman who possessed leadership skills and a positive attitude toward all that life's experiences brought her. Before her marriage to the renowned Swiss naturalist Louis Agassiz on April 25, 1850, she led the life of a cultivated gentlewoman, enjoying summers in Nahant, concerts, and the opera in Boston, but all that changed once she was married. She became a devoted stepmother to Agassiz's three children, Alexander, Ida, and Pauline, and a helpmate to him in his work. Although Agassiz was a professor of natural history at the Lawrence Scientific School, he had debts due to a publishing venture, and the family needed funds to supplement his salary, so Elizabeth opened a school for girls in their home, aptly named the Agassiz School. Agassiz supported the school and even lectured there. By 1862, the Civil War intruded, and Agassiz's salary had increased, so the school was closed, but Elizabeth's interest in the education of women was not over and figured largely in her life later on.

Elizabeth influenced Agassiz's professional decision not to take the chair of paleontology at the University of Paris. She felt he could do more for science in the United States than in Europe. She supported the establishment of the Harvard-affiliated Museum of Comparative Zoology in Cambridge that he founded in 1858. Though not scientifically trained, she became so deeply immersed in his work that she wrote her first book, *Actaea: A First Lesson in Natural History*, published in 1859. The book focused on anemones, coral, jellyfish, starfish, and sea urchins. A second edition appeared in 1879.

Louis Agassiz devoted himself zealously to lecturing and to developing the museum, and as a result, his health was affected. An ichthyologist, he had a long-time interest in Brazilian fossils, especially fish, and had connections with Emperor Dom Pedro II, so he proposed an expedition to Brazil and the Amazon River region to collect samples of fish and other small wildlife for the museum. The expedition was financed by Nathaniel Thayer, a wealthy Bostonian, who went along with six assistants and seven volunteers, including William James, the future psychologist and philosopher. The group planned to spend three months in Rio de Janeiro, ten months in the Amazon, and two months in the mountains near the coast. They boarded the steamship *Colorado* for Brazil on December 1, 1865.

The country that Elizabeth encountered was ruled by Emperor Dom Pedro II of the Braganza dynasty and his wife Teresa, a former Neapolitan princess. Independence had come peacefully to Brazil in 1822, when Dom Pedro I declared it. And as a result, the country never suffered the wars, death, and destruction that other nations in South America did. Once independent, the economy, based on slavery and the cultivation of sugar, coffee, and cotton, grew. By the middle of the 1850s, the importation of slaves ended as the anti-slave trade laws were enforced, thus dealing a death blow to its continuance. There was increasing pressure on the emperor and the government to abolish slavery in the ensuing decades, but it wasn't until 1888 that slavery was finally abolished by the emperor's daughter, Princess Isabel. When the Agassizes were in Brazil, slavery was an issue that divided the politically active republicans who demanded abolition and the landowners who opposed it.

Elizabeth joined the expedition as the clerk; her duties included keeping a journal, writing letters home, and copying Agassiz's lectures that he gave on the boat or to the public. Along with her other duties, Elizabeth kept a diary of her daily activities and made an effort to learn Portuguese. She was eager to explore her surroundings and took every opportunity to do so. When she first arrived in Rio, she went on horseback up Corcovado Mountain. She thought that Rio's harbor was beautiful and the woods and the views enchanting. She wrote a friend: "I have enjoyed every moment since I came to Rio." Brazil was a tropical paradise, and she thrived in the warmth of the Southern Hemisphere.

After his arrival, Louis Agassiz contacted Emperor Dom Pedro II, who was interested in his scientific work. Agassiz gave a lecture for the emperor and other interested parties, but no women were allowed to attend. Elizabeth attended, but had to ask permission to do so. She was surprised to learn that Brazilian women were not allowed to attend public events. Upon meeting Elizabeth at Agassiz's second lecture, Empress Teresa expressed envy that Elizabeth could travel and go about freely without a chaperone. As Elizabeth soon discovered, upper-class Portuguese women were uneducated and led greatly restricted lives; they did not go out unchaperoned, while Indian and Black women had much more freedom.

Elizabeth was not uncritical of Brazilian customs, people, and institutions during her travels; she commented on a wide range of topics, including the status of women, Indians, Blacks, slavery, and civic institutions. An intelligent observer, she praised the friendliness of the

Brazilians, but also noted their tendency to indolence and procrastination, and their indifference to the natural world around them. Nowhere did she find anyone who knew the name of a flower or an animal.

Brazil was home to four million Black slaves who worked on the sugar, coffee, and cotton plantations, and as domestics and tradesmen in the cities. Elizabeth thought that slavery was an obstacle to progress and had a pernicious effect on both the slaves and slave owners. Emancipation was not as divisive a topic as it was in the United States, and was openly discussed as inevitable. Even the royal couple thought that slavery would be abolished in time. The absence of racial prejudice was commendable, although she thought miscegenation resulted in an enfeebled population, deficient in energy and physical stamina, so she felt that the races should not intermarry. The Indian populations that she encountered in the Amazon were still in a state of nature and should remain so, as they would have difficulty adapting to an urban environment. However, Brazil was not Boston, and she was appalled at the morals of Indian women who cohabited with drifters and bore their children.

As a New England Protestant, Elizabeth brought her religious and moral values with her, and they informed her judgments. The Catholic clergy were immoral and ignorant, yet influential. Religious holidays and processions consumed time that was better spent working. She found the police corrupt. There was little support for education, and intellectual life was at a low level. Research was not funded, and museums and libraries were inadequate. Agricultural crops were raised for export, while food crops were not grown, thus depriving people of basic needs. Immigrants and a better class of white men were needed to develop Brazil. And she foretold that Amazonia would be populated and developed some day.

Although Elizabeth was critical of many aspects of Brazilian life, she also found much to praise during her fifteen months there. She liked the climate of the tropics, with its warmth and lush vegetation. It was a sharp contrast to the harsh New England winters that she experienced. The people were warm and welcoming, and she was delighted to receive the gift of a cacao cup from the ladies of Manaus upon her arrival there. Courtesy and civility were traits of the highest members of society to the lowest.

Once Elizabeth returned to Boston in June 1866, she wrote an article for *The Atlantic Monthly* on their trip to Brazil. Both she and Louis devoted their time to writing *A Journey in Brazil,* based on their experiences and his scientific work in the Amazon. The book was published in 1867 and sold out in three weeks. In 1868, Elizabeth accompanied Agassiz on a dredging expedition to Cuba and Florida, and again she wrote an article that was published in *The Atlantic Monthly.* The couple returned to South America in 1871–1872 to conduct a deep-sea dredging expedition aboard the steamer *Hassler.* The voyage took them to Rio de Janeiro, the Straits of Magellan, up the coast of Chile and Peru, to the Galápagos Islands, and Panama. Elizabeth kept a record of this expedition too, but no book was ever written about their discoveries.

Life changed for Elizabeth with the death of Louis Agassiz on December 14, 1873. She lost her companion, who had given direction to her life, but she soon immersed herself in writing Agassiz's biography and assembling his papers and correspondence for publication. His two-volume biography was published in 1885 and translated into French and German. When Alexander Agassiz's wife died that same year, he and his children came to live with Elizabeth. Again, she assumed the role of caregiver of his children and followed his progress as a naturalist. Emperor Dom Pedro II and Empress Teresa visited her in Boston in 1876. Their visit was a reminder of the past, one "so full of sad associations."

Elizabeth's long-standing interest in the education of women gave direction to her life in her final years. She was president of the Society for the Collegiate Instruction of Women, established in 1879, which sought to give women a Harvard education equal to men. Initially, there were no plans for a separate college for women, only a close affiliation with Harvard and instruction by Harvard professors. In 1894, the governor of Massachusetts signed the articles of incorporation of Radcliffe College, and Elizabeth became its first president. She resigned as president of Radcliffe in 1900 and was named honorary president, a title she held until 1903.

During her last years, Elizabeth lived in Boston in the winter, surrounded by family, her books, music, opera, and the theater, and in the summers in Nahant by the sea. She maintained an affiliation with Radcliffe College and attended events there. Elizabeth became an invalid and lived with her niece in Arlington Heights, where she died on June 27, 1907. She is buried in Mount Auburn Cemetery in Cambridge, Massachusetts, next to her husband.

Her publications include *Actaea: A First Lesson in Natural History* (1859), *Seaside Studies in Natural History* (1865), *A Journey in Brazil* (1868) and *Louis Agassiz: His Life and Correspondence* (1885).

Excerpts published here are from *A Journey in Brazil* and her biography, *Elizabeth Cary Agassiz,* by Lucy Allen Paton.

A JOURNEY IN BRAZIL

THE EMANCIPATION OF SLAVES

May 20 The subject of emancipation is no such political bugbear here as it has been with us. It is very liberally and calmly discussed by all classes; the general feeling is against the institution, and it seems to be taken for granted that it will disappear before many years are over. During this very session of the Assembly one or two bills for emancipation have been brought forward. Even now any enterprising negro may obtain his freedom, and, once obtained, there is no obstacle to his rising in social and political station. But while from this point of view slavery is less absolute than it was with us, it has some appalling aspects. The slaves, at least in the cities, are literally beasts of burden. One sees the most cumbersome furniture, pianos and the like and the heaviest trunks or barrels, piled one on top of the other, or bales of sugar and coffee weighting hundreds of pounds, moving about the streets on the heads of negroes. The result of this is that their limbs often become crippled, and it is common to see negroes in the prime of life who are quite crooked and maimed, and can hardly walk without a stick to lean upon. In justice I must add, however, that this practice, though it shocks a stranger even now, is gradually disappearing. We are told that a few years ago there were hardly any baggage wagons except these living ones, and that the habit of using the blacks in this way is going out of vogue. In this as in other matters the Emperor's opinions are those of an enlightened and humane man, and were his power equal to his will, slavery would vanish from his dominions at once. He is, however, too wise not to know that all great social changes must be gradual; but he openly declares his abhorrence of the system.

July 30 …Mr. Sinimbu tells us that here the result is on the whole in their favor; he say that the free blacks compare well in intelligence and activity with the Brazilians and Portuguese. But it must be remembered, in making the comparison with reference to our own country, that here they are brought into contact with a less energetic and powerful race than the Anglo-Saxon. Mr. Sinimbu believes that emancipation is to be accomplished in Brazil by a gradual process which has already begun. A large number of slaves are freed every year by the will of their masters; a still larger number buy their freedom annually; and as there is no longer any importation of blacks, the inevitable result of this must be the natural death of slavery. Unhappily the process is a slow one, and in the mean while slavery is still doing its evil work, debasing and enfeebling alike whites and blacks. The Brazilians themselves do not deny this, and one constantly hears them lament the necessity of sending their children away to be educated, on account of the injurious association with the house-servants. In fact, although politically slavery has a more hopeful aspect here than elsewhere, the institution from a moral point of view has some of its most revolting characters in this country, and looks, if possible, more odious than it did in the States.

SOCIALIZING WITH BRAZILIANS

LETTER OF ELIZABETH AGASSIZ TO MRS. THOMAS G. CARY, MANAOS, NOVEMBER 18, 1865

I have come to the conclusion that the Brazilians do not know either how to work or play. They have not that activity which makes life a restless force with us and gives it interest, neither have they that love of amusement that gives zest to the life of the Europeans. I have several times to make calls here with the Barras, and so stately and solemn an occasion you cannot imagine, though they are perfectly familiar with the people we go to see. I feel as if they were all tongue-tied, and stumble about in my poor Portuguese simply because I feel the silence so oppressive that I must break it or get up and run out of the house. One of the habits here is to send word beforehand when you're going to make a call: this in order that the lady of the house may have time to put up her hair and to put on her gown, which she never does, so far as I have found out except when company comes. If I could only command Portuguese enough, I think I should call all these unconscious sufferers together and tell them what benighted , colorless, crippled lives they are leading surrounded by beauties which they never see, all nature tempting them to walk, to row, to open their eyes only and look; and they sit speechless and stupefied putting on their fine things Sundays and feasts to show themselves in the streets for a few minutes. They are more to be pitied than blamed for it all. A woman is exposed to every sort of scrutiny and scandal who goes out unattended, and her only safety is to stay at home. I believe I am looked upon as a very extraordinary specimen but everything is forgiven to a stranger, so I go on my way unmolested. When I am walking in the woods here, as I constantly do, I often meet Indian women (whose life is perfectly free and a thousand times pleasanter than the ladies' life here), and they always express their wonder at meeting a "senhora" alone and asked me if I am not afraid. To which, I always answer, "No, why should I be? The senhoras in my country walk and row and ride and are perfectly safe, and I think it's a great pity that your ladies never go out."

VISIT TO A COFFEE PLANTATION

June 30th--Before leaving, we rode with Mr. Lage through his plantation, that we might understand something of the process of coffee culture in this country. I am not sure that, in giving an account of this model fazenda, we give a just idea of fazendas in general. Its owner carries the same large and comprehensive spirit, the same energy and force of will, into all his undertakings, and has introduced extensive reforms on his plantation. The Fazenda de Fortaleza de Santa Anna lies at the foot of the Serra de Babylonia. The house itself, as I have already said, makes a part of a succession of low white buildings, enclosing an oblong square divided into neat lots, destined for the drying of coffee. The drying of coffee in the immediate vicinity of the house, though if seems a very general custom, must be an uncomfortable one; for the drying-lots are laid down in a dazzling white cement, from the glare of which, in this hot climate, the eye turns wearily away, longing for a green spot on which to rest. Just behind the house on the slope of the hill is the orangery. I am never tired of these golden orchards, and this was one of especial beauty. The small, deep-colored tangerines, sometimes twenty or thirty in one cluster, the large choice orange, "Laranja selecta," as it is called, often ten or twelve together in a single bunch, and bearing the branches to the ground with their weight; the paler "Limao dôce," or sweet lemon, rather insipid, but greatly esteemed here for its cool, refreshing properties, all these, with many others, for the variety of oranges is far greater than we of the temperate zone conceive it to be, make a mass of color in which gold, deep orange, and pale yellow are blended wonderfully with the background of green. Beyond the house enclosure, on the opposite side of the road, are the gardens, with aviary, and fish-ponds in the centre. With these exception, all of the property which is not forest is devoted to coffee, covering all the hillsides for miles around. The seed is planted in nurseries especially prepared, where it undergoes its first year's growth. It is then transplanted to its permanent home, and begins to bear in about three years, the first crop being of course a very light one. From that time forward, under good care and with favorable soil, it will continue to bear and even to yield two crops or more annually, for thirty years in succession. At that time the shrubs and the soil are alike exhausted, and, according to the customs of the country, the fazendeiro cuts down a new forest and begins a new plantation, completely abandoning his old one, without a thought of redeeming or fertilizing the exhausted land. One of the long-sighted reforms undertaken by our host is the manuring of all the old, deserted plantations on his estate; he has already a number of vigorous young plantations, which promise to be as good as if a virgin forest had been sacrificed to produce them. He wishes not only to preserve the wood on his own estate, and to show that agriculture need not be cultivated at the expense of taste and beauty, but to remind his country people also, that, extensive as are the forests, they will not last forever, and that it will be necessary to emigrate before long to find new coffee grounds, if the old ones are to be considered worthless. Another of his reforms is that of the roads, already alluded to. The ordinary roads in the coffee plantations, like the mule tracks all over the country, are carried straight up the sides of the hills between the lines of shrubs, gullied by every rain, and offering, besides, so steep an ascent that even with eight or ten oxen it is often impossible to drive the clumsy, old-fashioned carts up the slope, and the negroes are obliged to bring a great part of the harvest down on their heads. An American, who has been a great deal on the coffee fazendas in this region, told me that he had seen negroes bringing enormous burdens of this kind on their heads down almost vertical slopes. On Senhor Lage's estate all these old roads are abandoned, except where they are planted here and there with alleys of orange trees for the use of the negroes, and he has substituted for them winding roads in the side of the hill with a very gradual ascent, so that light carts dragged by a single mule can transport all the harvest from the summit of the plantation to the drying-ground. It was the harvesting season, and the spectacle was a pretty one. The negroes, men and women, were scattered about the plantations with broad, shallow trays, made of plaited grass or bamboo, strapped over their shoulders and supported at their waists; into these they were gathering the coffee, some of the berries being brilliantly red, some already beginning to dry and turn brown, while here and there was a green one not yet quite ripe, but soon to ripen in the scorching sun. Little black children were sitting on the ground and gathering what fell under the bushes, singing at their work a monotonous but rather pretty snatch of song in which some took the first and others the second, making a not inharmonious music. As their baskets were filled they came to the Administrador to receive a little metal ticket on which the amount of their work was marked. A task is allotted to each one, so much to a full-grown man, so much to a woman with young children, so much to a child, and each one is paid for whatever he may do over and above it. The requisition is a very moderate one, so that the industrious have an opportunity of making a little money independently. At night they all present their tickets and are paid on the spot for any extra work. From the harvesting-ground we followed the carts down to the place where their burden is deposited. On their return from the plantation the negroes divide the day's harvest, and dispose it in little mounds on the drying-ground. When pretty equally dried, the coffee is spread out in thin even layers over the whole enclosure, where it is baked for the last time. It is then hulled by a very simple machine in use on almost all the fazendas, and the process is complete. At noon we bade good by to our kind hosts, and started for Juiz de Forza.

INDIAN MEN AND WOMEN

August 30th-- As time goes on, we grow more at home with our rustic friends here, and begin to understand their relations to each other. The name of our host is Laudigári (I spell the name as it sounds), and that of his wife Esperança. He, like all the Indians living upon the Amazons, is a fisherman, and, with the exception of such little care as his small plantation requires, this is his only occupation. An Indian is never seen to do any of the work of the house, not even to bring wood or water or lift the heavy burdens, and as the fishing is done chiefly at certain seasons, he is a very idle fellow for a great part of the time. The women are said, on the contrary, to be very industrious; and certainly those whom we have an opportunity of seeing here justify this reputation. Esperança is always busy at some household work or other, grating mandioca, drying farinha, packing tobacco, cooking or sweeping. Her children are active and obedient, the older ones making themselves useful in bringing water from the lake, in washing the mandioca, or in taking care of the younger ones. Esperança can hardly be called pretty, but she has a pleasant smile and a remarkably sweet voice, with a kind of child-like intonation, which is very winning; and when sometimes, after her work is over, she puts on her white chemise, falling loose from her brown shoulders, her dark skirt, and a rose or sprig of white jessamine in her jetty hair, she is by no means unattractive in her personal appearance, though I must confess that the pipe which she is apt to smoke in the evening injures the general effect. Her husband looks somewhat somber; but his hearty laugh occasionally, and the enjoyment of the glass of cachaça which rewards him when he brings in a new lot of specimens, shows that he has his bright side. He is greatly amused at the value Mr. Agassiz attaches to the fishes, especially the little ones, which appear to him only fit to throw away.

Last evening, with some difficulty, we induced Laudigári to play for us on a rough kind of lute or guitar,--a favorite instrument with the country people, and used by them as an accompaniment for dancing. When we had him fairly *en train* with the music, we persuaded Esperança and Michelina to show us some of their dances; not without reluctance, and with an embarrassment which savored somewhat of the self-consciousness of civilized life, they stood up with two of our boatmen. The dance is very peculiar; so languid that it hardly deserves the name. There is almost no movement of the body; they lift the arms, but in an angular position with no freedom of motion, snapping the fingers like castanets in time to the music, and they seem rather like statues gliding from place to place than like dancers. This is especially true of the women, who are still more quiet than the men....After it was over, Esperança and the others urged me to show them the dance "of my country," as they said, and my young friend R and I waltzed for them to their great delight. It seemed to me like a strange dream. The bright fire danced with us, flickering in under the porch, fitfully lighting its picturesque interior and the group of wondering Indians around us, who encouraged us every now and then with a "Muito bonito, mia branca, muito bonito" (Very pretty, my white, very pretty). Our ball kept up very late, and after I had gone to my hammock I still heard, between waking and sleeping, the plaintive chords of the guitar, mingling with the melancholy note of a kind of whippoorwill, who sings in the woods all night. This morning the forest is noisy with the howling monkeys. They sound very near and very numerous; but we are told that they are deep in the forest, and would disappear at the slightest approach.

Sept 1st Yesterday morning we bade our friendly hosts good-by, leaving their pretty picturesque home with real regret. The night before we left, they got together some of the neighbors in our honor, and renewed the ball of the previous evening. Like things of the same kind in other classes, the second occasion, got up with a little more preparation then the first, which was wholly impromptu, was neither so gay nor so pretty. Frequent potations of cachaça made the guests rather noisy, and their dancing, under the influence, became far more animated, and by no means so serious and dignified as the evening before.

THE CONTRAST BETWEEN INDIAN AND BRAZILIAN WOMEN

Oct 29 Yet I must say that the life of the Indian woman, so far as we have seen it, seems enviable, in comparison with that of the Brazilian lady in the Amazonian towns. The former has a healthful out-of-door life; she has her canoe on the lake or river and her paths through the forest, with perfect liberty to come and go; she has her appointed daily occupations, being busy not only with the care of her house and children but in making farinha or tapioca, or in drying and rolling tobacco, while the men are fishing and turtle hunting; and she has her frequent festa-days to enliven her working life. It is, on the contrary, impossible to imagine anything more dreary and monotonous than the life of the Brazilian Senhora in the smaller towns. In the northern provinces especially the old Portuguese notions about shutting women up and making their home-life as colorless as that of a cloistered nun, without even the element of religious enthusiasm to give it zest, still prevail. Many a Brazilian lady passes day after day without stirring beyond her four walls, scarcely ever showing herself at the door or window; for she is always in a slovenly dishabille, unless she expects company. It is sad to see these stifled existences; without any contact with the world outside, without any charms of domestic life, without books or culture of any kind, the Brazilian Senhora in this part of the country either sinks contentedly into a vapid, empty, aimless life, or frets against her chains, and is as discontented as she is useless.

BRAZILIAN INSTITUTIONS

Nov 27 The hospitality we have received in Brazil, the sympathy shown to Mr. Agassiz In his scientific undertaking, as well as our own sentiments of gratitude and affection for our many friends here, forbid us to enter into any criticism of Brazilian manners or habits which could have a personal application. Neither do I believe that a few months' residence in a country entitles any one to a judgement upon the national character of its people. Yet there are certain features of Brazilian institutions and politics which cannot but strike a stranger unfavorably, and which explain the complaints one constantly hears from foreign residents. The exceedingly liberal constitution, borrowed in great part from our own, prepares one to expect the largest practical liberty. To a degree this exists; there is no censorship of the press; there is no constraint upon the exercise of any man's religion; nominally, there is absolute freedom of thought and belief. But in the practical working of the laws there is a very arbitrary element, and a petty tyranny of the police against which there seems to be no appeal. There is, in short, an utter want of harmony between the institutions and the actual condition of the people. May it not be, that a borrowed constitution, in no way the growth of the soil, is, after all, like an ill- fitting garment, not made for the wearer, and hanging loosely upon him? There can be no organic relation between a truly liberal form of government and a people for whom, taking them as a whole, little or no education is provided, whose religion is administered by a corrupt clergy, and who, whether white or black, are brought up under the influences of slavery. Liberty will not abide in the laws alone; it must have its life in the desire of the nation, its strength in her resolve to have and hold it. Another feature which makes a painful impression on the stranger is the enfeebled character of the population. I have spoken of this before, but in the northern provinces it is more evident than farther south. It is not merely that the children are of every hue; the variety of color in every society where slavery prevails tells the same story of amalgamation of race; but here this mixture of races seems to have had a much more unfavorable influence on the physical development than in the United States. It is as if all clearness of type had been blurred, and the result is a vague compound lacking character and expression. This hybrid class, although more marked here because the Indian element is added, is very numerous in all the cities and on the large plantations;...

Shooting Fish in the Amazon, Library of Congress

TRAVELING IN THE AMAZON

April 2d-Ceará. We left Pará on the 26th of March, in the evening, feeling for the first time that we were indeed bidding good by to the Amazons. Our pleasant voyages on its yellow waters, our canoe excursions on its picturesque lakes and igarapés, our lingerings in its palm-thatched cottages, belonged to the past; except in memory, our Amazonian travels were over. When we entered upon them, what vague anticipations, what visions of a new and interesting life, not, as we supposed, without its dangers and anxieties, were before us. So little is known, even in Brazil, of the Amazons, that we could obtain only very meagre and, usually, rather discouraging information concerning our projected journey. In Rio, if you say you are going to ascend their great river, your Brazilian friends look at you with compassionate wonder. You are threatened with sickness, with intolerable heat, with the absence of any nourishing food or suitable lodgings, with mosquitoes, with Jacarés and wild Indians. If you consult a physician, he gives you a good supply of quinine, and tells you to take a dose every other day as a preventative against fever and chills; so that if you escape intermittent fever you are at least sure of being poisoned by a remedy which, if administered incautiously, may cause a disease worse than the one it cures. It will take perhaps from the excitement and novelty of Amazonian travelling to know that the journey from Pará to Tabatinga may be made with as much ease as a reasonable traveler has the right to expect, though of course not without some privations, and also with no more exposure to sickness than the traveler occurs in any hot climate. The perils and adventures which attended the voyages of Spix and Martius, or even of more recent travelers, like Castelnau, Bates, and Wallace, are no longer to be found on the main course of the Amazons, though they are met at every step on its great affluents. On the Tocantins, on the Madeira, or the Purus, on the Rio Negro, the Trombetas, or any of the large tributaries, the traveler must still work his way slowly up in a canoe, scorched by the sun or drenched by the rain; sleeping on the beach, hearing the cries of wild animals in the woods around him, and waking perhaps in the morning to find the tracks of a tiger in unpleasant proximity to his hammock. But along the course of the Amazons itself, these days of romantic adventure and hair-breadth escapes are over; the wild beasts of the forest have disappeared before the puff of the engine; the canoe and the encampment on the beach at night have given place to the prosaic conveniences of the steamboat. It is no doubt true of the Amazons, as of other tropical regions, that a long residence may reduce the vigor of the constitution, and perhaps make one more liable to certain diseases; but during our journey of eight months none of our large company suffered from any serious indisposition connected with the climate, nor did we see in any of our wanderings as many indications of intermittent fever as are to be met constantly on our Western rivers. The voyage on the Amazons proper has now become accessible to all who are willing to endure heat and mosquitoes for seeing the greatest river in the world, and the magnificent tropical vegetation along its shores. The best season for the journey is from the close of June to the middle of November,--July, August, September, and October being the four driest months of the year, and the most salubrious throughout the region.

ART AND EDUCATION OF WOMEN

July 7th- Yesterday we visited the Mint, the Academy of Fine Arts, and a primary school for girls. Of the Mint it is scarcely fair to judge in its present condition; a new building is nearly completed, and all improvements in machinery are wisely deferred until the establishment is removed. When this change takes place, much that is antiquated will be improved, and its many deficiencies supplied.

There is little knowledge of, or interest in, art in Brazil. Pictures are as rare as books in a Brazilian house; and though Rio de Janeiro has an Academy of Fine Arts, including a school of design and sculpture, it is still in too elementary a condition to warrant criticism. The only interesting picture in the collection derives its attraction wholly from the circumstances connected with it, not at all from any merit in the execution. It is a likeness of a negro who, in a shipwreck off the coast, saved a number of lives at the risk of his own. When he had brought several passengers to the shore, he was told that two children remained in the ship. He swam back once more and brought them safely to the beach, but sank himself exhausted, and was seized with hemorrhage. A considerable sum was raised for him in the city of Rio, and his picture was placed in the Academy to commemorate his heroism.

Of the public schools for girls not much can be said. The education of women is little regarded in Brazil, and the standard of instruction for girls in the public schools is low. Even in the private schools, where the children of the better class are sent, it is the complaint of all teachers that they are taken away for school just at the time when their minds begin to develop. The majority of girls in Brazil who go to school at all are sent at about seven or eight years of age, and are considered to have finished their education at thirteen or fourteen. The net step in their life is marriage. Of course there are exceptions; some parents wisely leave their children at school, or direct their instruction at home, till they are seventeen or eighteen years of age, and others send their girls abroad. But usually, with the exception of one or two accomplishments, such as French or music, the education of women is neglected, and this neglect affects the whole tone of society. It does not change the general truth of this statement, that there are Brazilian ladies who would be recognized in the best society as women of the highest intelligence and culture. But they are the exceptions, as they inevitably must be under the present system of instruction, and they feel its influence upon their social position only the more bitterly.

Indeed many of the women I have known most intimately here have spoken to me with deep regret of their limited, imprisoned existence. There is not a Brazilian senhora, who has ever thought about the subject at all, who is not aware that her life is one of repression and constraint. She cannot go out of her house, except under certain conditions, without awakening scandal. Her education leaves her wholly ignorant of the most common topics of a wider interest, though perhaps with a tolerable knowledge of French and music. The world of books is closed to her; for there is little Portuguese literature into which she is allowed to look, and that of other languages is still less at her command. She knows little of the history of her own country, almost nothing of others, and she is hardly aware that there is any religious faith except the uniform one of Brazil; she has probably never heard of the Reformation, nor does she dream that there is a sea of thought surging in the world outside, constantly developing new phases of national and individual life; indeed, of all but her own narrow domestic existence she is profoundly ignorant.

On one occasion, when staying at a fazenda, I took up a volume which was lying on the piano. A book is such a rare sight, in the rooms occupied by the family, that I was curious to see its contents. As I stood turning over the leaves (it proved to be a romance), the master of the house came up, and remarked that the book was not suitable reading for ladies, but that here (putting into my hand a small volume) was a work adapted to the use of women and children, which he had provided for the senhoras of his family. I opened it, and found it to be a sort of textbook of morals, filled with commonplace sentiments, copybook phrases, written in a tone of condescending indulgence for the feminine intellect. Women, being after all, the mothers of men, and understood to have some little influence on their education, I could hardly wonder, after seeing this specimen of their intellectual food, that the wife and daughters of our host were not greatly addicted to reading. Nothing strikes a stranger more than the absence of books in Brazilian houses. If the father is a professional man, he has his small library of medicine or law, but books are never seen scattered about as if in common use; they make no part of the daily life. I repeat, that there are exceptions. I well remember finding in the sitting-room of a young girl, by whose family we had been most cordially received, a well-selected library of the best literary and historical works in German and French; but is the only instance of the kind we met with during our year in Brazil. Even when the Brazilian women have received the ordinary advantages of education, there is something in their home-life so restricted, so shut out from natural contact with external influences, that this in itself tends to cripple their development. Their amusements are as meagre and scanty as their means of instruction.

In writing these things I but echo the thought of many intelligent Brazilians, who lament a social evil which they do not know well how to reform. If among our Brazilian friends there are some who, familiar with the more progressive aspect of life in Rio de Janeiro, question the accuracy of my statements, I can only say that they do not know the condition of society in the northern cities and provinces. Among my own sex, I have never seen such sad lives as became known to me there, lives deprived of healthy, invigorating happiness, and intolerably monotonous, a negative suffering, having its sources, it is true, in the absence of enjoyment rather than in the presence of positive evils, but all the more to be deplored because so stagnant and inactive.

Behind all defects in methods of instruction, there lies a fault of domestic education, to be lamented throughout Brazil. This is the constant association with black servants, and worse still, with negro children, of whom there are usually a number in every house. Whether the low and vicious habits of the negroes are the result of slavery or not, they cannot be denied; and it is singular to see persons, otherwise careful and conscientious about their children, allowing them to live in the constant companionship of their blacks, waited upon by the older ones, playing all day with the younger ones. It shows how blind we may become, by custom, to the most palpable dangers. A stranger observes at once the evil results of the contact with vulgarity and vice, though often unnoticed by the parents. In the capital, some of these evils are fast disappearing; indeed, those who remember Rio de Janeiro forty years ago have witnessed, during that short period, a remarkable change for the better in the state of society. Nor should it be forgotten that the highest authority in the community is exerted in the cause of a liberal culture for women. It is well known that the education of the Imperial Princesses has been not only superintended, but in a great measure personally conducted, by their father.

Lady Florence Dixie

An Aristocrat in Patagonia

Lady Florence Dixie was the daughter of aristocrats on both her parents' side. She was born on May 25, 1855, in Dumfries, Scotland. Raised a Roman Catholic by her mother, who had converted to Catholicism, she was educated at home and in convent schools. As a child, she participated in physical sports and excelled in riding, hunting, and swimming alongside her brothers. In 1875, at age nineteen, she married Sir Arthur Beaumont Churchill Dixie, whose wealth and position allowed them to live grandly, but his gambling and drinking resulted in the sale of his family's ancestral estate, and the couple moved to her mother's former home.

Shortly after the birth of her second son, Edward, in 1878, the couple; Florence's two brothers, Lord Queensbury and Lord James Douglas; and Julius Beerbohm, a friend who served as their guide, left for Patagonia. Why Patagonia? According to Florence, it was an area not well traveled by men and few, if any, European women had ventured there. She wanted to escape the busyness of modern life and chose Patagonia "precisely because it was an outlandish place and so far away." Florence wanted a unique experience and was an intrepid and hardy traveler. She hunted ostriches and guanacos and killed several, as the group depended on these animals for their food. She rode horseback throughout the trip, slept on the ground during rainstorms, admired the Andes Mountains, endured hunger, swam in the cold waters of the Straits of Magellan, searched for lost horses, experienced an earthquake, met Indians and an Argentine gaucho,and shot a guanaco.

Her six months in Patagonia resulted in two books for children published in 1890, *The Young Castaways* and *Aniwee.* Both took place in Patagonia and had strong, capable female characters. *Across Patagonia,* describing her experiences there, was published in 1880 in Edinburgh. An accomplished author, she wrote eight other books and numerous articles.

Lady Florence was a war correspondent in 1881, where she covered the Boer War and the end of the Anglo-Zulu War. She was a prominent feminist and supported suffrage for women, as well as equality between the sexes, coeducation, and wanted the professions open to women. A liberal and progressive in politics, she supported Scottish and Irish home rule.

Lady Florence died on November 7, 1905, and was buried on the Kinmount estate.

The excerpts here are taken from *Across Patagonia.*

ACROSS PATAGONIA

PATAGONIA AT FIRST SIGHT

Whilst we were threading the intricate passage of the First Narrows, which are not more than two miles broad, I scanned with interest the land I had come so many thousand miles to see—Patagonia at last! Desolate and dreary enough it looked, a succession of bare plateaus, not a tree nor a shrub visible anywhere; a grey, shadowy country, which seemed hardly of this world; such a landscape, in fact, as one might expect to find on reaching some other planet.

BARRENNESS OF PATAGONIA

The country we were now crossing was of a totally different character to that we had left behind us. Not a tree or a shrub was to be seen anywhere, and while to the left of us lay the rugged range of the Cordilleras, in front and to the right an immense plain stretched away to the horizon, rising and falling occasionally in slight undulations, but otherwise completely and monotonously level. The ground, which was rather swampy, was covered with an abundance of coarse green grass, amongst which we could see flocks of wild geese grazing in great numbers. We passed several freshwater lakes, covered with wildfowl, who flew up very wild at our approach. A hawk or two would occasional hover over our heads, and once the dogs started off in pursuit of a little grey fox that had incautiously shown itself; but except these, there was no sign of animal life on the silent, seemingly interminable plain before us.

PATAGONIAN INDIANS

We had not gone far when we saw a rider coming slowly towards us, and in a few minutes we found ourselves in the presence of a real Patagonian Indian. We reined in our horses when he got close to us, to have a good look at him, and he doing the same, for a few minutes we stared at him to our hearts' content, receiving in return as minute and careful a scrutiny from him. Whatever he may have thought of us, we thought him a singularly unprepossessing object, and, for the sake of his race, we hoped an unfavorable specimen of it. His dirty brown face, of which the principal feature was a pair of sharp black eyes, was half-hidden by tangled masses of unkempt hair, held together by a handkerchief tied over his forehead, and his burly body was enveloped in a greasy guanaco-capa, considerably the worse for wear. His feet were bare, but one of his heels was armed with a little wooden spur, of curious and ingenious handiwork. Having completed his survey of our persons, and exchanged a few guttural grunts with Gregorio, of which the purport was that he had lost some horses and was on their search, he galloped away, and, glad to find some virtue in him, we were able to admire the easy grace with which he sat his well-bred looking horse, which, though considerably below his weight, was doubtless able to do its master good service.

Continuing our way we presently observed several mounted Indians, sitting motionless on their horses, like sentries, on the summit of a tall ridge ahead of us, evidently watching our movements. At our approach they disappeared over the ridge, on the other side of which lay their camping-ground. Cantering forward we soon came in sight of the entire Indian camp, which was pitched in a broad valley-plain, flanked on either side by steep bluffs, and with a little stream flowing down its centre. There were about a dozen hide tents, in front of which stood crowds of men and women, watching our approach with lazy curiosity. Numbers of little children were disporting themselves in the stream, which we had to ford in order to get to the tents. Two Indians, more inquisitive than their brethren, came out to meet us, both mounted on the same horse, and saluted us with much grinning and jabbering. On our arrival in the camp we were soon encircled by a curious crowd, some of whose number gazed at us with stolid gravity, whilst others laughed and gesticulated as they discussed our appearance in their harsh guttural language, with a vivacious manner which was quite at variance with the received traditions of the solemn bent of the Indian mind. Our accoutrements and clothes seemed to excite great interest, my riding-boots in particular being objects of attentive examination, and apparently of much serious speculation. At first they were content to observe them from a distance, but presently a little boy was delegated by the elders, to advance and given them a closer inspection. This he proceeded to do, coming towards me with great caution, and when near enough, he stretched out his hand and touched the boots gently with the tips of his fingers. This exploit was greeted with roars of laugher and ejaculations, and emboldened by its success, many now ventured to follow his example, some enterprising spirits extending their researches to the texture of my ulster, and one even going so far as to take my hand in his, whilst subjecting a little bracelet I wore to a profound and exhaustive scrutiny.

Whilst they were thus occupied I had leisure to observe their general appearance. I was not struck so much by their height as by their extraordinary development of chest and muscle. As regards their stature, I do not think the average height of the men exceeded six feet, and as my husband stands six feet two inches I had a favourable opportunity for forming an accurate estimate. One or two there were, certainly, who towered far above him, but these were exceptions. The women were mostly of the ordinary height, though I noticed one who must have been quite six feet, if not more. The features of the pure-bred Tehuelche are extremely regular, and by no means unpleasant to look at. The nose is generally aquiline, the mouth well shaped and beautified by the whitest of teeth, the expression of the eye is intelligent, and the form of the whole head affords a favourable index to their mental capabilities. These remarks do not apply to the Tehuelches in whose veins there is a mixture of Araucanian or Fuegian blood. The flat noses, oblique eyes, and badly proportioned figures of the latter make them most repulsive objects, and they are as different from a pure-bred Tehuelche in every respect as "Wheel-of- Fortune" from an ordinary carthorse. Their hair is long and coarse, and is worn parted in the middle, being prevented from falling over their faces by means of a handkerchief, or fillet of some kind, tied around the forehead. They have naturally little hair on the face, and such growth as may appear is carefully eradicated, a painful operation, which may extend even to their eyebrows. Their dress is simple, and consists of a "chiripá," a piece of cloth round the loins, and the indispensable guanaco-capa, which is hung loosely over the shoulders, and held round the body by the hand, though it would obviously seem more convenient to have it secured round the waist with a belt of some kind. Their horse-hide boots ae only worn, for reasons of economy, when hunting. The women dress like the men except as regards the chiripá, instead of which they wear a loose kind of gown beneath the capa, which they fasten at the neck with a silver brooch or pin. The children are allowed to run about naked till they are five or six years old, and are then dressed like their elders. Partly for ornament, partly also as a means of protection against the wind, a great many Indians paint their faces, their favourite colour, as far as I could see, being red, though one or two I observed had given the preference to a mixture of that colour with black, a very diabolical appearance being the result of this combination.

The Tehuelches are a race that is fast approaching extinction, and even at present it scarcely numbers eight hundred souls. They lead a rambling nomadic existence, shifting their camping places from one region to another, whenever the game in their vicinity gets shy or scarce. It is fortunate for them that the immense numbers of guanaco and ostriches makes it an easy matter for them to find subsistence, as they are extremely lazy, and, plentiful as game is around them, often pass two or three days without food rather than incur the very slight exertion attendant on a day's hunting.

But it is only the men who are cursed or blessed with this indolent spirit. The women are indefatigably industrious. All the work of Tehuelche existence is done by them except hunting. When not employed in ordinary household work they busy themselves in making guanaco capas, weaving gay-coloured garters and fillets for the hair, working silver ornaments, and so forth. Not one of their least arduous tasks is that of collecting firewood, which, always a scarce article, becomes doubly hard to find, except by going great distances, when they camp long in one place.

AN OSTRICH HUNT

His prediction was speedily verified, for on reaching the summit of a little hill, up which we had slowly and stealthily proceeded, two small gray objects suddenly struck my eye. I signed to François and my brother, who were riding some twenty yards behind me, and putting spurs to my horse, galloped down the hill towards the two gray objects I had perceived in the distance. "Choo! Choo!" shouted François, a cry by which the ostrich-hunters cheer their dogs on, and intimate to them the proximity of game. Past me like lightning the four eager animals rushed, bent on securing the prey which their quick sight had already detected.

Guanaco, Library of Congress

The ostriches turned one look on their pursuers, and the next moment they wheeled round, and making for the plain, scudded over the ground at a tremendous pace.

And now, for the first time, I began to experience all the glorious excitement of an ostrich hunt. My little horse, keen as his rider, took the bit between his teeth, and away we went up and down the hills at a terrific pace. On and on flew the ostriches, closer and close crept up "Leona," a small, red, half-bred Scotch deerhound, with "Loca," a wiry black lurcher at her heels, who in turn was closely followed by "Apiscuña" and "Sultan." In another moment the little red dog would be alongside the ostriches. Suddenly, however, they twisted right and left respectively, scudding away in opposite directions over the plain, a feint which of course gave them a great advantage, as the dogs in their eagerness shot forward a long way before they were able to stop themselves. By the time they had done so the ostriches had got such a start that, seeing pursuit was useless, we called the dogs back. We were very much disappointed at our failure, and in no very pleasant frame of mind turned our horses' heads in the direction of our camp.

A HERD OF GUANACOS

The next day found us once more in the saddle, jogging along over the plains with the hopes of a speedy arrival at the Cordilleras to cheer us, under the depression of spirits which the dreary monotony of the country could not fail to produce. The character of the landscape was what we had been accustomed to since leaving Cabo Negro, being in this region, if anything, possibly more barren than usual.

This day's ride was memorable for the immense number of guanacos which covered the plains in all directions. On arriving at a broad depression we were surprised by the sight of a herd of these animals, which could not have numbered less than five thousand. This enormous living mass defiled past us up the side and over the brow of the escarpment which bound the depression referred to, occupying a space of time of about ten minutes—although they were going at a very quick pace—and once or twice before the day was over we met an equally numerous herd. How such an extraordinary number of animals can find subsistence on the barren plains, which they even seem to prefer to the grassy ravines, is a matter difficult of explanation. Certain it is that the withered pampa grass must contain great nourishing properties, as the guanacos thrive and grow very fat on it. Although they are generally rather shy, we passed one herd composed of some unusually tame animals. As we approached them, instead of running away, the whole herd came slowly trotting towards us, staring at us with naive unconcern, which showed that they were innocent of the chase. As it chanced we had plenty of meat, so we left them unmolested. It was not often that we found them so tame, especially when we happened so be short of meat; in such cases, with the usual perverseness of things, they would scarcely allow one to approach within rifle-range.

A LONG, DREARY MONOTONOUS RIDE

After another day's sojourn at this encampment we resumed our journey. We took a good supply of fuel with us, as we were now entering on the barren, woodless region, during our transit over which we should have to rely solely on the provision we now made.

Leaving the beechwood behind us we rode up on to a plain, on whose edge we could distinguish what appeared to be a little black cloud. In reality it was a peak, or rather clump of peaks of the Cordilleras, at the foot of which we were one day to camp, and towards which for the next few days we directed our horses' heads.

This day's ride, and it was a long one, was by far more monotonous and dreary than any of the preceding ones. The immense plateau over which we rode for six or seven hours was remarkable for its gloom and barrenness, even in a region where all is sterility and dreariness. There was no sun, and the sky, lowering and dark, formed a fit counterpart to the plain, which stretched flatly away to the indistinct horizon, gray, mournful, and silent.

We could not help being affected by the aspect of the scenery around us, and I do not remember ever to have felt anything to equal the depression of spirits to which I, in common with all our party, fell a prey, and to whose influence even the guides succumbed.

SIGHTING A CONDOR

The next day was passed in idleness. It was extremely hot, scarcely a breath of wind stirring, and in the evening we were rather bothered by mosquitos, this being the first acquaintance we made with them in Patagonia. During the day a bird was seen hovering over the camp at an immense height, which we were told was a condor. It was so high up that it looked scarcely bigger than an ordinary hawk. Taking advantage of a moment when it hung perfectly motionless, my husband had a shot at it, and by a marvelous fluke, the ball took effect, and down the creature came, growing bigger and bigger as it fell, till at last, reaching the earth with a loud thud, there it was, the most gigantic bird I had ever seen. We found it measured twelve feet from wing to wing. The most distinctive feature of the condor is the white down ruff which encircles the neck two or three inches below the head, which latter is completely bare of feathers and repulsively ugly. In the female bird the colour of this ruff is black.

AN ARGENTINE GAUCHO

We rode down a broad valley, which lead to the Gallegos River, where we were to camp for the night. On reaching its farther end we were suddenly surprised by the sight of an Indian camp, composed of three tents, which were pitched on the other side of the river. Having little curiosity to make the acquaintance of their inmates, we continued along the river to our intended camp, but Gregorio and Mr. B. rode over to see them. They rejoined us an hour afterwards; Mr. B. had found an old friend, an Argentine Gaucho, named Isidoro, who had accompanied him on a former trip, and whom, curiously enough, he had parted from a year before, on exactly the same spot where he now met him. I was glad to hear that Isidoro was going to pay us a visit the next day, as I had heard a great deal about him, and was anxious to make his acquaintance. We camped near the river, seven or eight miles away from the Indian camp, and consequently, we hoped, rather too far to attract a call from these people, the disagreeable experience of their visit whilst we were at Cape Gregorio being still fresh in my mind.

Early in the morning we saw a man riding in the direction of the camp, who, I was told, was Isidoro. He presently appeared among us, and except for his moustache and beard, and the superior cleanliness of his dress, he might have been taken for an Indian. He was warmly welcomed by the guides, amongst whom his unequalled proficiency in all that pertains to the pampa craft, and his personal character, had gained him great prestige. Isidoro did not stop long, as he was going to hunt with the Indians that day; so, after taking a few cups of maté, and smoked a pipe or two in silence, he said good-bye, and took his departure.

As he rode away, I could not help admiring his manly bearing and his perfect seat on a splendid well-bred looking horse, which seemed not unworthy of its master. He wore his guanaco capa with a certain foppish grace that one might have looked in vain for in Gregorio or any of the others, and every article of his accoutrements, from his carefully coiled lasso to the bright coloured garters round his potro-boots, was perfectly finished and natty.

Mary Lester

A Teacher in Honduras

LITTLE IS KNOWN OF MARY Lester's background. She was a British citizen, born in the Pyrenees, where her father was a soldier; hence, she grew up speaking Spanish fluently and English. Orphaned as a young woman, she boldly obtained a position as a governess to a planter's family in Fiji. Mary then moved to Sydney, Australia, where she taught school. Somehow she made contact with a supposed Roman Catholic priest who wanted to establish a school for the children of colonists in San Pedro Sula, Honduras. Mary was promised a good salary as a teacher and a plantation of 160 acres. Desirous of settling down and having a home, she accepted the offer and left Sydney for Central America in May 1881.

Mary began her 219-mile journey overland at the port of Amapala, Spanish Honduras. As a woman traveling alone, she faced difficulties obtaining mules and muleteers. Ever the optimist, Mary bravely faced the weather conditions of heat and rain, swollen rivers, poor accommodations and food, and endured being taken advantage monetarily along the way. As she neared San Pedro Sula, she heard rumors that the school did not exist, and once she arrived, she discovered that the alcoholic priest had been defrocked and left town. Mary, unfortunately, was duped by a charlatan and arrived in San Pedro Sula almost penniless. Her only choice, at this point, was to return home. She took a steamer to New Orleans and then made her way back to Europe. Mary was not bitter about her journey; she was grateful for the help she received along the way and thought well of the Honduran people.

Mary, under the pseudonym of Maria Soltera, wrote a book about her six-month experience, entitled *A Lady's Ride across Spanish Honduras,* which was published in London in 1884. In 1889, she coauthored a handbook on South America.

The following excerpts are taken from *A Lady's Ride across Spanish Honduras.*

TRAVELING ALONE

The captain was standing on board as we ascended. "I have not had time to say much to you," said he, addressing me; "but I hear you are going to Honduras. Surely it is a terrible journey for you to take alone!"

"I do not fear a little hardship," said I, perhaps too confidently. "I am the daughter and sister of English soldiers, and my bringing up has never been luxurious. Circumstances in later years have compelled me to depend on myself"

"It is a wonder to me," continued the captain, "that your relatives allow you to go."

"I have no near relations, and I go to make a home of my own. We have all of us troubles, captain; do not discourage me. Hitherto I have got on very well, and the world in general is kind to lone female travellers."

"Yes, the civilized world." The captain here shook his head.

ADVICE ON TRAVELING ALONE

"La Libertad is the next port that we stop at," I say, in order to ward off any further reference to this gentleman's annoyance.

"Yes; I get off there, as I have to go up into the interior on business. You will have a terrible time of it going across to San Pedro. I have often thought of going there; but from what I have heard about the roads, and the starvation, and the chances of attack (chances, mind, I say-for I don't want to frighten you, but there is nothing really to eat), and other discomforts, I have decided to give up the idea. I should like, however, to accompany you," he added, after a short pause.

"Why not?" say I, catching at the opportunity of securing a travelling companion. "You and your servant and mules joined with mine (for I am to hire a lad and muleteer at Amapala), would make quite a respectable company. We should protect the one the other, if needs be. I have little fear, and surely there must be something to eat. How do the people live themselves?"

"A plantain and a cigarillo is all they require," replied Mr. Z. "you will suffer very much from want of food. Take what you can with you. For myself, I could not do without my dinner more than twice a- week. I have always been accustomed to live well. No, no—at my time of life it would not do. Glad the consul at Amapala will look after you. Have you got a revolver?"

"A revolver! No. I never fired one in my life," I replied in terror. " I would much rather be without one."

A MULE THAT BOLTED

Eduardo had ridden a good deal in advance; as he neared the road turning to the left, we saw the baggage-mule suddenly break loose from his hold, and dart at full speed among the trees, Eduardo following as hard as he could gallop.

This made the mare a little restive, but Abel's strong arm subdued her. "Let us turn into the left path," said he; "you will have to dismount and wait whilst I go on. The baggage mule has bolted."

Turning into the road on the left, which was little more than a bridle-path through shrubs and nice soft grass, the man dismounted me, at the same time tying the mare to a low bush. There was plenty of grass, and so this one of the party, at least, was very much at ease.

"You won't mind being left a short time," said Abel; "It is quite safe. I had better follow Eduardo quick. Ah, it was time," he said, returning with something in his hand.

It was my dressing-comb, in two parts, and full of dirt and sand.

I accompanied him a little way, and had the pleasure of picking up one of my slippers, part of a little book, and many other things with which my handbag had been packed. Further on lay my long tin box, unfastened, indeed, but stove in by what was unmistakably a violent kick in the wrong direction.

"Ah," said Abel, contemplating this, "the mule is wild; he has rushed against the trees, and the baggage has got loose; I hope there is no accident. Señora, I am sorry to leave you alone, but I had better get on to Eduardo."

So he sped away at a flying swing-trot, and I was left literally to pick up the pieces.

SCENIC RIVERS OF HONDURAS

The painter of river scenery can nowhere in the wide world find more charming subjects for his brush than the lovely water-courses of Spanish Honduras. The cascades among the mountains are simply magnificent, and deserve to be classed among the finest in any land. The lowest and dirtiest of villages in the interior can generally show a beautiful running stream in its midst; and it is, I think, in consequence of this, that typhoid fever and blood poisoning are unknown.

THE MOUNTAINS OF HONDURAS

I may write, perhaps, with some partiality; for what the sea is to many, the mountains are to me. I was born amongst them, in the grand Pyrenees, and so I am their daughter. When sickness of body and sorrow of heart fall upon me, I will arise and flee to the mountains. My strength surely comes from them.

We ascended higher, and in the elastic air the men became refreshed, and as hunger and noonday approached, we agreed to halt. There was a *hacienda* picturesquely built in a cleft of the ranges. To this we wended our way, and were glad to see the chestnut-trees stretching grandly in front of this demesne. Here was shelter for the animals, since the grass and shade were deep all around; and we human beings could sling a hammock on the lowest branches of the fine trees.

ACCOMMODATIONS AT ARIMESINE

Reached Arimesine at seven. Passed a fairly good night, as the woman of the house possessed some notions of propriety. Quite in clover, for I had a railed-off space wherein to swing my hammock, divided from the public room by my travelling rug and shawl hung on a high clothes-horse. The men slept in the verandah. There was a white basin in the establishment, and Eduardo got this filled with water, and in a manner I managed to wash.

TRAVELING THROUGH THE MOUNTAINS

Our journey, after some miles of travel, began to be on the ascent, and shortly we were far up the mountains. Here, losing the luxuriance of herbage and grass, we came upon rock, and cedar and pine trees. Clumps of these last grew in great profusion, scenting the air with the peculiar healthy smell of the Aleppo fir, which, alternating with masses of the elegant deodara tree gave a magnificent clothing to tracts of land which might otherwise be bare. The mountain was not a high one, but the descent on the other side was so abrupt that I was glad to get off and walk, notwithstanding that the path was little less than an assemblage of loose stones, mingled with gravel and dust. Gradually this path narrowed, and we entered a high defile, so full of rock, and holes, and enormous roots of trees, that every step had to be picked with care, and our wary baggage mule slipped for the first time...

A CONFRONTATION WITH A MULETEER

I had just settled myself for the night, when, to my surprise, Marcos lifted the latch and walked in.

"Señora" said he, "I want half a dollar, please."

"What for? Why do you come at this time?"

"I have put the mules into the stable of the place, and I want the money to pay for them." This with a very decided air.

"No, Marcos," I replied, "I will not give you the money. In the first place, you had no business to put the mules in the public stables without consulting me; in the second place, you know you expressly promised never to do so unless there were a scarcity of grass and water here."

"There is scarcity of grass and water here."

"That is strange, Marcos; the schoolmaster told me that there was an abundance of both; besides, I saw Luisa feeding in a meadow not an hour ago."

"Then you will not pay for stabling, Señora."

"Most certainly not; you can do if you choose," I replied.

"Señora," answered Marcos, "if you do not give me the money, I will leave you and go home when we get to Comayagua."

"No, Marcos; if you leave me, you will go tomorrow morning. We can settle at the office of the *alcalde* here; you will have broken your engagement, and so I must place the papers before the *alcalde*, and he will arrange what I am to pay you. Good night; shut the door behind you, and don't come in here till I call. Now go."

The man stared at me, but said nothing. After waiting a moment, he turned on his heel and went out, shutting the door with a clang.

The situation was uncomfortable enough, but I was determined not to be victimised. The matter certainly was small, but to accede to this demand would only be to open the way to further extortion. I plumed myself, too, on the way I had dragged in the *alcalde,* as I had not the faintest idea whether such a functionary existed in the place or not.

CROSSING A RIVER

"No hay vado; y mas, no hay canoa:" (no ford; and worse, no canoe). Eduardo remained silent, and walked to and fro, looking at the water as if he had a personal quarrel with everything around, and with it in particular. At length I said, "There ought to be a canoe here; where, I wonder, is the man who owns it?"

A shrug of the shoulder and a flourish was the only reply, and then Marcos solved the difficulty with the usual Hondureian Platonism, "No hay remedio" (there is no remedy). The action that accompanied these words further intimated—"There is nothing for it but sink or swim: the river must be crossed, ford or no ford, and the sooner we go the better." Obviously there was no remedy; and the men turned up their drawers up to their knees, folded their jackets on their heads, and prepared to walk into the water. The elder of the two Indian women now came towards me. Placing one small brown hand on the mule's neck, and almost caressing my knee with the other, as I sat humped up to keep clear of being wet, she said, "Es muy peligroso, señora, muy peligroso; no anda": (it is very dangerous, lady; do not go).

I knew instinctively, and as well as she did, that it was very dangerous; but what could be done? And I turned to Marcos with this inquiry.

The man replied in his usual incisive and somewhat peremptory tones, " We must cross at once, Eduardo, and I will go first; he will lead the baggage-mule, and I will follow on the *macho*. When Louisa see the *macho* well into the water, the creature will follow at once. Now stick on hard", this being expressed as (apargate muy fuerte). With this admonition he seized the hem of my dress, and began to roll it up in a rough fashion, to prevent it being immersed in the water.

The Indian interposed: "Let me do that for the lady,--you must not touch her in that manner;" and pushing Marcos aside she arranged my garments most comfortably. Then she said, with oh! such pathos in her voice, "The river is so strong—it is very dangerous. You will go; but'ay di mi, you have much courage."

Much courage! Had she felt my throbbing pulse; could she but know, kind soul, the struggle that was going on in my proud English heart not to appear to be afraid! True, my words were measured, and I smiled because I felt I must not give way one inch; but if this were courage, it was merely the desperation of "no hay remedio": nothing more nor less.

The men, meanwhile, had driven their beasts into the water. The mules here went straight enough; and having got them safely to their work, Marcos turned round and hailed to me to follow close on. I patted the woman on the shoulder, saying as I did so, "Adieu, good friend—all will be well," and gathered up the reins to ride away.

A MISERABLE NIGHT

The rain had driven the mosquitoes into the dwelling, and at a later hour these pests became intolerable. A stir from without arrested my attention, and presently a lad with an iron brasier entered, lighted a candle which was stuck against the wall, and returning to the brasier, seemed to stir it up. At that instant a smoke and a most fearful smell pervaded the whole room, suffocating and nauseous in the extreme. I drew my net over my head, and lay wondering what this could mean; but nobody else seemed to be annoyed, or even to take notice of the nuisance. A more miserable night I never passed; and it was with the greatest thankfulness that I saw a gleam of the morning's light through the door which opened to let the first riser out.

A TRIP IN VAIN

"I, John Frederic De Brot, Her Britannic Majesty's Consul at Puerto Cortez:"--

"Whereas Miss Mary------------and the Rev. Dr. W. L. Pope have consented to submit to my arbitration the question in dispute between them, about the unnecessary expenses accrued to the former in a useless voyage to this country; and whereas I declared myself willing to accept the office of arbitrator in this matter, I have come to the following decision, based on the letters and other documents presented to me;

That the Rev Dr. Pope pay to Miss Mary---------the half of the expenses she has incurred in her voyage to and from this country."

"Given under my hand and seal, this tenth day of October 1881."

(Signed) J.F. De Brot

British Consul

"You will never get a penny from Pope, I am sure," said Mr. De Brot, when I called to thank him for this document. " Still, I think it will be a satisfaction to you to have your own statements thus, as it were, publicly substantiated; I only wish that you had insisted upon a legal agreement before you started, but in the face of such a letter as Pope's last one to you, I do not wonder at this idea not occurring to you."

"The matter at this point, Mr. De Brot," I replied, "just resolves into this: nothing succeeds like success. Had this matter turned out fortunately, every one would have said, What an enterprising woman "Soltera" is! so sensible to go abroad, where there is so much more opening for employment,--and all the rest of it. As it is, I am considerably out of pocket, and many of my friends, I feel sure, will be more ready to blame than to sympathise with me in the matter. However, the world on the whole is kind, and I shall be able to work the lost money back in some way; you know "Voy con Dios" is my motto."

Mr. De Brot asked if I had thought of putting the affair into the law-courts of Honduras, in the case of Dr. Pope's refusing to pay.

"Certainly not," I replied; "it would be a degradation not only to myself, but also to my family. Your decision establishes my claim and my honour; for the rest, I am content to let this unworthy man go his way." As I said this, the quaint old Italian proverb ran through my mind—"Evil does not always come to do hurt."

"I am glad to hear you say this," replied the consul; "but I boil with indignation when I think of this man. However, you are better off than many."

"May I ask if you have seen Dr. Pope since he received his copy of the arbitration?"

"He came to my office last night, but he was in such a state that I refused to see him. Depend upon me, if I can get any money out of him for you, I will do so."

"I suppose," continued Mr. De Brot, his handsome kind face lighting up with a smile, "after this experience you will never believe more in anything or anybody?"

"Not quite so bad as that," I replied:" has not the golden cord of others' kindness run like a string to hold me up through all my troubles? Believe me, I am not ungrateful, and I shall often think with pleasure of the people of Honduras."

Nellie Bly, Library of Congress

Nellie Bly

A Newspaper Reporter in Mexico

NELLIE BLY, THE PSEUDONYM OF Elizabeth Cochrane Seaman, was born in Cochran's Mills, Pennsylvania, on May 5, 1864. Of Irish descent on both sides (her grandfather had emigrated from County Londonderry at the end of the eighteenth century), she spent her youth in Cochran's Mills until her mother moved the family to Pittsburgh after her father died in 1871. It was in Pittsburgh that the outspoken Elizabeth caught the attention of the editor of the *Pittsburgh Dispatch,* when she responded critically to a column in the paper that stated a woman's sole purpose in life was to be a housewife and mother. She wrote her rebuttal under the pseudonym "Lonely Orphan Girl," and, upon hearing from the editor, she identified herself and was offered a job writing a column. An early feminist, she wrote about life issues that affected women, including divorce, which her mother had recently experienced, and she advocated a change in divorce laws. Elizabeth selected the pen name Nellie Bly, after the Pittsburgh-born Stephen Foster's song "Nelly Bly," which was popular at the time. She, unlike many women writers, did not adopt a masculine pen name so as to hide her real identity in order to get published. Nellie bravely chose a female name.

In the early stages of her career, she was an investigative reporter, writing about the issues that women factory workers faced. When complaints from factory owners came to the newspaper because of her criticisms, she was transferred to the women's section, assigned to write on topics of interest to women: gardening, housekeeping, and fashion. But Nellie soon became frustrated with her new assignment, and she arranged to go to Mexico as a foreign correspondent for the *Dispatch.* She traveled to Mexico with her mother in 1886, where she spent nearly half a year reporting on all aspects of the country and the people (both rich and poor), including courtship, marriage, bullfighting, smoking, religion, food, the Indians, travel by rail, the Mexican press, and social life. Although she did not speak Spanish, this was not an impediment. She found it easy to get around and get by knowing only a few words. Her reports to the *Pittsburgh Dispatch* were eventually published as a book, *Six Months in Mexico,* in 1889. She dedicated the book to the newspaper's editor, George Madden, who sponsored the trip.

When Nellie arrived in Mexico, Porfirio Díaz had been in power for ten years. Díaz ruled Mexico unopposed until 1911, as he amended the Constitution to continue his time in office. He supported economic development and courted foreign capitalists and landowners whose investments helped to develop the country, but at the price of the loss of freedoms, electoral fraud, press censorship, suppression of dissent, and the welfare of the peasants. The army, church leaders, and the landowners, who benefited from acquisitions of Indian lands, supported him.

Nellie was forced to flee Mexico or face arrest when she wrote an article, published in the United States, about a reporter who criticized the lack of freedom of the press under the dictator Porfirio Díaz. Apparently the Mexicans got a hold of the article, and since she did not look forward to spending time in a Mexican jail, she returned to the United States, where she accused Díaz of muzzling the press and being a tyrant. Nellie continued working for the *Pittsburgh Dispatch*, but unable to write on topics of interest to her, she left for New York City in 1887 to try her fortune there.

That year, Nellie talked herself into a job with Joseph Pulitzer's newspaper, *The New York World*, where she offered to feign insanity to expose conditions in the Women's Lunatic Asylum on Blackwell's Island. After ten days there, Pulitzer asked for her release. Bly's reports were published as *Ten Days in a Mad-House* in 1887, and the deplorable conditions that she exposed created a sensation that led to reforms. In turn, the book also made her famous.

Bly's next adventure and publicity stunt, sponsored by the newspaper, was to beat the round-the-world record of Phileas Fogg, Jules Verne's hero in *Around the World in Eighty Days*. On November 14, 1889, Nellie started out around the world, traveling lightly, with just the dress she wore, money, and toiletries. The newspaper sponsored a contest whereby a reader who guessed the exact date and time of her return would be given an expense-free trip to Europe. But not to be outdone, the *Cosmopolitan*, another New York newspaper, sent Elizabeth Bisland around the world to challenge Nellie. Nellie traveled alone by ship and railroad across Europe and into Asia, sending reports home by telegraph and cable. She arrived in New Jersey on January 25, 1890. She had traveled over forty thousand miles in seventy-two days and set a world record, only to have it eclipsed just a few months later. Bisland came in second, as she arrived in the United States four days after Nellie. Another book, *Around the World in Seventy-Two Days*, published in 1890, resulted from Nellie's adventure. Peeved because she did not receive a bonus or salary increase after her famous exploit, she left the newspaper, traveled in Europe, and remained out of public view for the next three years.

In 1895, at the age of thirty, she married Robert Seaman, a seventy-year-old millionaire and owner of the Iron Clad Manufacturing Company, which made steel containers. After Seaman's death in 1904,

Nellie took over the company, but due to embezzlement by employees and her inattentiveness to the financial aspects of the business, the company went bankrupt, and she was in financial straits. Nellie was an inventor and had designed a milk can and a garbage can; by 1905, she had registered some twenty-five patents. Now a widow with limited funds, Nellie went back to reporting on the women's suffrage convention (she predicted women would receive the vote in 1920), the Democratic and Republican conventions of 1912, and Woodrow Wilson's inauguration for the *New York World.* With creditors after her, Bly fled to Europe in 1915 and was in Austria when World War I began. She remained there until 1919 and reported on wartime conditions, visiting the Austrian, Russian, and Serbian battle zones and supporting the Austrian people, especially the widows and orphans.

For the last three years of her life, Bly returned to reporting at *The New York Evening Journal*, writing a column on the social issues of the day: impoverished women, the poor and destitute, orphans, capital punishment, and the treatment of American seamen. Always compassionate and socially conscious, she turned to dispensing advice and saving souls at the end of her career

Nellie Bly died of pneumonia on January 27, 1922, at age fifty-seven in New York City. She is buried in Woodlawn Cemetery in the Bronx, New York. But her name and exploits have lived on, as she has been portrayed in film, plays, television, and books. In 1998, she was inducted in the National Women's Hall of Fame, and in 2002 the United States government honored her with a postage stamp, one of four journalists selected.

The selections published here are from Bly's book *Six Months in Mexico.*

THE FUTURE OF MEXICO CITY

The City of Mexico makes many bright promises for the future. As a winter resort, as a summer resort, a city for men to accumulate fortunes; a paradise for students, for artists; a rich field for the hunter of the curious, the beautiful, and the rare. Its bright future cannot be far distant.

Already its wonders are related to the enterprising people of other climes, who are making prospective tours through the land that held cities even at the time of the discovery of America.

STREET CHILDREN OF MEXICO

Nine women out of ten in Mexico have babies. When at a very tender age, so young as five days, the babies are completely hidden in the folds of the *rebozo* and strung to the mother's back, in close proximity to the mammoth baskets of vegetables on her head and suspended on either side of the human freight. When the babies get older their heads and feet appear, and soon they give their place to another or share their quarters, as it is no unusual sight to see a woman carry three babies at one time in her *rebozo*. They are always good. Their little coal-black eyes gaze out on what is to be their world, in solemn wonder. No baby smiles or babyish tears are even seen on their faces. At the earliest date they are old, and appear to view life just as it is to them in all its blackness. They know no home, they have no school, and before they are able to talk they are taught to carry bundles on their heads or backs, or pack a younger member of the family while the mother carries merchandise, by which she gains a living. Their living is scarcely worth such a title. They merely exist. Thousands of them are born and raised on the streets. They have no home and were never in a bed. Going along the streets of the city late at night, you will find dark groups huddled in the shadows, which, on our investigation, will turn out to be whole families gone to bed. They never lie down, but sit with their heads on their knees, and so pass the night.

WOMEN TORTILLA MAKERS

Tortilla is not only one of the great Mexican dishes but one of the women's chief industries. In almost any street there can be seen women on their knees mashing corn between smooth stones, making it into a batter, and finally shaping it into round, flat cakes. They spit on their hands to keep the dough from sticking, and bake in a pan of hot grease, kept boiling by a few lumps of charcoal. Rich and poor buy and eat them, apparently unmindful of the way they are made. But it is a bread the Americans must be educated to. Many surprise the Mexicans by refusing even a taste after they see the bakers.

SMOKING IS A PASTIME

There is but one thing that poor and rich indulge in with equal delight and pleasure—that is cigarette smoking.

Those tottering with age down to the creeping babe are continually smoking. No spot in Mexico is sacred from them; in churches, on the railway cars, on the streets, in the theaters—everywhere are to be seen men and women of the elite-smoking.

SUNDAYS

This is the busiest day in the markets. Everything is booming, and the people, even on their way to and from church, walk in and out of the thousands of stalls, buying their marketing for dinner. Hucksters cry out their wares, and all goes as merry as a birthday party. Indians, from the mountains, are there in swarms with their marketing. The majority of stores are open, and the "second-hand" stalls on the cheap corner do the biggest business of the week.

Those who do not attend church find Mexico delightful on Sunday. In the alameda (park) three military bands, stationed in different quarters, play alternately all forenoon. The poor have a passion for music, and they crowd the park. After one band has finished, they rush to the stand of the next, where they stay until it is finished, and then move to the next. Thus all the morning they go around in a circle. The music, of which the Mexican band was a sample, is superb; even the birds are charmed. Sitting on the mammoth trees, which grace the alameda, they add their little songs. All this, mingled with the many chimes which ring every fifteen minutes, make the scene one that is never forgotten. The rich people promenade around and enjoy themselves similar to the poor.

In the Zocalo, a plaza at the head of the main street and facing the palace and cathedral, the band plays in the evening; also on Tuesdays and Thursdays.

SUNDAY AT THE THEATER

Sunday is the most fashionable theater day. Every person who can possibly collect together enough money goes, from the poor, naked person to the Spanish millionaire. On Monday all amusement houses are closed and many are only open every other day throughout the entire week; they are not at all particular about fulfilling engagements. A play may be billed for a certain night and on arrival there the servant will politely inform you it is postponed until manana (to-morrow), and all you can do is to go back home and await their pleasure.

The National Theater is a fine building with accommodations for 4,500 persons. The first entrance is a wide open space faced with mammoth pillars. Going up the steps you enter, through a heavily draped doorway, the vestibule or hall. Along the sides are racks where gentlemen and ladies deposit their wraps. The orchestra, or pit—the fashionable quarter in American theaters—is known as the "Lunetas." The seats are straight-backed, leather- covered chairs of ancient shape and most uncomfortable style. They were evidently fashioned more for durability than beauty, being made of very heavy, unpainted wood. Narrow passageways intersect each other, and wooden benches are placed along the seats to serve as foot-rests. Down in front of the stage is the orchestra, flanked at either end by long benches running lengthwise of the stage. Boxes, six stories in height, look out upon the stage, and balconies circle the room. The balconies are divided into compartments holding eight persons. Common, straight chairs, with large mirrors on the door and walls, are the only furnishment. The "Lunetas" command seventy-five cents, to $1.50, Palcos (boxes) $2 a chair, and the Galeria (the sixth row of balconies) twenty-five cents.

At 8:30 the orchestra strikes up, people come in and find their places, and about 9 o'clock the curtain goes up and silence reigns; the enthusiasm which is manifested in bull-fights is absent here. Everything is accepted and witnessed with an air of boredom and martyrdom that is quite pathetic. More time is spent gazing around at the audience than at the players. Everybody carries opera glasses, and makes good use of them.

Without doubt you would like to know how they dress; the men—who always come first, you know—wear handsome suits, displaying immaculate shirt-front and collar that would make Eastern dudes turn green with envy. Generally the suit is entirely black, yet some wear light pantaloons. High silk opera-hats and a large display of jewelry finish the handsome Spanish man.

The ladies wear full dress, always light in color—pink, blue, pea green, white, etc.-trimmed with flowers, ribbons or handsome laces. Their hair is arranged artistically, and the dresses are always cut very low, displaying neck and arms such as only Mexican women possess. Very handsome combs and pins generally grace the hair. Young girls sometimes wear flowers, but it is considered better taste to wear the artificial article, because the real are so cheap, and the former, unsurpassed by nature, command very high prices. A Mexican woman would not be dressed without the expensive fan which she flits before her face with exquisite grace. The prevailing style is a point lace fan, which adds beauty to the face and, at the same time, does not hide it from beholders, for, let it be whispered, Mexican girls are fond of being looked at. A lady considers it the highest compliment she can receive from a man to stare at her for a long time, and the men come quite up to the point of being extremely complimentary.

...so between acts the ladies visit one another, and the men rise in their seats, put on their hats, turn their backs toward the stage, and survey the people, English fashion. They smoke their cigarettes, chat to one another, and discuss the women. The cow-bell rings again, people commence to embrace and kiss, and when the third bell rings again, hats are off, cigarettes extinguished, and every one in place in time to see the curtain, after being down for thirty minutes, rise.

Theaters close anywhere between 12:30 and three o'clock. The audience applaud very little, unless some one is murdered artistically. If a few feel like applauding other fine points, they are quickly silenced by the thousands of hisses which issue from all quarters of the house, and a Mexican hiss has no equal in the world. Ladies do not applaud, never look pleased or interested, but sit like so many statues, calmly and stupidly indifferent. After the play every one who can afford it goes to some restaurant for refreshments. Mexicans are not easily pleased with plays; and the only time they enjoy themselves is when they have a "Zarzuela"—a cross between a comic opera and a drama. Then they forget to hiss, and enter into the spirit of the play with as much vim as an American.

LARGE FAMILIES

Mexico is the hotbed of children; the land is flooded with them, and a small family is a thing unknown; they greet you at every window, at every corner, on every woman's back; they fill the carriages and the plaza; they are like a swarm of bees around a honeysuckle...A man died the other day who was followed to the grave by eighty-seven sons and daughters, and had buried thirteen, more than you can count in three generations in the States, so he was father to the grand total of one hundred children. There is another man living in Mexico who has had two wives, and who had living forty-five children. Down in a small village, out from Vera Cruz, is a father with sixty-eight children. Allowing the small average of five to a family, one can see how numerous the grandchildren would be. I am acquainted with a gentleman whose mother is but thirteen-and-a half years older than he, and she has eighteen more of a family. It is a blessed thing that the natives are able to live in a cane hut and exist on beans and rice, else the lists of deaths by starvation would be something dreadful.

MEXICAN WOMEN

On the street a woman is not permitted to recognize a man first. She must wait until he lifts his shining silk hat; then she raises her hand until on a level with her face, turns the palm inward, with the fingers pointing toward the face, then holds the first and fourth fingers still, and moves the two center ones in a quick motion; the action is very pretty, and the picture of grace when done by a Mexican senora, but is inclined to deceive the green American, and lead him to believe it is a gesture calling him to her side. When two women walk along together the youngest is always given the inside of the pavement, or if the younger happens to be married, she gets the outside—they are quite strict about this; also, if a gentleman is with a mother and daughters, he must walk with the mother and the girls must walk before them. A woman who professes Christianity will not wear a hat or bonnet to church, but gracefully covers her head with a lace mantilla. No difference how nicely she is powdered and painted, to the height reached only by chorus girls. Four years ago, the Americans tell me, the Mexican women promenaded the streets and parks and took drives in ball-dresses, low neck, sleeveless, and with enormous trains; this has almost been stopped, although the finest of dresses, vivid in color, and only suitable for house or reception wear, are yet worn on Sundays.

COURTSHIP AND MARRIAGE

When parents notice a"bear," if they are favorably inclined, they invite him in, where he can see the object of his adoration hemmed in on either side by petticoats of forbidding aspect. When he once enters the house it means he has been accepted as the girl's husband, and there is no "backing out." The father sets a time for a private interview and when he calls they settle all business points: As to what the daughter receives at the father's death, when the marriage shall take place, where the bride is to live and how much the intended husband has to support her; the lawyer finishes all arrangements and escorts the engaged pair to a magistrate, where a civil marriage is performed---that their children may be legal heirs to their property. Even after this they are not permitted to be alone together; the intended bridegroom buys all the wedding outfit, for the bride is not allowed to take even a collar from what her father bought for her before.

The final ceremony is performed in a church by a *padre,* who sprinkles the young couple with holy water and hands an engagement ring to the groom, which he puts on the little finger of his bride, then the *padre* puts a marriage ring on both the bride and groom. After which, holding on to the priest's vestments, they proceed to the altar, where they kneel while he puts a lace scarf around their shoulders and a silver chain over their heads; symbolic that they are bound together irrevocably, as there is no such thing as divorce in Mexico. After mass is said the marriage festivities take place and last as long as the husband cares to pay for them, anywhere from three days to a month, and then, like the last scene on the stage, the curtain goes down, lights are put out, and you see no more of the actors who pleased your fancy for a short time.

The husband puts his wife in his home, which is henceforth the extent of her life. She is devoted, tender, and true, as she has been taught. She expects nothing except to see that the servants attend to the children and household matters—and she gets only what she expects. He finds divers amusements, for, according to the custom of the country, his "illusion:" (what they call love) dies after a few days spent alone with his bride, and he only returns at stated intervals to fondle or whip his captive—just as fancy dictates. The men discuss at the club the fact that he has more loves than one, but they all have, and it excites no censure. But the world can never know what the bride thinks; private affairs are never made public. He can even kill her, as did their predecessor Cortes, and it will excite little or no comment. When matured years come on, she loses what good looks she had; three hundred pounds is nothing for weight, and on her lip grows a heavy, black mustache. She cares for nothing but sleeping, eating, drinking, and smoking the perpetual cigarette. And in this way ends the fair Mexican's brief dream of the *grande passion.*

MEXICO IS NOT A DEMOCRACY

Very few people outside of the Republic of Mexico have the least conception of how government affairs are run there. The inhabitants of Mexico—at least it is so estimated—number 10,000,000 souls, 8,000,000 being Indians, uneducated and very poor. This large majority has no voice in any matter whatever, so the government is conducted by the smaller, but so-called better class.

My residence in Mexico of five months did not give me ample time to see all these things personally, but I have the very best authority for all statements. Men whom I know to be honorable have given me a true statement of facts which have heretofore never reached the public prints. That such things missed the public press will rather astonish Americans who are used to a free press; but the Mexican papers never publish one word against the government or officials, and the people who are at their mercy dare not breathe one word against them, as those in position are more able than the most tyrannical czar to make their life miserable. When this is finished the worst is yet untold by half, so the reader can form some idea about the government of Mexico.

THE MEXICAN ARMY AND THE CAMP FOLLOWERS

The standing army in Mexico is said to number forty thousand men, but it is believed to be more. Every little village of a few hundred people has its army, and every day that army is being increased; the officers range from those who have gained experience and fame on the battlefield to the young ones reared and trained in military colleges; they are mostly all of what is considered the highest class of people in Mexico.

The rank and file are mostly half-breeds or Indians, who are not by any means volunteers. They are nearly all convicts. When a man is convicted of some misdemeanor he is enlisted in the regular army, separated from his home, and to serve the rest of his natural life. This life is not a bed of roses—there is no bed at all, and out of a medio (61/4 cents) a day, he has to furnish his food and comforts. The dress uniform is made of coarse woolen goods, with yellow stripes on the sleeves; and the undress uniform, which is worn constantly except on review days, is but white muslin, pants, waist, and cap.

Some of the Indians are stolen and put in the army, and they immediately resign themselves to their fate, for there is no more escape for them than there is from death.

The wives of these poor fellows are very faithful, and very often follow the regiment from one place to another; they live on what nature grows for them and what they can beg or steal; the men are called in Spanish "soldados," and the women, because they cling to their husbands, "soldadas." It looks very pitiful to see a poor Indian woman with a babe tied to her back and one clinging to her skirts, dusty, hungry and footsore, traveling for miles through the hot sun with the regiments.

These soldadas are wonderfully hardy; they can travel for a week through the hot sun, with nothing to drink and but a spoonful of boiled beans and one tortilla—a small flat cake—for two day's rations, sleep on the ground at night, and be as fresh for service as a well-kept mule.

...The soldiers have an herb named marijuana, which they roll into small cigaros and smoke. It produces intoxication which lasts for five days, and for that period they are in paradise. It has no ill after-effects, yet the use is forbidden by law. It is commonly used among prisoners. One cigaro is made, and the prisoners all sitting in a ring partake of it. The smoker takes a draw and blows the smoke into the mouth of the nearest man, he likewise gives it to another, and so on around the circle. One cigaro will intoxicate the whole lot for the length of five days.

THE MEXICANS MAY OVERTHROW DIAZ

The Mexican have a good deal of suppressed wrath bothering them at the present day; they know that Diaz is a tyrannical czar, and want to overthrow him. It may be readily believed that Diaz knows they are bound to get rid of this superfluous feeling, and he would much rather have them vent its strength on the Americans than on himself; thus he stands on the war question. He is a good general, and has many good, tough old soldiers, the best of whom is ex-President Gonzales, to aid him, besides the convict soldiers and the Rurales.

THE MEXICAN PRESS

The press of Mexico is like any of the other subjects of that monarchy, yet it is a growing surprise to the Americans used to free movement, speech and print who visit Mexico with the attained idea that it is a republic. Even our newspapers have been wont to clip from the little sheets which issue from that country, believing them untrammeled, and quoting them as the best authority, when, in truth, they are but tools of the organized ring, and are only capable of deceiving the outsider.

In the City of Mexico there are about twenty-five newspapers published, and throughout the empire some few, which are perused by the smallest number of people. The Mexicans understand thoroughly how the papers are run, and they consequently have not the slightest respect in the world for them. One can travel for miles, or by the day, and never see a man with a newspaper. They possess such a disgust for newspapers that they will not even use one of them as a subterfuge to hide behind in a streetcar when some woman with a dozen bundles, three children and two baskets is looking for a seat.

All the papers which I know of are subsidized by the government, and, until within several months ago, they were paid to abstain from attacks on the government. The subsidy has stopped, through want of funds, but the papers say nothing against the government, as they care too much for their easy lives; so they circulate among foreigners misrepresenting all Mexican affairs, and putting everything in a fair but utterly false light. The Mexicans have nothing but contempt for the papers, and the newspaper men have no standing whatever, not even level with the government officials, whose tools they are. If a newspaper even hints that government affairs could be bettered, the editors are thrown in prison, too filthy for brutes, until they die or swear never to repeat the offense. The papers containing the so-called libelous items are all hunted up by the police and destroyed, and the office and type are destroyed. These arrests are not unusual; indeed they are of frequent occurrence.

....even a foreigner does not write about Mexico's doings as they really are. I had some regard for my health, and a Mexican jail is the least desirable abode on the face of the earth, so some care was exercised in the selection of topics while we were inside their gates. Quite innocently one day I wrote a short notice about some editors, who received no pay from the government, being put in jail. The article was copied from one paper to another, and finally reached Mexico. The subsidized sheets threatened to denounce me and said in Spanish, "One button was enough;" meaning by one article the officials could see what my others were like, but by mean of a little bravado I convinced them that I had the upper hand and they left me unhurt.

MEXICANS ARE MISREPRESENTED

I dread the return and reports of such people in the States, for although there are good and bad here, the Mexicans have never been represented correctly. Before leaving home I was repeatedly advised that a woman was not safe on the streets of Mexico: that thieves and murderers awaited one at every corner, and all the horrors that could be invented were poured into my timid ear. There are murders committed here, but not half as frequently as in any American city. Some stealing is done, but it is petty work; there are no wholesale robberies like those so often perpetrated at home. The people are courteous, but of course their courtesy differs from ours, and the women—I am sorry to say it—are safer here than on our streets, where it is supposed everybody has the advantage of education and civilization. If one goes near the habitation of the poor in the suburbs, they come out and greet you like a long lost friend. They extend invitations to make their abode your home, and offer the best they own. Those in the city, while always polite and kind, have grown more worldly wise and careful.

NORTH AMERICAN TOURISTS SHOULD VISIT MEXICO

How much I would like to paint the beauties of Mexico in colors so faithful that people in the States could see what they are losing by not coming here.... Business men who wish to rest from their labors find perfect quiet in this paradise. All cares vanish. Some strange magic seems to rob one of all care, of every desire to hurry. Railways furnish comfortable and safe transportation; the people are attentive and polite, and as many comforts are attainable as at any other place away from the States. People who have any desire to see Mexico in all its splendor should come soon, for civilization's curse or blessing, whichever it may be, has surely set a firm foot here, and in a few years, yielding to its influence, all will be changed.

Marguerite Bates Dickins

A Naval Officer's Wife in Uruguay and Paraguay

Marguerite Bates Dickins was the wife of United States naval officer Francis William Dickins who commanded the USS *Tallapoosa*, a steamer of the United States Navy's South Atlantic Squadron from 1887 to 1889. For two and a half years she sailed with him along the east coast of South America. Having a woman aboard a naval vessel—especially the wife of the commander—was not unusual in the United States Navy or the Royal Navy in the nineteenth century. Marguerite prepared for her adventure by studying Spanish and reading everything she could on the countries they were to visit. As a result, she had some familiarity with the area. She documented her travels by writing letters home, and these letters were published in her hometown newspaper. Eventually, her letters became a book entitled *Along Shore with a Man-of-War*, which was published in 1893.

The *Tallapoosa* stopped at the major ports in Brazil, Argentina, and Uruguay, and went upriver 1,100 miles to Asunción, Paraguay, as well. Marguerite described each city she visited, with its buildings, homes, hotels, churches, streets, and shops, as well as the local population. She always made a point to comment on the women of each country—their dress, their looks, education, and manners—and the men as well. Festivities, Carnival, balls, bullfights, and meetings with dignitaries and political leaders filled her narrative. She was a careful observer of her surroundings and local ways.

Most of the selections represented here are Marguerite's observations of Uruguay and Paraguay, countries that were not normally on the female traveler's agenda. Uruguay, the smallest republic in South America, was invaded by Brazil in 1817, but a small band of Uruguayan exiles revolted against Brazilian domination, and a war ensued, with Argentina's United Provinces involved. By 1828, the war now a stalemate, Uruguay's independence was guaranteed by Great Britain to ensure that the country would not fall under the domination of its powerful neighbors and British trade would not be interrupted. Montevideo emerged as the nation's capital and was the country's economic and cultural center. In the 1870s, Italian and Spanish immigrants came to Uruguay, where they worked in small factories or established estancias on the grasslands where beef cattle and wheat were raised. The nineteenth century saw the emergence of two political parties; the liberal *Colorados* were pitted against the conservative *Blancos*, as each party vied for electoral control of the country. When Marguerite arrived in Uruguay in 1886, the country was being transformed economically and socially, and the military, which had been the power brokers, was being replaced by politicians that resulted in increased civilian participation in government.

The USS *Talapoosa* went up both the Paraná and Paraguay Rivers to the remote capital of Asunción, where few foreigners ventured to visit or trade. The capital was founded in 1537 by Argentine settlers fleeing Indian attacks on Buenos Aires. Paraguay, a landlocked and isolated country, was independent by 1811 and ruled by José Gaspar Rodríguez de Francia until 1840. Rodríguez reduced the power of the Catholic

Church and created a mestizo society by outlawing marriage between Caucasians. The López dynasty ruled Paraguay until 1870 and treated the country as their own fiefdom. Carlos López assumed power in 1841 and worked to modernize Paraguay, improving communication, building an army, supporting education, promoting industry, and opening the country to trade. His son, Francisco Solano López, led the country during the disastrous Paraguayan War that lasted from 1864 to 1870. A conflict between Brazil and Paraguay escalated into a war, with Brazil, Argentina, and Uruguay forming an alliance against Paraguay. The war dragged on for five years and ended with the death of López in battle. Paraguay lost territory to the aggressors, 50 to 60 percent of its population was killed, and the country was forced to pay reparations. In the aftermath of war, Brazil, as the occupying power, supported López's former generals as leaders of the country. They sold lands and businesses to foreign interests; as a result, Paraguay lost its economic and political independence. When Marguerite Dickins visited Paraguay, the country was still in the process of recovering from the war.

Once the cruise was over, Marguerite's name dropped out of history (she died in 1899 due to an explosion of naphtha in her home), but her husband's name did not. He was an 1865 graduate of the United States Naval Academy, was promoted to rear admiral in 1904, and retired from the navy in 1906. He died in 1910 in New York City and was buried in Arlington National Cemetery. The *Tallapoosa*'s days were over too, as she spent six years as a station ship in South America before being sold in Montevideo, Uruguay, in 1892. By that time, the ship was old, falling apart, and no longer seaworthy.

The following selections are from *Along Shore with a Man-of-War.*

Plaza de Constitutión, Montevideo, Uruguay, Library of Congress

URUGUAY AT FIRST SIGHT

Uruguay—or, as it is officially called, Republica Oriental del Uruguay, from its being on the oriental bank of the river—is a small but wonderfully fertile and rich country, which only needs more people, law, and order to flow with milk and honey.

In the northern and eastern parts there are mountains, and the rest is what looked to us with our memoires of Brazilian mountains, a dead, monotonous level, but in reality it is a rich, rolling plain, covered with fine succulent grasses, on which the herds of cattle thrive and fatten. One never gets to the mountainous regions, because there is no grand river highway to lead the people and commerce to them, and they are comparatively undeveloped. Only a few adventurous spirits or miners take the long stage coach and horseback rides, and the reports they bring back are not such as to tempt one, yet they report the country as beautiful and the mines rich. In short, the little republic can boast of a well-watered land, rich soil, good climate and the landscapes; in fact, it is a land where every prospect pleases and only man is—well, he is not exactly vile, but certainly not pleasant to live with, for his ways are not ours. A republic in name and without some of the bad features of a monarchy, but personal politics, arms at the polls, good laws badly enforced, revolutions, and a state church, all combined, make anything but an ideal republic. Of course I am now speaking of the people as a nation, for individually the *gente decente,* or better class, are delightful. Their country is still young and they had a bad start. Fancy what our country would have been if only the poorer class of Spaniards had settled here and intermarried with the Indians, and we had only these people to form our republic!—what a fine mess we should have made of it!—instead of which we had English, Dutch, French, and Spanish blood and all sorts of creeds, each one holding the other in check and forming a common front against the Indians, and then when we had formed the nucleus of a nation and accomplished our independence, in our hour of need we had patriots and statesmen to start us on the right road, and we have grown until our nation is the guiding star of all republics and a menace to all monarchies.

On the morning of our sixth day out from Rio we arrived at Montevideo, and what a peculiar picture it was that greeted us as we came on deck to see the city. Everything was gray; the sky covered with heavy gray clouds, the city of gray adobe, the water breaking against the shore, the surrounding country, all gray, and looking so cold and dreary. The chill wind of early spring whistled through the rigging and we got ashore as soon as possible to look for something cheering, as this was to be our headquarters for several years.

On the point of the bay opposite the city is the mount from which the city gets its name of Montevideo or Mount I see. It is a base grass-grown hill, with an old fort and lighthouse on its summit, while at its feet cluster the houses and saladeros of the suburb known as Cerro. The wharves are good, and lead directly up to the narrow streets of the old port of the city, which is built on the point. As I said before, the wind was cold, so every one stepped along briskly and there was color in their cheeks, quite cheering to look at after the pale faces of Rio; and oh! How pretty the Montevideo girls are! especially when about fifteen or sixteen. Such plump little pigeons with large dark eyes, sweet smiles, and perfectly fitting gowns—a little too fond, perhaps, of covering their pretty skins with cosmetics, but very pretty, sweet, and attractive, all the same.

THE LOTTERY

The lottery is a government institution, and the proceeds are used for the support of the big charity hospital on the Twenty-fifth of May Street. It built the hospital originally, and has also paid for the insane asylum, besides other small buildings for charitable purposes, such as lying-hospitals. Men and boys are the chief vendors, and you are assailed by them at every corner, but especially on the plazas. There are three different lists of prizes, headed by a grand prize which is either $50,000, $25,000 or $12,500. If it is the first mentioned, a whole ticket costs $10, if the second, $5 and if the last named, a ticket is $2.50. The tickets are divided into fifths; on the face of each fifth is a list of the prizes offered, a description of the ticket to let you know what color it ought to be, and on the back the date of drawing. The vendors get 6 per cent, and they always have in their pockets an official printed copy of the numbers of the last drawing, and you constantly see people stopping and taking tickets out of the pockets to compare with the list, and see what they have drawn. Every one buys, from the street vendors of fruits and cakes, porters, and laborers up. Drawings are frequent, and prizes are always promptly paid in silver coin.

MATE

Mate, generally called Paraguayan tea, is made from the leaf of a small tree of the holly species—*ilex paraguayensis*—which flourishes in parts of Paraguay. The leaves are gathered, prepared and then carefully packed in fresh hide bags, which contract when drying and make a package as hard as a stone. It is yellowish green in color, and teaspoonful of mate powder is put into the gourd, a small lump of sugar also if you like it, and then the cup is filled with boiling water, the bombilla inserted, and the infusion sucked through it. Fully three-fourths of the natives of Uruguay and the Argentine drink mate, and the quantity they consume is astonishing. A silversmith in the town of Paysandu told me he only drank thirty to forty cups in a day, and I have often seen a dozen emptied one after the other, and the cup sent out for more. Officers and soldiers standing at the barrack doors are drinking mate, and there is generally a gourd passing among the guard at the palace. Women and girls run to the door to see something pass, or stand there talking, with the inevitable mate gourd in one hand. In small stores a man will imbibe mate while attending to your wants. In short, you see it used everywhere except in the houses of fashionable people in the cities, where it is no longer stylish to drink it, tea having taken its place. I have often tasted it, as it is the universal custom to offer some refreshment to callers, and when mate was passed of course we partook. It tastes like weak green tea, and would not be disagreeable were it not that in a group of people only one gourd and one bombilla is used, being passed to each person in turn, and one has to put in their mouth in the unwiped end of a metal tube that has been in more or less mouths present.

CORPUS CHRISTI DAY IN MONTEVIDEO

To see the plaza at its gayest one must go in the evenings, especially on warm summer ones, when a military band plays and numerous pretty senoritas of the city and Buenos Aires are sitting demurely at the tables, with papa and mamma, pretending to eat ices or drink beer, while the young men wander about speaking to those they know. On Corpus Christi day it is crowded, packed with people who assemble to see the great religious procession of the year, when all the priests and societies of the city meet together in the cathedral, and issuing from it march in solemn procession around the square, singing, carrying lighted candles, and showing to the multitude the great treasure of the country, which is a small piece of the true cross. I saw the procession one year and it was a beautiful sight. The people in the surrounding houses brought out silk hangings and embroidered cloths and hung them on the front of their houses. Every balcony was filled with people, and all in and about the plaza the people were packed so close that it seemed a sea of heads as one looked down on them—a sea that swayed and surged as each one strove to better his position. The curbstones on each side of the street were lined with soldiers in full uniform, and there was a military band at each corner. There was some delay, but finally the procession issued from the church, and it was so long that it reached nearly around the square. First came the boys destined for the priesthood, then those who were training for missionaries; next a veiled host on the top of a long pole, the veil stiff with embroidery, borne by a priest. It was followed by a long line of them; next the big white satin gold embroidered banner of the bishop; behind that a banner of cloth of gold, with a small glass case hanging in the center of it. In this case was the piece of the true cross, and at its approach the soldiers and people all knelt. Next came a veiled host, then a pennant, which was so heavily embroidered with gold that it stood out straight and stiff. Just behind was a double row of Jesuit priests in robes- as well as others—their candles being in lanterns. Priests of the cathedral, dressed in the robes of the mass, followed, the priests walking backward and burning incense before the bishop, who walked beneath a yellow brocade canopy, dressed in gorgeous robes and surrounded by attendants. After he passed, all those who were kneeling arose and watched the priests of different parishes, headed by veiled hosts, file by. The procession closed with numerous societies, all dressed in ordinary dress and distinguished by the ribbons around their shoulders. When all had paced slowly around the square they entered the cathedral and a long service followed, but as soon as they had disappeared behind the doors the band struck up a march, the soldiers fell into line and marched off to their barracks, while a few people went in to attend the service and the majority went home.

It was a lovely spectacle… and to Roman Catholics, who understood the meaning of all the details, it must have been especially attractive.

BEACHES OF URUGUAY

There are two favorite places Ramirez and Pocitos, either only to be reached by a long ride in the street cars.

Ramirez is the nearer, and after a twenty minutes' dash along the streets, through soft warm air and clouds of dust, one arrives at a long pier, the shore end of which has a restaurant, band-stand, and little tables set about on a platform. At the other end are bath-houses, with ladders leading down into the water, and these were the favorite resorts for those who could swim. On one side of the pier were a number of bathing machines, which were drawn in and out of the water by mules, and into these the pretty girls, with their dainty, gayly-colored gowns would flock, be drawn out into water, and when pulled in again, would emerge with everything thing in perfect order and their crimps intact. It was a puzzle, until I was told that they never went into the water at all, but made the excuse to go to the beach and afterward sit around the tables, taking some light refreshment and having their toilets and themselves admired by the men, old and young, who flocked there, and who are obliged to bathe on quite another part of the beach.

CARNIVAL IN MONTEVIDEO

The three days before Ash Wednesday ushers in Lent are given over in Montevideo to the delights and license of carnival, but many days before that the city was filled with preparations, and the daily papers with announcements and comments.

The store windows all displayed a goodly assortment of *pomitos,* which are lead tubes with caps, like those that oil paints come in, only very much larger. They are filled with cheap scented water, and by giving them a good squeeze one could throw a jet of the water, with considerable accuracy, about six feet. Everything, except those and flowers, it was strictly forbidden to throw, yet we were advised to seek the seclusion of our rooms, and stay there during King Folly's reign, as dirty water and ancient eggs would be used as much as ever. That, however, was not our idea of seeing foreign people and their ways, so Sunday we put on some old clothes and sallied forth. First we took a ride around in the street cars, and saw groups of maskers in their Sunday best, all laughing and having a good time. Here and there were rooms where societies, in fancy dress, were gathering before joining the procession; but beyond one small boy, who was filling a rubber squirt at a mud-puddle in the street, there was nothing alarming, so we got out, and making our way to the Eighteenth of July Street, found the broad thoroughfare crowded. Prizes had been offered for the finest decorated house along the route, while in the procession the finest ornamented car belonging to a society, the best decorated carriage, the finest horses, and prettiest costume were all to be rewarded. The crowd was good-natured and merry; the maskers were quite plenty, very few in fancy dress, nearly all wearing dominos; *pomitos* were quite plentiful and freely used, the neck and face being the favorite points of attack, and woe to any one who wore eyeglasses; they were wet as quickly as dried and the wearer helpless most of the time.

Every house has one or more balconies, which were all more or less gayly decorated, one family having brought out all their parlor furniture, hanging the curtains on the outside of the windows, the pier mirrors between, and placing ornaments here and there as they were usually displayed inside. Mounted police and soldiers tried to keep a passageway open down the center of the street, and finally the procession came. First marched a band of music, and then the managers, mounted on fine horses; after these many societies with bands of music here and there.

There were numerous Italian societies and a band of bull fighters—the bull, two men encased in an old hide—and whenever the procession halted they gave a most comical burlesque of a bull fight. One tall red wagon was filled with men dressed as butterflies, their red bodies and gracefully waving golden gauze wings being beautiful. A band of Spanish students were noticeable; and finally came the citizens, in carriages, headed by the President's wife, in full evening dress, the vehicle decorated with the national colors. Many of the ladies were simply in evening toilets, with tiny black velvet masks, while others were in fancy costume, some of the latter being especially striking. That evening the illuminations were very fine, all the gas arches and lanterns being alight and all the public buildings outlined with tiny flames. There were crowds of people in the streets, afoot and in carriages, all good-natured, all using *pomitos* and all having a charming time.

Monday was a repetition of Sunday, except that we went in the evening to a fine ball given by the Spanish Club in their roomy quarters on the Eighteenth of July Street. All the clubs give balls every night of the carnival, and there are besides many private and public balls, but we were advised to accept our Spanish Club invitation as being the most exclusive and best club at that time. Their lofty rooms are entirely decorated in the national colors—red and gold—which make them very brilliant; and large as they were, by one o'clock they were filled to suffocation, so the fine band, hidden among palms, played dance music to no practical purpose. There were handsome toilets, but not among the maskers. Only ladies were allowed the privilege of hiding their faces, and as those who took advantage of it never uncovered them, nor removed their dominos, there was no incentive among them to fine gowns. They prefer dominos, as they cover hair, neck, and ears, making identification more difficult. Supper and fine wines were served all evening, and one could easily see where the club spent $13,000 on their three balls.

The third evening we passed at the Italian legation, the Duke and Duchess of Lieignano inviting their friends and throwing open their house to receive maskers. Many of the latter came, and among them a company of Morescas, who danced an old Italian sword dance for our edification, and then we danced ourselves until Lent came in. Lent should have caused the cessation of masks and mummery, but it did not; groups in odd attire went about the streets, and there were balls every night until the following Monday, when the decorated wagons—with their flowers faded—were brought out once more to escort the dying King of Carnival to his grave in the Prado. A figure lay upon a couch in one of the carts; one doctor leaned over him with a fan, while another stood by with a lot of instruments in his hands, but both were shaking their heads dolefully, and by the end of the journey he was supposed to be dead, and unceremoniously hustled into a hole in the ground. The next day the decorations were removed, the city resumed its quiet gray aspect, and our ears were no longer tortured by the shrill falsetto tones assumed by the maskers to add to their disguise. The whole public cost was $17,000, $15,000 of which was paid by the Government.

SEEING PARAGUAY FOR THE FIRST TIME

When the town of Corrientes faded from our sight I gazed up stream with increasing ardor and impatience, for we were nearing the goal of my desire—the land of dictators and of a war whose history reads like a grand, bloody romance in five volumes, one for each year in which the little land bound republic of Paraguay held at bay its proud and powerful neighbors, its people copiously watering the soil of their native land with their blood in order to preserve their autonomy and their rights. What matters is that they fought under and at the command of a tyrant? What if Francisco Solano López was unnecessarily unjust? And all the braver their fight if there were brightness neither at home nor abroad. Think of that little nation fighting for so long Brazil, Argentina, and Uruguay, yet at the end preserving most of its country; and who ever head of their complaining? Nine-tenths of her people fell, men, women, and children in battle, of wounds, hunger or disease; the country was untilled; money, jewelry, all, even the most desperate resources for raising money exhausted, yet they took up the burden and began again unknown, unnoticed. One hundred thousand people alone remained in 1870; but their country is wonderfully rich in gifts of nature. The mountains and plains are covered with valuable forests; many streams water it; the climate is tropical, and cultivation of the soil easy. So when the people increase once more and develop their natural riches there seems no reason why they not take a prominent placed in the sisterhood of republics.

ASUNCIÓN, PARAGUAY

There are about 25,000 inhabitants in Asunción, and we found several good wharves, back of one of which they are building a custom-house that promises to be quite a fine one. Steamers run up twice a week from Buenos Ayres to this city, and when one was in I liked to frequent the wharves to see the bales of mate and tobacco, boxes of cigars, ferns, palms, orchids, and other living plants; parrots, parroquets, small birds, deer, monkeys, and many small animals that were always brought down to be shipped to the lower river ports. There are two street railways, and between their tracks the ground is paved; otherwise and elsewhere the streets are full of sand, which gets into one's shoes and seems unpleasant, but I heard several people complaining that it was proposed to pave the streets, which they thought would make the city unhealthy, as all of those impurities which now sank into the sand would rest on top of a pavement and poison the air!

Walking along one of the streets, near the river, we came to López's palace, which he had to abandon in an unfinished state and fly before the allies to the northward, retreating until he met death on the banks of the Aquidiban River, not far from the Brazilian frontier. The government is now finishing the building for its own use and it will be a very fine affair. The ground floor and that above are spacious and roomy, with a grand staircase, while a view from the tower takes in the city and surrounding country for miles in every direction. Below ground—in the basement—were numbers of tiny cells for prisoners, some without even a ray of light, and one which was only to be reached by a passage about six feet long, four feet from the ground, and just large enough to shove a man's body through; it gave one the horrors just to look at these places.

THE MARKET IN ASUNCIÓN

The market was a perpetual source of delight, and I went there every day of our stay. Raised two and three steps from the street was the tall, square building, occupying a square, and surrounded by a double row of columns reaching to the roof, the whole colored a deep, dark red. Crouched among the columns were groups of women and children, their bronze skins showing plainly each outline where the pure white garments parted, jet black hair falling down their backs in two braids or caught up into a careless cluster by a big comb with gold top.

These gold combs were much prized formerly, and the women divided into two classes, those who had gold combs and those who had not. These groups were guarding piles of yellow maize, yams, potatoes and mandioca. Coming and going were numbers of white-robed figures bearing burdens on their heads, from tiny bundles to big red earthen jars filled with water. Inside was a large, square, open court filled with low tables covered with merchandise, and all, even those where meat was cut up, served by women for the war took so many of the men that women do all the work and fill all sorts of unaccustomed places; a male child being a treasure beyond price in their eyes, the little naked fellow bare faced around as you pass that you may notice the sex, and envy the mother accordingly. Here we found meat, vegetables, monkeys and other pets, breads of all kinds, and among them a crescent-shaped roll of bread and cheese baked together; lace of the different kinds and native-made jewelry stands, where we purchased gold beads, combs, and ear-rings. There were piles of native cigars--excellent tobacco they are made of—and every one smokes. The best brand is Papa Lucas and they cost $2 a hundred. Just back of the market is a large barren plaza, where one of the Presidents was assassinated.

THE NATIVE PARAGUAYANS

The native Paraguayans are tall and bronze skinned. The women are generally clad in white cotton skirt and *manta*, and the folds falling in straight lines and draping them from head to foot were very picturesque, and the burden carried balanced on the head gave them erect carriage and even gait. When we met a woman with a bundle that looked like cloth on her head we would say *Nanduti* in a questioning tone, and then, if she had any, the bundle would be lifted from her head and placed anywhere in the sandy street, and we all would sit down to enjoy a trade.

Nanduti is Guarani for spider's-web and is used to specify a lace as fine as any made in Europe and more charming because of its novelty. It is made with a threaded needle, web and pattern being woven at the same time, and is generally made in wheels, hence the name, and these wheels are put together to form borders for handkerchiefs, fans, yokes for chemises, trimming by the yard, and a coarse variety for sofa pillows, bed covers and towel ends. The thread used or fine pieces is about No. 300. The workwoman stretches a bit of muslin on a hand frame, threads a needle, and weaves her spider-web wheel, attaching it at the edges of the muslin. When finished, she cuts it loose and begins another.

A BALL ON PARAGUAYAN INDEPENDENCE DAY

The present government building of Asunción is just beyond the unfinished palace of López, on the river bank. It stands apart, surrounded by grass, and is rather an old-looking, two-storied affair. We first saw it on the 14th of May, which is Paraguayan Independence Day. All the windows were open and the people passing in and out, and two bands playing outside gave the whole a properly festive air properly festive because President Escobar was holding a reception within. Many military personages were coming and going, and some civilians in broadcloth, but none of the people, none of the masses. They failed to take any interest except in the music, which was continuous, for as soon as one band stopped to take breath the other one piped up. Near-by was a goodly monument, on which we read, "Foundation of Paraguay, 15th of August, 1536. First shout of liberty, 14th of May, 1811.Oath of the Constitution, 25th of November, 1870. Independence Day, 25th of December, 1842." Just beyond was a stretch of green turf in front of the cathedral, which is a fine large old structure with roomy interior, two of the windows being of stained glass. The high altar is covered with plates of silver, and many ornaments of the same precious metals were about it.

The night of the 14th we were invited to a ball given by the Club Familiar to celebrate the day, and I was all the more anxious to go as it was whispered in the air that the adherents of the political party named "Blue" or "Conservative", had agreed to assassinate the ex-secretary of state, Senor Caravallo, that evening at the same ball. He belonged to the Radicals, or "Reds," and it was determined to strike him because he was believed to be a modern Warwick, the true power behind the throne. As we approached the scene of festivities we noticed double guards at every corner, and at the entrance a file of soldiers was seated, with another file concealed behind a screen of trees in the patio. Either precautions were too well taken or they were ashamed to have a scrimmage before so many naval officers of the mother Republic, whose Stars and Stripes were floating from a war-ship in their harbor for the first time for over thirty years. Anyway the evening passed off quietly, and but for the guards and the absence of some Paraguayan officials and friends, who told me they considered discretion the better part of valor, one might have fancied all at peace.

THE WOMEN OF SOUTH AMERICA

The women of South America are often spoken lightly of, and it seems to me quite without reason. If their men were like ours, if the women had our education and chances they would be as famous for their morality and beauty as is the girl of the United States. There, as everywhere, it is the one lamb who goes astray that is told of in song and story, not the ninety and nine in the sheepfold. After four years spent in South America, I am a warm defender of the women there. They are pretty, sweet, gentle, and pure, and their intellects good. What more can one ask?

Alice Marland Wellington Rollins

A Lover of Nature in Brazil

ALICE ROLLINS WAS A CHILDREN'S author, an essayist, poetess, novelist, and travel writer. She was born in Boston in 1847 and attended the Everett School and LaSell Seminary. She taught for several years, and in 1876 she married Daniel Rollins, who worked for firms that traded with South America. Together, they traveled to South America and lived in Brazil for a period of time. In the 1880s, the couple went to the Caribbean, Alaska, and Brazil. In 1892, *From Palm to Glacier, with an Interlude: Brazil, Bermuda, and Alaska,* an account of her travels, was published by G.P. Putnam.

The couple visited Pará, Maranham, Bahia, Pernambuco, Rio de Janeiro, and the mountainous retreat of Tijuca during their time in Brazil. Alice described the Amazon as muddy and unimpressive, while Pernambuco was dazzling with its white building and canals. According to her, Rio de Janeiro boasted few fine public buildings or beautiful streets. She was not delighted with the city. Since yellow fever was prevalent in Rio, the Rollinses left for the mountain resort of Tijuca, about two hours away and 1,200 feet above sea level. They stayed in an English hotel for six weeks until the epidemic was over. Surrounded and enveloped by the natural world of beautiful flowers and trees, Alice described her time in Tijuca as an exile in paradise.

However, the monotony of her residence in Tijuca soon became wearing. Although she delighted in the gardens and the profusion of flowers and trees, they stifled thought, and she was reduced to being a mere spectator of a silent landscape. The heat and humidity were inimical to serious thought and physical activity. Once the yellow fever epidemic was over, the Rollinses returned to Rio but went back to Tijuca several times.

The world of nature was the focus of Alice's travel writings, but she also commented on aspects of Brazilian society and customs that she found strange as a North American. For example, during the hot summer months, the Brazilians wore flannel and donned shawls, and refused to drink or eat anything cold. The elite dressed in velvet, satin, and fur to distinguish themselves from the poorer classes, who wore white to deflect the sun's rays. The rise of republicanism was threatening the emperor's rule, and she cautioned him to not flirt with democracy but continue to be imperial.

Alice was a romantic by nature. She was endowed with a vivid imagination and was entranced by the beauty of the natural world that surrounded her. At the same time, she was both attracted and repelled by the lush and verdant environment of the tropics, so different from her native New England. Nature was triumphant in Brazil and dwarfed the human element so dominant in the United States. Brazil was truly an Eden, a natural paradise in Alice Rollins's eyes.

Alice lived the last part of her life in Lawrence Park, Bronxville, New York, where she died in 1897. During her lifetime, she wrote magazine articles, novels, children's books, and poems. She contributed to the *North American Review, The Ladies' Home Journal, The Century,* and other periodicals. Her published works include *Aphorisms for the Year 1895*, *Dr. Oliver Wendell Holmes in Beacon Street* (1885), *Little Page Fern and Other Verses* (1895), *Mrs. Jackson (H.H) in Colorado Springs* (1885), *The Ring of Amethyst* (1878), and *The Story of Azron* (1895). Her novel entitled *Uncle Tom's Tenement* (1888) drew attention to conditions in the slums and may have influenced reforms. It was her best-known work.

The excerpts here are from *From Palm to Glacier, with an Interlude: Brazil, Bermuda, and Alaska.*

VISITING PARÁ

So we go ashore cheerfully, to investigate Pará under the happiest circumstances, having friends on shore in whose large, cool, spacious apartment, delightful with fruits, orchids, and iced lemonade, we have our first glimpse of a Brazilian home. And almost the first thing to strike the eye in this Brazilian home is a copy of the *St. Nicholas* on the library table!

We have only a few hours on shore "after the rain," but every experience is novel. I have a confused recollection of a wonderful garden of orchids; of picturesque blue heron; of great balls of India rubber just as it is brought from the great forest farther up the Amazon, so heavy, so solid, so tough and brown that it is hard to realize its having dripped from a tree in colorless, white sap. Riding out into the suburbs in the horse-car, we have our first experience of Brazilian money. Their smallest coin is an imaginary one, the rei, of infinitesimal value, and the rest are enormous multiples of it. For instance, in the horse-car one offers for our party of four a bill of 1,000 reis, receiving in change 600 reis. Much of the currency is in big copper, so heavy to carry about that the story is told of a man coming into an office to pay a bill of $250 in copper which it required ten men to carry. Even in the horse-cars the conductors have large travelling satchels in which to carry their change.

PARÁ, BRAZIL, LIBRARY OF CONGRESS

Ah! Such flowers as we carry back to the ship; purple, and crimson, and white, and gold. It is quite dark as we row across the river, and glide past one of the big boats that go up the Amazon a thousand miles or more, very picturesque in the half light of its own lanterns, with its hammocks swung on three decks almost to touch each other, for passengers to sleep in rather than in the close cabins-a sort of airy improvement for a sleeping-car.

There is an evening of tropic moonlight, then a day of delicious and grateful coolness, when we recover our lost strength and feel once more like northern people, with prejudices and convictions. Another cool, delightful evening that seems like summer yachting over northern seas, and we are at Maranham.

PERNAMBUCO

Three more days of azure and gold, three more nights of white and silver, with the phosphorescence so glorious that if often seemed as if great lighted cities were in the horizon, and we are up early in the morning for the first glimpse of Pernambuco, the Venice of the South. It is a superb day; not a fleck of anything but gold on the blue of sea and sky. Then slowly, slowly, slowly, the silvery city rises from the sea, her gleaming white walls glowing, and yet cool, fresh and dainty as Aphrodite herself. There is not a glimpse of verdure, of hill or tree or any land at all, until long after the white walls and domes and towers fill the horizon. The effect is as if the city, like Hans Andersen's little Daŭmelinchen had danced out upon lily-pads to meet us. At Pará and Maranham we had our first experience of entire houses tiled as our fireplaces are at the North, with color and design. Delicate tracery of pink and blue and chocolate, in tiny squares of white, had cover the entire outer wall; but at Pernambuco the buildings are all of a white stucco over brick or stone, which in the distance has all the effect of marble. It is in the unanimity of color and design that produces the unique effect. An entirely white city would be impressive anywhere; and here, set in a sapphire sea, on land so low that you are scarcely conscious of land at all, and under a dazzling sky, the result is fairy-like, with architecture which, simple as it is, seems magical. No ugly docks, or projecting piers, or unsightly warehouses, line the edge of the town. There is a waving fringe of cool trees on the very shore as we draw near, stirred refreshingly by the trade-winds that make Pernambuco one of the pleasantest residences on the coast, and everything is white from the beginning. Then the city spreads back into the country, subdivided with an effect as of many canals by its broad river, spanned with innumerable bridges. Here, too, we are at home; here some of us have lived in years gone by, and here some of us are going to live.

TASSO'S GARDEN

And then we step across the road into Tasso's garden. How fortunate, when, as the possessor of such a garden, your name is romantic enough to suit it! For Tasso's garden out-gardens Cruz das Almas, as Cruz das Almas outstrips the pale gardens of the North. There is not a square inch of it but seems to have been stretched to its utmost to hold its handful of flowers. There is a row of splendid palms, and under them—ask me not what; I could not tell. I am only conscious of flowers, flowers, fountains, perfume, color; the very sunshine seems tinted. But do you know what I wish: In the midst of all the wonder of blossoms, I catch myself wishing there were not quite so many!

For a strange oppression takes possession of me in all this richness of luxuriance. Already I am beginning to be conscious that in the tropics Nature is triumphant. We shall have to sacrifice both our humanity and our individuality, and the Puritan self-consciousness dies hard. "What is man, that I should be mindful of him?" is Nature's attitude towards the human in this land where vegetation is so massive, so luxuriant, so crowded, so strong, so all-pervading, that it actually seems sentient. Humanity, dominant at the North, seems crowded out, insignificant, merely tolerated by these magnificent and lazy trees, these indolent and superb flowers. It is not only that man evidently cannot patronize Nature any longer; it is doubtful whether he can get along with her at all. He will have to conquer, not merely her storms, but her sunshine. She is never his friend. Whatever he succeeds in doing, will be in spite of her. He has written poems has he? But Nature at the South is herself a poem. He has attained magnificent success, perhaps, after repeated failure, but without effort. She is not merely indifferent to what you can do, but she will not let you do it. Who but Nature could attain magnificent success in anything, with the thermometer at 98? If you should try to write a poem in Tasso's garden, you would soon find yourself in the position of a brilliant lady who apologized for being dull in a Queen Anne parlor: " I could not think of anything to say; there was so much to look at." As we leave the garden and go in to dinner, I can only reflect humbly: " When I am at the North again, I will write an essay about it"; which is the revenge I am trying to take now on Tasso's garden.

BAHIA

Bahia is the first port we have entered at night, and very beautiful is the magnificent bay ringed with brilliant lights. It is a big city, of two hundred and fifty thousand inhabitants, gloriously set on a superb bluff overlooking a superb harbor. If Pernambuco tempted us ashore by its dainty morning freshness in white and silver, Bahia lures us equally at night with its glittering golden lights like the apples of the Hesperides.

But we cannot go ashore till morning. Then after exploring the shops and looking at Brazilian diamonds and sapphires in the mercantile part of the lower city, we are lifted one hundred and eighty feet to the heights by an elevator in the street precisely like those in our hotels, and take a horse-car to the suburbs where the pretty dwelling-houses are, set in rich, glowing gardens. Here, too, the houses are covered with square tiles, usually of some color, though the most beautiful was one of pure white tiles, whose smooth and snowy surface gave the curious effect, not of marble, but of white satin. How such a surface can be kept so glitteringly white, so softly spotless, is hard to understand, even with the brief explanation, "You know we never have a frost."

GOING TO TIJUCA

For, as our driver, with the pardonable pride of drivers in all languages, spurs his horses to make a magnificent entrance through the flowery approach to our hotel, we catch glimpses of a wilderness of intricate charm, in which nothing can be identified or remembered except as beauty. Everywhere rich masses of fragrance and color break upon the sight in billows of bloom. We seem to see the results of care, without any of the care. At the North, laborious processes almost spoil one's delight in eventual achievement. At least we think so for the moment. There it is such hard work to make even an acre yield anything, that it is almost appalling to find here a square inch yielding so much voluntarily. The garden is a restless and rich mosaic, though without design of any kind, and without anything repeating itself. Everything that happens is the unexpected. Nothing is where it ought to be, yet everything is beautiful. As we whirl up the avenue there are photographed in turn upon the palimpsest of memory a splendid cluster of bamboos; an orange tree in blossom; a banana-tree laden with fruit; a Japanese pagoda; a vine of honeysuckle; a shallow brook slipping softly over it brown bed under arching trees, and looking like brown eyes full of tears; a little well, roofed over with glorious golden flowers; the brook again, but now in a sunny spot, where its brown eyes are full of laughter; a rose-arbor; two magnificent palms, over a hundred feet high, that seemed to say to us: " You have climbed high and well, but not so high or so well as we have climbed"; a little fountain under a purple passion-vine; a thatched summer-house; clusters of shining white azaleas; fragrance, as of jasmine out of sight, that could not find room to grow in earth, and so hangs as a disembodied spirit in the air; a great tree of rose-colored blossoms; a stone bridge; a picturesque rustic seat; a wooden bridge; steps leading down to some water; a little path winding up the mountain; a great bed of violets; a stone wall overgrown with maiden-hair fern; lilies; and then roses.

SIX WEEKS IN A GARDEN

Suns rise and set. There is absolutely nothing to give individuality to the days. The six silent, uneventful weeks in that loveliest of gardens are in memory but as one day-a day of flawless sunshine, of sky pitilessly blue, of intense silence punctuated with vivid flowers. Very, very, very quiet is the narrow court, the blossoming garden, the long, slow, winding, lazy stretch of road under the solemn mountains. Nothing happens. Occasionally, if I happen to look out at just the right moment, I see dreamily as in a vision a quiet donkey idling down the road adorned with picturesque paniers and accompanied by his master in vivid rags; but his unshod feet fall soundlessly upon the path, and I should never know he was there if I did not see him by accident. It is all like a silent panorama. At the North we are occasionally proud of putting a bit of real life on the stage—a "real" cow, a "real" load of hay, a "real" child; but in the tropics it seems to be the stage that is put into real life. Everything is theatrical; everything seems meant to be looked at. You have nothing to do; you only have to play your part as an interested spectator. And everything that is there to be looked at is exquisitely beautiful; there is not a blemish or a scar.

So I take refuge in the scenery, which alone is Brazilian; and as I step out on my balcony the first morning, I think that I have never known so fair a scene. The sun is just gilding the tops of the mountains; it will be a superb day; a stainless sky, and absolutely faultless sunshine. Under my window the brook is gliding swiftly and musically; Manuel is watering the strawberry-beds; the oranges on the tree just below are turning golden in the golden sun; humming-birds are darting in and out of the honeysuckles on the trellis; great blue butterflies are skimming over the beds of tall white fragrant lilies; everywhere there is splendid foliage and a glorious wealth of superb flowers. Surely an exquisite scene!

AN INTEREST IN POLITICS

As time goes on we begin to take an interest in politics. All unaware are we of the tremendous change to be wrought so quietly a few months later in the government, and yet there are signs of mental disturbance that we enjoy watching because it seems to create no dismay. I am indeed slightly out of patience with a dynasty that seems far too democratic for an empire. If I must have an empire, I want it to be imperial. In a land where there are duchesses, I should wish to be a duchess, and in land where the rulers are supposed to trample on the people, I should wish to be trampled on. I like not the republican simplicity of tarnished gilt on the royal carriages; they ought not to be gilded, but if they are gilded the gilt ought not to be tarnished. I like not to see the emperor's coachman sitting on the curbstone in his shirt sleeves, while his royal master is laying a corner-stone or listening to a *Te Deum.* There is much confusion of sentiment when Parliament meets, and evidently much republican feeling, as leaders change their party with incredible swiftness. I am a good republican, but in an empire I want to see the republicans put down. I like not the tolerance of which we read in the evening paper, when the new members of Parliament were to take the oath of allegiance. "One new member," it is written, "refused to take the oath of allegiance because he did not believe in imperial form of government, nor in the union of church and state union; whereupon," it is gravely stated, "the president of the Senate dispensed with the usual oath, and the new member took his seat"! No wonder that six months later the empire crumbled silently into oblivion.

Virginia Heim George

A YWCA Director in Brazil

Virginia Heim George was born in 1908 in St. Joseph, Missouri. She graduated from the University of Wisconsin in 1929, and for the next forty-two years she was involved primarily in YWCA work, both in the United States and aboard. From 1929 to 1940, with a brief interruption for graduate work in social work at Carnegie Institute of Technology (now Carnegie Mellon University), she was a YWCA program director in Kansas City; Utica, New York; and Pittsburgh, Pennsylvania, and served as a camp director as well. From 1940 to 1943, she was executive director of the YWCA in Rio de Janeiro, Brazil. Her delightful letters from Brazil, with her impressions of the country, the people, and her travels, are published here.

When her assignment in Rio de Janeiro was over, she worked as regional assistant director of the USO in Brazil and the Caribbean, with offices in Puerto Rico. Her YWCA organizational skills served her well in that position. Once the war ended, she was transferred to Europe, where she was a program consultant for the Czechoslovakian YWCA and worked with women's groups in Germany. In 1948, after eight years abroad, she returned to the United States and was on the national staff of the YWCA.

During the 1950s, she was a recreational leader at the YWCA in Oakland, California, and from 1953 to 1966 she was executive director of the YWCA in Yakima, Washington, and Utica, New York. In the late 1960s and early 1970s, she advised the YWCAs in Taipei, Taiwan; Lima, Peru; and Colombia. In 1971, she was appointed executive director of the YWCA in Omaha, Nebraska.

Virginia Heim George died in 2003.

Her letters are located in the Virginia Heim George Papers, Sophia Smith Collection at Smith College in Northampton, Massachusetts.

SUNDAY-AUGUST 8, 1940

Dearest,

Today is certainly a big day. I had 3 letters from you. I expected them Friday or yesterday but they didn't come so I went to the school today & they had arrived 3 from you, 2 from Martha, 2 from Will Baird. There may be others tomorrow. It took quite a while for the Barbados letter to get to you & any airmail will take you 7 or 8 days. It's 5 from here to Miami & by the time it gets home & delivered there is a couple more days. The letters dated Aug 13-18-19 were the ones to arrive. If all goes well maybe will get a letter a week. I got yours & Martha's last week--one can hardly tell. The Delta boat goes out at odd times-the regular boats every 2 weeks –airmail 3 times a week & now there is a new airline that makes it in 21/2 days instead of 4 or 5 so it shouldn't be so bad.

I'll try to answer all of your questions. Too bad about the fire-hope you get some bargains. Your dress material is pretty & should be nice on you. Am so glad you've gotten your new glasses- you've needed them badly & it was good of Mrs. Land to give you the frames. That was a big help. Glad, too, you got the watch fixed. Hope you got your coat.

Mrs. Smith needs to come down here where she can get cheap help. 'Tis terrible what they pay girls. So glad Jane got married & is happy –I hope she still likes her new home-give her my love & congratulations when you write and best wishes for her future.

I think I told you that your airmail was awaiting me when I arrived. I was so thrilled with it that I can hardly imagine having neglected to say anything about it.

The food here is good. They eat a tremendous amount of rice which I skip & lots of meat. The pastries & cakes are dry. Fruit is delicious—The oranges people eat by the dozens- You never eat just one & they cut them around leave a little stand & you cut it between the fibre to eat it. I've never tasted more delicious pineapple which are just coming into the regular season. They are as sweet as sugar & they sell big slices of them. They have a fruit called "mamão" which is similar to a cantapa but not as tasty & when green they boil it as a vegetable. I've eaten filet mignon almost every day-they tenderize it by pouring the juice of the "mamãos" in it (I think that's the way you spell it). Meat is not refined as it is in the States—it's freshly butchered stuff. The "guatara" I think that is a popular drink like our cokes at home. It's very good-makes me think a bit of ginger ale.

My clothes are all O.K. things are pretty much the same. They wear more sport clothes than I expected so I've been knitting a sweater to go with my skirts. Yarn is awfully cheap tho not as many varieties. My sweater will cost about .60 when finished.

Belo Horizonte is very informal in dress, etc. & I've had a hat on only once here. It's quite different in Rio-- So I'm going to wait until I get to Rio before I get more hats. They are cheap from $1.50 to $3.00 & you get a good looking hat.

The meals on the boat were not as bad-as well as the accommodations. I dressed for dinner only a nite or 2. The 1st class passengers dressed each nite & a few people but it looked out of place to me as second class was so informal. Eddy gave me $10 to pay you for my transportation to Utica & etc. to N.Y over the 11th that I told you. The dining room was nice but not luxurious.

Money here is getting a good exchange. People talk about "selling their checks" or buying some money. It sounds so funny. I got 21.8 milreis to the $ the last time I sold some money orders. Miss Corbett said that when she first came down years ago she was getting 8 to the 1.00 so you see its good. Prices & things are very cheap for some things & expensive for others i.e. food is awfully cheap-I was with a girl the other day when she bought meat –she got over 2 pounds of the best veal steaks for about .13 cents. Fruit is cheap, in fact all foods but anything imported is awful-a ten cent box of Kleenex is 25 cents-some paper plates that would be 15 cents at home were 60 cents here. They are getting ready to wear clothes here but they are about 1/3 to 1/2 higher than at home. The cheapest kind of purses ($5 to 1.00 at home) are 2.00 to 3.00. The good leather kind of made of alligator are lovely & cost anywhere from $6 to $20. So you see-it all depends what you buy-if they are Brasilian made they are inexpensive & if Amer. made very expensive. I'm going to begin making a list of things I want you to bring over.

I don't know whether I wrote to you of the Equator ceremony or not. I was disgusted with it & that they could have done things much more clever. They had King Neptune of course & initiated people –thank heavens they didn't pick on me. They doused the men with eggs-spaghetti-had them smell bad fish & all that slap stick stuff. I felt it was terrible. I guess sometimes they have right class ceremonials but ours wasn't.

The weather here is perfectly delightful-warm during the day & cool enuf in the evening for a jacket or coat. Almost like the Denver summer weather. It's been grand ever since I arrived. They tell me the rainy season is starting in about a month and lasts for several months.

I think I've answered all your questions so will now write the news of the week.

This has been a week of holidays. Wednesday was "Youth Day" & they had a parade of all the school children in the city –they said there were 4,000 of them. All of the students wore their uniforms –each school has their own-the mission school had navy blue flared skirt jumper dresses with white blouses & navy blue (serge) pockets. They are very attractive. The Isabella Hendrie School is a new one, has only been here 2 or 3 years & very up to date & modern- one of the best of its kind around. The stores were closed on the morning of this day but open in the afternoon. They paraded in front of the Normal School –there was a band & a speech or 2. Just a demonstration of youth.

Yesterday was Independence Day celebrating Brazil's independence from Portugal in 1822. I went to the school to see their special assembly –they sang the national anthem-- which is very nice – had some readings & then a speech. Then there was a big military parade. Some of the soldiers wore green uniforms-others tan-the cavalry paraded- bands & some students. It was interesting to see some brigades with burros marching along carrying the pack which is so typical of Brasil. There were no fireworks as we celebrate July 4th & everything seemed very quiet. There were some dances last nite at the clubs, I guess. I spent most of the day at the school with Clyde & Verda-came home in the afternoon for a Portuguese lesson & read in the evening. About 9 Verda called & asked if I'd like to go out with them & get something to eat so we went out & had a fruit salad as they call it (really a fruit cup).

It's interesting how easy going the Brasilian people are & they are always taking time out for coffee. What we call breakfast in the morning they call coffee-- then at noon they may have another breakfast. About 9:30 they have a mid-morning snack-coffee & a bread & butter sandwich or something-this is breakfast. In the afternoon they have coffee or tea & at nite they have dinner.

It always gives them time to visit a bit & take time out for refreshments. On Tuesday I stayed to the assembly after my lesson at the school to hear a Negro boy play 12 instruments at one time. He had them tied on his hands & feet & on his guitar- 'Twas quite a feat but it would have sounded better if 2 or 8 of them had been left off. That afternoon I took a trip to the permanent exhibit of Minas Gerais (that is the state of which Belo Horizonte is the capital). It was very interesting- a miscellaneous display of stones. It shows the kinds of thing the state does-industries, etc. That evening Mary & Doyle Morton, a young missionary couple who are studying the language came over to have dinner with me. They are young & attentive & Mary is always doing nice things for people. I enjoyed them a lot.

Mother-you would love living here. Everyone gets up early. Classes at the school begin at 7 A.M. & they do in most schools. That is because they have 2 or 3 sessions as there are not enuf schools to accommodate everyone but it seems to be the life of the community here to get going early. I find myself getting going earlier than usual.

Thursday nite Margaret & Richard Waddell had a dinner party for Mary & Doyle Morton. The Waddells are also missionaries. They are a young couple too & not, either of these couples, missionaryish. Richard spends most of his time in the interior trotting along on mule back. I'm sure he has dozens of interesting tales to tell which I've not heard about as yet. The party was a 1st wedding anniversary party for Mary & Doyle. A Mr. Ellis-also a missionary who is here for awhile, had a birthday so they told Mary & Doyle it was to celebrate Mr. Ellis' birthday & told him it was to celebrate their anniversary so it was a grand surprise all around. Mary had a dandy dinner with her biscuits & everything. We played some games & all in all had a very nice evening. There were 9 of us all together. The American crowd here is so small & it is really centered around the missionary bunch-its quite different in Rio. But they have been grand to me & I'd have died probably without them. They're all so thoughtful in including me in all of their doings & I've really enjoyed them lots.

Friday morning I get up early & over to Mary Mortons by 9 A.M.to go to market. The market gets going good between 7 & 8 & I wanted to see things so off we went with a market basket. You will love the markets here, Mother- they are really fascinating & there is everything imaginable in them. They had tiny little monkeys in this market, birds of various kinds, guinea pigs-dresses- dress material-fish-vegetables-flowers-meat, etc. They are all in the open. That was where Mary bought here 21/2 pounds of meat for 13 cents. Beautiful huge calla lilies were 7 cents a dozen. The flowers are perfectly immense here and are beautiful. Daisy I saw 3 or 4 inches in diameter & dahlias about 6 or 8 inches. It was lots of fun –then I went to Mary's & had a good ole American breakfast with bacon, eggs, fruit and toast, none of which they ever heard of for breakfast here. Breakfast here consists of a roll and coffee. I ask for pastries -they don't eat it for breakfast but they eat it at other times of the day. I came home after my lesson on Friday and studied all afternoon. One afternoon I took a walk in the park with one of the Brasilian teachers-We had quite a time trying to converse but she was really a great help. The Portuguese is coming along. It's a long hard, pull, 'tho, & there is so much to absorb but now & then I can get myself understood. It hasn't been over 3 weeks yet that I've been working on it & the vocabulary now stands at about 900 words. I'll be so glad when I can understand & speak it.

I'm knitting socks for the British at the present moment & am working on my sweater which is the hard work at the present time & am reading & am reading "The Conquest of Brazil" by Ray Nash which is perfectly splendid. It's a big book but if you can get it at the library you'd probably be very much interested in it. Everyone recommends it as the best book out on Brasil.

Today I got up about 10-washed my hair-did my nails & invited Clyde & Verda for dinner. They didn't stay late-until about 2 A.M. & here I am writing letters. I've completely caught up on my correspondence with the exception of 6 letters which I hope to get off this week- that is really something.

Today I got my Sept. check from National-I hadn't expected to get it till the end of the month. They sent on to you $30.00 & $50.00 to be deposited on my checking account. I had just written them to keep this check-to send $85.00 to you, Mother & after insurance deductions to send the rest to myself so my October check will be sent that way.

The $85.00 Mother, I wanted you to spend this way:-

30.00 to you

35.70 Einlender

12.09 Heiches

7.21 or the remains as a birthday present

Then, I wonder if you'd pay the following-Never mind-I'll send the checks from this end & see if they get through to the addresses, etc. Anyway, I'll be entirely cleaned up financially except for the extra $150.00. I borrowed from you & my school debt is about to close-that is really wonderful. Next month or the next after should finish up on my school debt. I will continue to send the regular monthly check but I'll be so happy mentally to know 'tis over with. It should be after all of these years. I had a big head today when I received my letter the National Board. I began on my field rate today. Tis really wonderful because it makes a difference of about $10 more cash a month which will very nicely set you to sail to South America. It's a find of about $300, not bad, eh? Honestly, for the first time since I've been working 'tis money left at the end of the month. I can't tell you what a grand feeling it is. Maybe for once in my life I can get a bit ahead of myself. I'll be so glad when you get here & we can enjoy it all together.

I've spent practically all afternoon writing this letter. It's about 6 p.m. and as the sun is setting; it is making the most beautiful picture of shadows on the tower of the library across the street. The hills in a distance look hazing & are beautiful tones of blue & lavender & in the foreground stand the stately palms.

I'm enclosing a picture taken from my hotel window & one taken from the boat at Barbados showing the Negroes who came out & dove for coins & sold their wares. If you look closely you can see, in the first boat, a basket with a man holding on to a string that ran from the boat to the ship where they would send up their wares to passengers in the boat who wanted to buy things.

Much love to you,

Boots

P.S I've loved wearing the clip & pin. It is such a pretty one & I know I'll wear it lots in the future. So far there has been no long dress affairs even in Rio-We will see-maybe I've too many of the "fancy "dresses. One never knows till they get here.

Love again,

Boots

AUGUST 19, 1940

Dearest Mother,

This letter is being taken to the States to be mailed so I can talk freely. There are many things I've wanted to say but have hesitated to do it when I was afraid that the letters might be censored. I'm writing this letter too, so that it may be sent on to some of the folks—I'll list them at the end of the letter & MYL can either make carbon copies & send it so you can send it around.

This has been one of the most interesting days I have spent, in order to see what Brazil is really like politically. I have been saying that I've been held up because of my registration so perhaps I'd better explain a bit. Every foreigner who comes into the country has to be registered so a week ago I went to the American Consulate to register. The signed a paper saying that I had registered there and suggested I get a "despachante" to continue with it. A despachante is a person who does nothing to get things thru public officials that are to be done. I thought it was a silly idea to pay close to $10.00 just to get registered but every one advised it. You have no idea the amount of red tape there is to be hurdled. In the first place the letter at the consulate had to be taken to a notary or some such place and a "swearing " take place that the signature was correct.

Thursday we hired a despachante who came over and took the consulate letter then he started out to the police, etc. and came back and said all the gov't officials were closed because it was a church holiday so nothing could be done and then on Friday they would all be busy because they hadn't worked on Thurs. that he couldn't do anything. Saturday the offices were only open a couple of hours so he couldn't do anything says he—be ready promptly at 11:45 Monday all will be ready so-we were all set to go yesterday at 11:45 but he didn't come we called his office but he wasn't there –we waited until 5pm & finally after dozens of calls got him & he had forgotten all about us but alibied by saying he was held up in court etc. but he'd be here for sure to-day at noon. Anyway, I had my first Portuguese lesson yesterday afternoon & one this morning by Dona Camina –one of the staff who speaks Portuguese beautiful.

Today was the day for the despachante and at noon we were ready again. About a half an hour late he arrived and apologized profusely about yesterday –piled us in his car off we went to the police station. There were hundreds of people there –you see, last year a law was passed that all aliens had to be registered & it was all supposed to be done by last Dec. It is typical of the Brazilians to make laws but they don't think thru them enuf & so they have no set up for carrying them out. All these people were trying to get registered. Then, the gov't offices only finger print from 11 till 2:30 & they don't have nearly enuf people to do it. So we were told today people sleep on the street so that they can be first in line the next day. The despachante has a "drag" –he bribes a bit & "get you thru". We passed up all the line-he paid the "chief'" a little extra & had him sign some papers so I could get it thru. It's a terrible situation really-everything is done by a "drag" you find someone who knows someone else & has done a favor to someone else & so you get by without having to go thru the red tape that the rank & file have to go thru. I have no idea what all had to done but there were loads of papers with one person or anothers' signature on it. I had my finger prints taken twice-once at the police station & by the way we just walked up in front of a whole line of people waiting & I got mine done. One woman who was more important-the wife of one of the police or something got in in front of me- my despachante gave way to her-a favor you see. Then we went a mile to another place. By that time it was after 4 and the gov't office was supposed to be closed but some way or other my despachante got it thru and I had my finger prints taken again. How these people do it by themselves is a mystery. I can understand why it would be 3 or 4 months to go thru all the red tape.

We finally got it fixed up & were just leaving when we met Miss Corbett's despachante from the Panair. She is going to Paraguay in a couple of weeks & was trying to get things fixed up. T'was all set-says he-but she'll have to be vaccinated again. She was vaccinated 4 years ago in Amer. & last Jan in Bahia but "no" she'd have to do it again. My despachante invited her to come along with us & together they'd see what they could do. She would have to be vaccinated at the public health clinic & she says it is awful-dirty & unsanitary & of course she doesn't want to have it done. So went to see if we could fix that up but it was closed so they said they'd see someone & get the paper signed that she was ok & she'd not have to do it. "Just leave it to them." It's all so dishonest & corrupt-you can't imagine how it is—we know nothing of such things & its this way in every single line. Everything is bribing & pull and if you don't have it you are out of luck.

After the day standing and waiting we decided that perhaps I could get my ticket and get off tomorrow. The train leaves at 6AM and it takes ages to get things checked, etc. so we began a hunt for a car that could take my trunk and bags to the train today and get them checked today. We finally found an open air model that would carry the trunk on the rear. Went to the hotel and picked up my stuff and down to the station we went. The trains are terrible here. I am looking forward to an interesting ride tomorrow seeing real Brazilian life. We're supposed to get in at 9 PM but the trains are never on time. The dining cars are terrific, they tell me, so Miss Corbett is putting up a lunch for me. No one ever travels with trunks & I'm only taking my wardrobe trunk but had to pay over $3.00 excess baggage-imagine that! After much tadoo there we got things checked & got on a bus to come home. About half the way home the bus broke down-just stopped. They all sound as if they are falling to pieces & I guess this one did. So out we piled & get into a cab to come on to the hotel. What a day it was but it was certainly an eye opener as to the way the life of Brazil is run. I've gone into much detail about this but it's nothing as to the detail of everything one touches here. My job is going to be working with one detail after another.

The thing that bothers me is what fundamentally is happening to people-everything is downright dishonest & you can hardly be honest in such a set up. If I'd done all of this business by myself I'd never get it done or it would have taken days and days of worry & time. To have the despachante do it meant his bribing officials & pulling all strings. And there are hundreds of these men who do nothing else—it's a profession. Today he said "Some people are meant to be Drs others lawyers but I was meant to be a despachante."

As to the international here—it looks to me pretty much like the U.S. People generally seem to be pro-ally and many are bitterly opposed to the Germans but the army is pro-German and one is very careful with whom they talk and you do not air your opinions out in the open because there definitely is a 5th column here. Vargas has done many fine things for the working people. There is minimum wage law now of 249 miliers a month. In our money that is 12.00 a month. Girls were working for 100 and 120 miliers a month previously 5.00 and 6.00. In Brazilian it means more than Amer. Money but even then you can see how little its. Then there has been an old age insurance plan put in effect –the worker-employer and gov't was each to put in 4%of the workers wages but the gov't has never done its share. The ideas are good but somehow or other they miss a point in getting laws enforced. However, Vargas is well liked by the masses, but not liked by the moneyed people. He's really tried to do things. There is a very much a feeling of the wealthy that everything should be for them and the under dog doesn't matter anyway. You see a great disregard for personality.

One striking thing to me is the carelessness with which people drive their cars. The pedestrian doesn't count and if a person is knocked down the driver goes ahead because if he is not caught in 24 hours he is entirely free. And anyway it was the pedestrian's fault. So believe me it doesn't pay to take any chances around here. You are out of luck in more ways than one if you are run down.

Things look fairly clean around about. Twas amazed at the cleanliness of the market-yet other places are filthy and they have no conception of sanitation. The drug stores are terrible. I've not been in any of the hospitals but they say they are awful-one doesn't want to go there if it's possible to stay away.

I saw two lepers yesterday begging for the first time in the street. In fact, I almost fell over one. One's foot was eaten off and it looked like a petrified stump. They have been doing a great deal to rid the country of leprosy, and I understand. In Belo Horirzante there is a leper colony and they are doing treatments and fine work with them. If they catch it soon enough they can cure it so I am told.

All my letters up to this one has shown the rosy part of the picture of Rio & it is all that I have said but it does have it's awful spots, too, as you can see.

There is terrible poverty around about- whole sections where people live in awful shacks- logs filled with mud- no sanitary facilities at all- not even outhouses. There is always wild bananas for food & they don't freeze but that's the best one can say. Illiteracy is terrific. There is compulsory education law but there aren't nearly enuf schools so it can't be enforced & people just have to go without schooling as yet.

My conclusions & impressions are only surface ones at present. What I've heard or observed as I've gone along but I think I can say- that a dictator isn't all that it's cracked up to be from their point of view & that I'll stick to a democracy & struggle thru the difficulties of that.

I've rambled enuf but now & then when I get a chance I'll try & send this kind of a letter home. Don't write anything that wouldn't go thru the censor all right. One never knows when a letter might be opened & there is no use taking chances. There is too much dynamite about these days.

I'm off for Belo Horizonte tomorrow morning. Mail will have to be forwarded to me but I'm hoping for a big bunch on the boat that comes in tomorrow. I'm surely looking forward to news from home.

My love to all,

Boots

FRIDAY, OCT. 11, 1940

Dearests.

As I sit on my bed writing this letter I can hear the laughing gaiety of young people on the streets below and in a distance the singing of Brazilian music. Until a little while ago there were dozens of young people walking along the avenida not in couples but a group of boys and a group of girls. It is the recreation and the custom in the Brazilian communities such as Ouro Preto. Yes, we arrived here today one of the most interesting towns I have seen after traveling about ten hours to come 100 miles—our train was 41/2 hours late. It was a very eventful trip as you can imagine. Mary, Doyle and I got up at the crack of dawn, 4 a.m. to be exact, in order to catch a 5 a.m. train. It seems as though all Brazilian trains leave early in the morning. The trip started out to be like any other trip although it was still new and interesting to me to see the men plowing the land, panning for gold in the river, digging for iron in the hills, the bamboo and mud houses with grass roofs and dozens of people around each house. We were on the road (or tracks) for about two hours when we stopped at a town for 40 minutes. There was little to do but we walked around, saw mules by tens and twelves carrying loads, mud streets-general stores with everything imaginable in them-a typical inland small town. There was no place to eat-coffee was served on the platform and awful looking "doces" –cakes, cookies, etc., so we didn't partake. We finally got on our way for about 15 or 20 minutes when everyone was told to get off bags and baggage. A train which apparently uses the same track coming toward us had been derailed. It was a coal train and apparently had been derailed sometime previously because there was no engineer on it at the time. So here we are in Brazil some place between Belo Horizonte and Ouro Preto although we weren't sure where. We took our bags, walked the rails, sat on our bags, looked at the scenery, which was beautiful-mountainous, a nice stream etc., and waited. It was a sight to behold-babies, people, bundels, bags-everything, dumped by the railroad tracks. We waited for about an hour and a half until another train came to pick us up, and on our way we went. There were only two cars-first class and second class. Personally, I can't see much difference. They are both pretty bad. One realizes what perfect transportation we have in the States after riding in these. There were lots of amusing things. Everyone eats on the train and we were aghast when we saw a man devour six bananas in about six minutes. Another man had his pan of rice-manious flour and chicken right with him. Our next stop was in a small town for lunch. It was then 12:30 and we were supposed to arrive in Ouro Preto at 10:30 a.m. The one and only hotel in town was jammed but we managed to get a ham sandwich and a glass of guarana. We were off again, in hopes that this would be the home stretch and it was until we were about 20 minutes out of Ouro Preto when we heard an awful racket and a sway and realized that our car was derailed. Believe you me, there were some seconds that were really thrilling. We didn't know what would happened-fortunately we stayed upright but spent about three-fourths of an hour getting the wheels back on track. At 3 PM we rolled in Ouro Preto feeling mighty glad to get the two feet down on firm ground again after an eventful trip up and seeing a bit more into the life of Brazil this time the inland life and the way the great majority of people live. There is never a dull moment.

As we got off the train we gazed around at the oldest city in Minas Gerais-the oldest capitol of the state-an historical place because it was here that plans were made to free Brazil from the Portuguese domination. It is a very picturesque town. Narrow winding streets of cobblestone, with the grass growing in between-the houses situated right on the sidewalks with overhanging wrought iron balconies-the pastel houses and burros going along the streets- I have never seen such high hills which are difficult to walk over because of the steepness and the cobblestones.

When we got off the train we came directly to the best hotel in town-it looks fairly clean. The sheets and beds are anyway-though in good form as well as the hardness of Brazilian beds. We spent little time getting cleaned up before we started sightseeing. Our first venture was to one of the oldest churches built in 1712-very ornate and full of gold. They say some of the gold has been painted over so as to lighten the church –beautiful carved wooden doors were in this church and some man took us to another part of the church to show us some carved wooden tables-drawers-drawers about 20 feet long-carved wooden figures and so forth, and then the priests'robes of gold and embroidered robes for special occasions. It was all extremely interesting. As we were heading for another church, we met a girl that Doyle knew who is the daughter of a well-known family here-in fact her father owns the two hotels in town. She insisted that we come into the house. It was certainly a "break" for us for it proved to be a perfectly fascinating visit. They have a very large home, but the living room had all the stiffness of a Brazilian home with the pictures hanging practically on the ceiling. However, there were pillows everywhere-on every chair-settee and three big ones on the floor. One was made entirely of chicken feathers. I have seen better Brazilian artist! After a visit Senora Toffalo asked us to see her flowers and garden. She has a tremendous collection of cactus-dozens of little pots with all varieties. On the tree just as you enter the house is a gorgeous orchid with five big blossoms on it. She showed us her large collection of orchids, then she had all varieties of ferns-and then to the garden, acres and acres of land, a banana orchard (if one calls it that) and gorgeous flowers of all kinds and descriptions. It was a perfectly fascinating visit and they were delightful people. They are giving a piece of land to the Methodist people on which to build a church. Senora Toffalo has had 17 children-11 or 12 are living!!!

We came back to the hotel to have a real Brazilian dinner-black beans and rice-two kinds of meat-two vegetables which I hadn't met before and a cheese custard for dessert! A bit heavy but typical and very good.

Tomorrow looks like a big day. I'll tell you of that tomorrow night. Much love.

Boots

MONDAY, FEBRUARY 17, 1941

Dearest Folks,

Once again comes a letter from Rio---this time to stay pretty much put as it was—at least for awhile. There may be some short trips hither & yon—weekend trip-driving etc. But the language study period is about to close & 2 weeks from today will be my final day on the job. I boarded the train Saturday nite heading for Rio & landed in the apartment as I'd left it with out painting & cleaning as I expected would be done later—that's one of the things we learn to accept here—"paciencia"as it were. The other really important word in the language is " amanhã "—tomorrow. I couldn't get too concerned about it as it seemed good to have a place to call my own—to unpack my things & get settled. It's fun to wander but one misses the hominess when wandering. So yesterday & today I've had a grand time unpacking my baggage, arranging things, etc. Last nite Katherine Briggs, the Mexican (American) invited me to her hotel for dinner. I met a delightful woman from Rochester, a dental hygienist who is here for 2 or 3 months or so. She & Katherine have been chasing each other about S. America & have landed here as the same time. They were my first guests tonite for dinner in the apartment & Annetta did herself proud on the dinner which was really delicious—shrimp cocktail, filet mignon, salad, carrots & cauliflower, hot biscuits & a dessert of fresh oranges & brownie which I made but they didn't taste like the brownies as the chocolate was sweetened & it was funny, it wouldn't even melt. Anyway, it tasted good & the table looked pretty. For 2 to 4$ –12 cents I decorated the entire room with flowers & to be able to have flowers all of the time—such a joy and it gives the place a nice festive look.

There are lots of things I want to do to the apartment –a few fresh curtains, a dab here and there will fix it up right nice, but so far nothing of course, but it will get fixed up gradually. One chair needs caning badly. I'm hoping I can find someone who can do a good job cheap so it will be clean and fresh looking. The other overstuffed chair can ride along for awhile, but one has holes in it.

Last week was a terrifically hot one & a very busy one. I tried to get done all the things I wanted to do in Sao Paulo. I didn't quite complete the list but almost.

On Monday we went visiting one of the organizations in the community –the Liga Senhora Catolicas. The have an extensive piece of land—all kinds of departments. We visited the nursery, tiny babies up to 2 yrs old-most of them are abandoned children, the majority hopelessly diseased. It was rather a depressing sight to see 50 or 60 children, undernourished with skin irruptions, etc. The Pres. of this organization took us around in one of their cars. From there we went to their vocational school for girls training to be maids, for girls who want to learn how to run a home and for some who are going into the teaching field of home econ.,etc. Then they took us to the headquarters, a beautiful old house—high ceilings, lovely rooms etc., which was used by the Bd of Directors & members. We had tea there & then visited another section of their work-similar to a woman's exchange as we know it. They have a boarding house for women, & a nursery type of school neither of which we visited. The next day, however, we visited the "Cidade do Meninos- It is a city of boys from 7 to 18 years of age, Boys from broken homes etc. & was a tremendously interesting piece of work. Every boy is studied from the point of view of mental ability, physical ability & psychological problems. Then after 2 months of observation he is placed in a family type of situation. There are houses in this place –with a couple at the head & 3 boys in each house. Each house has a plot of land, gardens, fields etc & each one takes responsibility in some way or another. He has an opportunity to earn a little money outside, if he is ambitious so he can save or spend it as he likes. There is a big football field, a store, a hospital, a church –everything there, an elementary school, & then a trade school. The director is a man with real vision, an educator & very progressive in his thinking. He is trying to see that the boys have every opportunity available to prepare them to enter society. It was a fascinating & thrilling afternoon to see such a splendid piece of work being done. All of the work of the Liga Sehnora Catolicos is with poor children, those of broken homes, etc. quite unlike the work of the Y.W.C.A.

One morning we visited a social work school which is very small & very nice. They are the only social work school in Sao Paulo & there are few any place around here. We met with 3 of the directors there who were young, interesting & elite.

Oh, yes, we had lunch at the Restaurante Feminino which is also a part of the work of the Liga S. Catolicos. They serve very cheap meals to working girls etc. There are 2 sections-one section for those who just want soup & a roll & they serve it for 600 reis or 3c in our money. The other section serves a full lunch for 1200 or 6 c in Amer. Money. They have no church work or anything like that-church services-Catholic –every two weeks.

One afternoon I started out for the department of labor to see what was there & had a very interesting time in the department of women & minors—children under 14 are not allowed to work here & those between 14 to 18 must have permission from their parents, a statement from the employer as the type of work they are to do & that it isn't dangerous, a health exam and a school diploma. If they haven't the latter, they must take an intelligence test & if they do not pass it—of reading, writing & arithmetic, they can start work but must go to nite school & after 6 months take another test & so on for 3 years. If after 3 years they don't pass it, they have to quit working. For women there are many regulations-one interesting one is that she has 3 months off to have a baby-2 months before & one month afterward and ½ salary. Then the employer must make arrangements to take care of the children afterwards so that factories are now having nurseries, preschools, etc. I haven't seen those yet, but have only heard of them. One afternoon I had a long conference with an educator here & heard about one of the schools of sociology & they are doing work on statistics, etc. Sao Paulo is such a fascinating city, because it is so big & increasing at such rapidity that it's hard for everything to grow as fast as it is growing. 50 years ago it had a population of 70,000, now it is estimated to have a population of 1,200,000 to 1,500,000. Factories have built all over the place in the past 10 years-of all descriptions-textiles being on the major industries. Women are working in stores & factories & are having more freedom all the time, but it is not like our girls, as yet, in Amer.

One afternoon I went to see the work of the Salvation Army here. They have 2 divisions—evangelization & rescue work. We visited their piece of work of the latter field. A Norwegian woman is in charge, really a lovely person. They take care of the girl who has had difficulties, is having a baby and after the baby arrives or after a baby is abandoned. They had about 15 children, 13 or 14 girls in the house. I was impressed by how healthy looking these youngsters were- who come from some of the poorest, most diseased types of background. They have religious services & all of that, of course. They are planning on expanding some to take care of more children, to set up a craft work shop for Mothers, etc & to have one section for old people.

With all this running around I've seen a bit of the types of work that's being done here-some of it is extremely interesting-Rio is the next place to take on.

Besides the visiting I did last week, a few interviews thrown in, I had a Portuguese lesson every day & got lots of Portuguese on these travels as most of it was in Portuguese conversation.

For diversion—Monday nite Maristella & Maria do Lourdes, the cute young thing with whom I've been exchanging lessons, were over for dinner. We had lots of fun, fooled and danced the Samba till late. Tuesday nite Eliz. Peterson, whom I visited in Piracicaha came over & then my Portuguese teacher & his brother who is an Episcopalian minister came over, the latter with a vest & funny collar & all of that. It was a very interesting evening but I' m afraid I shocked the minister who thinks carnival is very wicked, dancing bad, much less all the other little things. I never wanted to pull out a cigarette so bad in all my life & really shock him. I had some other people over on Friday nite who had (been) very nice to me so the week flew by. Life never ceases to be interesting & varied.

The trip back here Sat.nite was my first experience of traveling in an upper berth. I was awakened all during the night with the lurch of the train feeling sure that one of the times I'd take a headlong plunge to the floor, which would have been a tumble as I clung tighter and tighter to the wall. There is no security of a curtain in one of the cabins-you either stay on top or else!! The girl in my cabin was an Argentine so we talked a mixture of Spanish, Portuguese, and English- such a business.

Saturday of this week, Carnival begins. It's practically begun already. One hears carnival songs every place. The elite of Rio have flown to Petropolis, Terezapolis, Pongas do Carlos & other resort places. Those who remain are those who can't possibly get away, the masses who adore carnival & its gaiety & the tourists who are coming in by the 100s. I'm anxiously waiting to see this much talked of, written about, thing called carnival.

Guess I've rambled enuf for now & the hands of the clock are pointing to 1 A.M.. I think the Utica, Pittsburgh, Dinner & K.C. lunch might be interesting in this letter-as well as the St. Joe gang. I can certainly not rewrite it all so if someone –May or Martha could copy it & send it along--'twould be swell. My love to all of you wherever you are-

Jinny, Virginia, Heimie & Boots

RIO DE JANEIRO, BRASIL

(FEBRUARY 1943)

My Dear Friends,

This is a lazy man's way of writing a letter-having it mimeographed but I've been threatening to do it ever since I left the States and with mail so irregular, I think you'll be sure to get this letter if it's mailed from the States and I want to tell so many of you the thrilling vacation I had-so I'm killing a lot of birds with one letter.

First of all I'm including a crude map of Brasil divided into states so you can see how vast this country is. You'll have to fit it into the map of S.A. Then too you can see that it doesn't look as tho we traveled far into the interior when you see it in relation to all of Brasil but one must remember that large proportions here are still undeveloped and most of the development is right along the coast.

Perhaps I am getting ahead of my story, I decided I wanted to see a bit of Brasil this summer outside of the big, modern cities of Rio, Sao Paulo and Belo Horizonto that I already know and then found an American geologist who was here and interested in a similar trip-so-off the two of us went. No one gave us much encouragement-2 girls traveling alone-poor means of communication, and all of that but we were determined to go. We started off to-gether in Belo Horizonto and visited a quartz mine and a diamond mine on our way to Pirapora where we could start sailing down the river. These two mines were both fascinating. I'd always heard of rock crystals but still hardly believed that they came out of the ground-often looking as tho they had been perfectly cut. The diamond mine was fun too. One could hardly imagine that there were "diamonds in them thar hills" but after it was washed down-put thru various processes etc. I actually picked one out-not "for keeps" but the thrill was there nevertheless.

This was only the beginning of our trip. We were lucky to get the biggest boat on the Sao Francisco river and were delightfully pleased with it. It was like an Old Man River boat-with a big turning wheel in the back, but it was comfortable and we had a nice room. The fun came as we stopped several times during the day to load on wood that was burned in the boat, or to load or unload cargo in the little towns. Always some of the boys of the crew would pole vault off the boat and pull it to the shore. Our stops were varied-from 15 minutes or some times just to pick up or let off a passenger-to several hours, so we felt very much acquainted with all the towns along the way. We had 8 grand days along the river and hundreds of interesting experiences-seeing swarms of butterflies, birds and an interesting church built in a cave and the various cargo we picked up was always interesting to mo-pinga, the Brasilian whiskey, tobacco, cotton, hides, fiber, a wax made from palm trees, molasses sugar, and dozens of other things. This area is dry and there is little fruit and vegetables so we ate rice and black beans, the national Brasilian food, dried meat and dried fish most of the way.

When we reached the end of our 8 day trip we wanted to go on further to see the famous Paula Alfonso falls on the same river but the river was too rapid to continue on the same boat so we hunted for other ways to go and finally went by truck, station wagon and a cute toy train- 3 days travel but it was an experience. We slept in a truck one nite- in hammocks, bathed and washed our clothes in the river but were thrilled with our trip. The country was dry and there was a great deal of cactus but the birds, I've never seen anything like it-thousands of small parrots and paroquets, wild canaries, hundreds of varieties of all shapes and sizes. We saw wild fox, ostriches, huge camoleans and thousands of goats and nary a snake did I see. It was worth all the discomfort in travel to see the falls. They were simply breath taking. The muddy water-getting creamier and creamier until the sprays were pure white, falling over the reddish brown rock and edged with green trees and foliage was some thing long to be remembered.

From there we decided that we were so close to Recife that we should go there for Carnival. We spent several days getting there-stopping to see the hand looms and the workers weaving elaborate hammocks and then to see a large modern textile mill in the heart of the interior- a beautiful fruit fazenda with cajus, oranges, mangos, cocoanuts, goiabas and every conceivable variety of fruit.

Recife was interesting-again we felt modernized-big buildings, a comfortable modern hotel, beautiful beaches and carnival was fun. The nites were exciting-every one out in elaborate costumes, singing and dancing the "frovo" –a very vigorous dance peculiar to Pernambuco and very different from the "samba" and "marcha" of Rio. There is no carnival quite like Rio's but it was interesting to see it in another part of the country.

Probably the biggest thrill of our trip was between Recife and Maceo, the capitol of the state of Alagoas. We took a station wagon and rode along the ocean-in fact three times we rode on the beach and crossed bays by running the car on a raft. I've never seen anything in my life more beautiful than this section-miles and miles of cocoanut groves, houses built of palm leaves and a shallow coral beach with the most gorgeous colors you can imagine-aquamarines to blues and dashes of pastel shades and in the distance the jangadas, the raft like fishing boats with their little white sails.

Bahia, Brazil, Library of Congress

Before we got to Baia (San Salvador) we'd gone by bus, sail boat, and train stopping in cities and taking in as much as we could absorb. Baia was a perfect ending to our trip. It's lovely in it's oldness yet there was the contrast of the big modern city. There is the upper and lower city connected by a tremendous modern elevator. We browsed around antique shops, loved the wharfs with the picturesque fishing boats with the huge sails, the old-old churches and monasteries and the beautiful beaches. The big market was exciting. We spent hours there looking around buying baskets, trinkets, pottery and - a monkey-called a micho here- a very tiny little monkey, only about 4 inches long and as cute as can be-named Pudge-because she's just that! Five days were not long enuf for Baia-it's one of the places which I must return some day.

You can imagine what we looked like when we got off the boat in Rio after our three day ocean voyage from Baia-loaded with duffle bags, baskets, knick knacks plus a monkey in a cage. We were a sight-black as could be from the sun and wind, yellow from the pills we took as a malaria preventive, but happy as could be over our thrilling five week trip. I'd completely forgotten about my job- a real vacation-as it were, but probably the most interesting one in my life. A letter is rather an unsatisfactory way of telling about it. You can imagine that there were all kinds of things that happened that one cannot put down on paper. Some day perhaps I'll be able to tell you all about those things. We were followed in some of the small towns by crowds, as women rarely travel alone in the interior and two foreigners was a sight to behold, but every place the people were marvelous the most cordial in the world, I'm sure and they would do any thing to make us happy. It's the people, I know who can make one have the happiest experiences in one's life.

I hope you've not been bored with this long letter, but there was so much to say. I was going to write P.S.'s to many of you, but that will be impossible now that I am sending this to the States to be mimeographed-so please consider this a personal letter to each and every one of you and know that I'm thinking of you and inquiring about your families and am interested in what you are doing and how the war situation is affecting you all.

I'm hoping this will bring many replies as to what you are doing and how you are getting along. My best wishes to each and every one of you.

Always,

Heimie-Jinny-or Virginia Heim

P.S. Please pass this letter along to any one that would be interested.

Josephine Hoeppner Woods

In the Mining Camps of Bolivia and Peru

JOSEPHINE HOEPPNER WOODS WAS BORN in 1881 to German immigrant parents and enrolled in Washington State College in 1897, where she received a bachelor's of science in chemistry in 1902 and was secretary of her class. Six years later, she received a master's of science in German from Washington State. Josephine was the first woman to receive an advanced degree from that university. She went on to teach German at her alma mater and later at the University of Washington. Some years later, she taught at a high school in Tuolumne, California. There she met Clarence E. Woods, her future husband. With the beginning of World War I, Josephine left teaching and moved to Washington, DC, where she worked for the Ordnance Department while Clarence was in New York doing wartime mineral work. The couple married November 24, 1918, at her brother's home in Hastings, Nebraska. Their honeymoon was spent in Arizona, Mexico, and Honduras.

The Woodses settled in Orland, California, where they operated a forty-five acre farm as part of the Orland Irrigation Project. There they raised chickens and turkeys, stacked hay, learned to milk cows, irrigated the land, and worked from dawn to dusk. Josephine taught in the district school and assumed all the other household chores, as well as helping with the farm work. After three years on the farm, Clarence received a three-year contract as superintendent at the Huanchaca Silver Mine in Pulacayo, Bolivia. The couple decided to accept the offer and made plans for their departure. Clarence left first for the mine, some 13,600 feet above sea level and 1,500 miles from the equator, in 1923. Josephine left a month later.

In the 1920s, when Josephine settled in the mining camp, Bolivia was a poor, mountainous, landlocked country with a large Indian population of Incas, Aymaras, and Guarani, who had little education, and no political rights. The Indians worked as farm laborers on the estates or in the tin mines, but they were not passive. The Indians defended their language, their land, and tribal culture and revolted in 1921 and 1927. The Indian tin miners were mobilized and struck over wages and working conditions. The elites and the military controlled the government; it would not be until the early 1950s that a revolutionary movement emerged that gave Indians political rights, land, and dignity.

In 1925, the Woodses moved to Chojñacota, a tin mine, where Clarence was manager; they stayed there for three years. The Woodses ended up living in Bolivia for five years. From Bolivia, the couple moved to the Santo Domingo gold mine in southern Peru, where they lived from 1928 through the early 1930s. Clarence obtained a two-year concession in the mine from the owners, which enabled him to move to a lower altitude for health reasons. Eventually, the Woodses purchased the mine, and they profited handsomely from it.

During their residence in South America, the Woodses traveled to La Paz, Cochabamba, Lima, and Arequipa; they returned to the United States several times, as they were allowed a vacation every six months.

Josephine's life and adventures in three different mining camps were recounted in chatty and descriptive letters written from 1931 to 1933 to two friends, Byrdie and Iva, and circulated to other relatives in the United States. Her letters describe the mines, a miner's strike, her homes, the natural world, the Indians, their customs and superstitions, the people she met—including dinner with the president of Bolivia—the cities, and daily life in the mining community in a time period when few North American women had the opportunity to live in such remote and isolated areas. At times, she was the only woman in the mining camp. Josephine was an intrepid, resourceful, and fearless woman who adapted to difficult living conditions without complaining. Her letters were published as *High Spots in the Andes: the Peruvian Letters of a Mining Engineer's Wife* in 1935.

The Woodses eventually returned to California, where Josephine died in 1967.

The selections here are from *High Spots in the Andes: the Peruvian Letters of a Mining Engineer's Wife.*

OCTOBER 22, 1930, PRESIDENT SÁNCHEZ-CERRO OF PERU

Clarence and I went to the United States Embassy, where we were cordially received by Ambassador Dearing, thence to see our lawyer, who has been trying to secure a concession for Clarence, a large section of territory in southern Peru, to prospect and exploit for gold; Dr. Fernandez, figuratively and almost literally, embraced us with tears of joy, as he was to cable Clarence to return as soon as possible; with him, we went to the Minister of Mines, the only member of the Leguia cabinet who survived (his office) the Revolution, and while visiting here, there came a telephone call that the President would receive us. So the three of us hurried to the President's and were ushered into an elegantly richly furnished room, into which almost immediately entered a dapper, well-groomed, short, very dark complexioned forty-two year old, but younger looking, alert soldier, dressed in a Lieutenant Colonel's uniform; I was introduced to his Excellency, Sánchez Cerro, President of Peru, who kissed my hand in true Spanish fashion. The three men with courteous apologies to me, began at once to discuss the concession to which I was a most interested listener and in little more than a half hour the interview ended, and the President again kissed my hand. So now I have talked with two Presidents—you remember, I wrote you about sitting at the right of President Saavedra of Bolivia at a memorable banquet.

AUGUST 10, 1931, SANTO DOMINGO MINE

The *Cholas* in the market place and use of *Coca.* The *Chola* is a woman with some foreign blood, be it ever so little; although ninety per cent Indian, she is no longer Indian but *Chola.* Here, in the plaza, which was also the market place, the *Chola* sits on the ground, usually a sheepskin under her, and her many, many voluminous skirts become useful as well as picturesque; whatever she has to sell is spread out in front of her; generally, a certain *Chola* sells only eggs, another onions and still another slices of pumpkin. But the two coca vendors were, however, the busiest and most prosperous—every morning and night as the shifts went to work, every man stopped to buy a handful of coca. He will not go to work without his coca and many a man has a lump of coca the size of a turkey egg in his cheek; it seems forever, because every time I saw these men, they had the same swelling (looks like mumps) on one side of their face. ....Men, women and children use it; I have seen a six year old boy with a hen-egg lump in his cheek but usually the children are not addicts until they reach the age of fourteen or sixteen. Coca deadens the pangs of hunger and as a result almost all the chewer of coca are undernourished; many a miner goes to his shift with but a hunk of bread and a handful of coca.

Chola, Library of Congress

HALLOWEEN

Todos Santos (All Saints), our Halloween of childish pranks is a two-day commemoration, November 1st, the Day of the Living, and the following day, the Day of the Dead. The first is a wild, wild play day but on the morning of the second, there is a decorous procession to the cemetery, almost every man, woman and child bearing candles and breads, which are placed on the graves by the relatives; numerous prayer boys are in attendance, who receive a small stipend for reciting prayers at designated graves (and I think they swipe the food and drink afterwards). The priest reaps a big harvest but following these religious rites, the celebration deteriorates into a drunken orgy, almost as bad as, if not worse than, the worst features of Carnaval.

INDIAN CARRIERS

Every Indian, man, woman or child, always has a load on his back. It is a badge of servitude, handed down from the Incas; the nobility carry no burden. Even to this day, the toddling Indian child has its diminutive cargo, perhaps a few little sticks, and this load is increased as the child grows, hence he is literally trained to be a "beast of burden"; a man will carry more than a hundred pounds on a paved or good road (eight pounds is an average load) and in the mountainous, rough trails, he will uncomplainingly carry fifty pounds all day long.

OCTOBER 11, 1931, DAILY ACTIVITIES

How did we pass the time when there were no fiestas? Ah, my dear, even with no household cares, the time did "fudge it." At first I made myself read Spanish instead of English and after while I really preferred the Spanish; I conscientiously did my hour of Spanish every morning and you, of course, remember my propensity for walking so I rarely missed a daily walk of three or four kilometres (a kilometer is six tenths of a mile) and here on the "roof of the world" I learned to play golf. We had a nine-hole golf course and we claimed to have the highest links in the world but I think this was challenged by Cerro de Pasco of Peru. At Chojñacota, where we later lived, and now here at Santo Domingo, the camp is so steeply located it would be difficult to play "Ring around the Rose". Most of our time in Pulacayo there were six *gringas* in camp, four of whom played bridges so we had "Bridge Teas," the non-bridge players dropping in for tea. Letter-writing became a restored art: I began writing "round robins" of anything special, such as fiestas or the strike, and a round robin was passed around our many relatives—you know my large family and Clarence has seven sisters besides three brothers and parents—and generally a copy to different friends, who likewise passed it on, and in this way we received many replies to one letter.

JANUARY 3, 1932, TROUBLE WITH SERVANTS

The series of teachers, doctors, etc., remind me of my troubles with a succession of servants. I was so fortunate in Pulacayo with my "paragon" Marcelina and while at the American Institute of La Paz and Cochabamba the domestic machinery seemed to function almost automatically, so I expected no "servant problem" at Chojñacota. What a rude awakening! Julio, whom we inherited, a Bolivian, was an excellent cook, in fact, he had been "chef" on the Antofagasta-La Paz railway; his wife was supposed to keep the house clean and to do the laundering. The previous Manager was alone, his family living in La Paz for school advantages, but the young English millman took his meals at the Administration; so there were but the two to cook for. Julio's "woman" was given the privilege of doing the laundry for office men, in spite of the fact that she was receiving extremely good wages from the Company. Julio received twice as much salary as I have ever paid any servant before or since yet the house was never swept unless I usually demanded it; the woman did make the bed but never aired the bedding without a special request, she was too busy washing and ironing for others. Still, the meals were excellent, so tasty and Julio seemed so anxious to please—and I had not completely forgotten how to do things around the house myself—that we overlooked a lot of the woman's shortcomings. But when I saw the first month's statement of our household expenses, even though the Company did pay all the expenses, I immediately asked for the keys to the *dispensa* (storeroom) and when Julio asked for a second can of butter ... I wanted to know why he needed so much butter, for remember there were only two of us to cook for. Then he "in a huff" went to the office and complained to Clarence that I was interfering with his cooking. Clarence came over to find out what it was all about and soothe Julio's ruffled feelings but it was the "beginning of the end"—when he had to account for everything he used, he lost interest in preparing good meals and, very shortly, he received a letter that his mother was ill and he asked for *permiso* to visit her, Almost invariably when a servant or laborer want to quit work, he or she receives a letter that a father or mother or grandfather of someone is ill and he must go to the bedside as soon as possible.

VISITING THE CHOJÑACOTA TIN MINE

FEBRUARY 16, 1932

My first ride up to the mine was an event: I just couldn't see how a mule could cling to such a narrow trail and I admit I was badly scared, But I went so many times that I learned not to mind it at all and comfortingly assured every visitor whom I escorted over the trail that no mule had ever fallen off and that the trial was being widened every a time a mule went over it. The mine is a thousand feet higher than the mill, which is directly behind the offices and on the same level as the Administration House. The trail takes you through the miners', which is where the Mine Superintendent lives, too. At this camp was a boarding house, a cinema and a sort of an athletic field—think of it, an athletic field more than 16,000 fee high! About three quarters of the way up, there was a *cancha* where the ore is sorted by women, the waste ore being dumped over the mountain side. The women work in this open *cancha* in all kinds of weather, pushing wheelbarrows loaded with heavy ore, or sorting ore ready to be put in wheelbarrows; bundled up to their ears, yet barefooted! When I went up with Clarence, I usually waited here at the *cancha* for him...but visitors, of course, always wanted to go "clear up" to the mine.

By climbing a little farther than the mine, the summit of the ridge was reached and the view was well worth the effort or probable scare. In any direction snow peaks can be seen...the glaciers of Laramcota, Chojñacota, and Monte Blanco, and at least five beautiful lakes. ...Women folks could, of course, go to the summit but could go only to the portals of the mine—the inside of the mine was "verboten" to all "skirts"; as I wrote you before, the Indians have a queer notion that a woman entering the mine is a sure sign of an accident.

INDIANS PREPARE *CHUÑO*

Another time, on a Sunday, we picnicked part way down on this "hill" that leads to Tanapaca and watched the Indians preparing their *chuño;* the potatoes are spread out on the ground and left there during the night to freeze; if they are making *tunta* or white *chuño,* the following morning, before thes sun is up, the potatoes are covered with straw, but if it is to be the common or black *chuño* the potatoes remain uncovered. In either case, the men, women and children tramp, tramp, tramp on the potatoes with their feet, squeezing out all the juice possible; the potatoes are left to freeze and if to be the white variety, covered with straw again before sun-up. This process is repeated four or five times, until all the moisture is extracted then the potatoes are thoroughly dried.

The white *tunta,* as I understand it, first put in water, just enough to cover, for several days until "cured"and is then dried. Dried in this manner, the potatoes will keep for years and *chuño* is the main staple of the Indian diet.

APRIL 29, 1932

ONLY WHITE WOMAN IN THE SANTO DOMINGO MINING CAMP

Did I mind very much being the only white woman in camp? Well, not *very* much; whenever this particular phase of nostalgia manifested itself, I donned coat and hat and took a brisk walk, returning from the second lake and sometimes the third, I usually thanked my lucky stars that I was privileged to enjoy such magnificent scenery. I rode a great deal with Clarence and we had a well stocked library besides the great number of magazines from the states. We had a very good phonograph with several hundred records, the very best of the classics---one of the previous managers was a real musician, but nevertheless, I often wished for a woman-friend—many, many times I wished "Iva would drop in" for you were always a tonic to me. With the coming of Miss Krause, I used my German more and after Mrs. Karatieff arrived, well, she and I discussed and "settled" most of the problems of the world.

AUGUST 13, 1932, THE SANTO DOMINGO CAMP

...Our camp is relatively small, from 350 to 400 on the payroll, which seems small compared to the 1500 in Pulacayo, while Chuquicamata perhaps has three or four times as many as Pulacayo. Santo Domingo is the most compact of any of the camps I have lived in—building space is at a premium and the land here is terraced for buildings, just as the Incas terraced it for agriculture. Houses are perched on very available space and oftimes, more often than not rock walls are built along the sides, and at times on all four sides of the building, to make the foundation more secure. There are houses for the Gringo families—one double or should I say "duplex" house and an apartment house for three families. "Casa Santo Domingo", the boarding house, has accommodations for eight employees of the "white-collared" type, four more rooms for lesser employees, while the first cook has quarters off the first-class dining room, the second cook from the second-class dining room and the other servants are housed on the bakery floor.

JANUARY 15, 1933, THE SANTO DOMINGO MINE

And until 1905 the very location of Santo Domingo was in dispute; its discoverer was a Peruvian and all connected with the mine later had come in by way of Peru but Bolivian money was the only currency used, the workmen receiving their pay in Bolivian silver pesetas, and, until

Santo Domingo was discovered, the boundary between Peru and Bolivia was indefinite, the Inambari River being considered by some as the boundary.

From about May 1912 the mine did not produce so well and there occurred a bewildering change of personnel, from manager down to peons, but even during Mr. Brown's regime and on down to 1914 when the company was reorganized, Santo Domingo had more than its share of bad men, high-graders (those who steal high-grade ore) and lawless desperadoes: Mr. Spencer, inspector of the change-house, told me the mountain sides were dotted with the tents of the *comerciantes* (merchants or peddlers), who brought in alcohol with other things, and fighting affrays were frequent. So bad did the conditions become, that the management decided to put in a *cantina* (barroom) to try to regulate the drinking. Many are the amusing stories of the "bootlegging" that followed: bottles of alcohol cleverly tucked away in bundles of coca leaves and even in cans of rice and sugar. But there was an improvement for the apprehended bootlegger was not allowed to return. We have a dry camp with drinking troubles almost nil.

STEALING ORE AT THE SANTO DOMINGO MINE

Not all the high-graders were Indians or common workmen: an assayer who analyzed samples of ore and concentrates to estimate their value, made thin sheets of gold in his laboratory and sent them to his family in flat packages labeled photographs. One manager blew up the old mill (the so-called new is the one we are now using) with dynamite, appropriated S10,000 ($4,000) and left for Bolivia without leave. High-grading is always a serious problem in any gold mine and constant, unremitting vigilance is necessary. Just the other day Clarence found a beautiful gold specimen near the track—it contained at least three ounces of gold ($60). He thinks it must have been thrown off by a carman during the night and a confederate was to have picked it up; but Clarence, always an early riser, made his usual rounds somewhat earlier this morning; and it was in this way that he found reason to suspect Mamani, a carpenter, one of the original thirteen who was here when we arrived. Clarence met him on the track several times, too early to be reporting for work; his house was searched and, sure enough, more than $300 worth of ore was found under the kitchen floor.

Wilma Jerman Miles

An Admiral's Wife in French Guiana and Nicaragua

WILMA MILES SPENT THREE YEARS traveling and living in Latin America as a navy wife. Her youth and family life in Washington, DC, gave no indication that she was to spend many years of her life in foreign countries. Wilma's father, a grocer and real estate salesman, was from Virginia and her mother from Keokuk, Iowa. Her mother moved to Washington, DC, to study music and met and married the enterprising Charles Jerman in 1902. Wilma was born two years later, on March 20, 1904.

Wilma's growing-up years were spent in the nation's capital. She attended the city's public schools. When the United States entered World War I in 1917, her life changed, as her mother went to work for the government. Wilma assumed some of the household duties and took a job as a cashier at a government cafeteria. But her life was about to change again as she and her mother vacationed at their cottage at Arundel on the Bay in September 1919. There she met her future husband, Milton Miles. He and two classmates from the US Naval Academy were on leave, and pulled their sailboat up to their pier. Milton and his friend stayed for dinner, and he soon began to correspond with Wilma.

Theirs was a long courtship, as Wilma was very young and still in high school. In 1921, she entered Cornell University, where she majored in nutrition. Milton graduated from the US Naval Academy and was commissioned ensign in 1922. While Milton went on navy cruises and duty in China, Wilma finished her studies at Cornell and graduated in February 1924, having finished half a year early. The couple was married on September 2, 1924, in Hong Kong, just one day after she arrived. For the next two years, the couple lived in China, seeing each other when Milton was off duty. They traveled extensively and immersed themselves in the history, culture, and language of China.

The Miles family returned to China in 1936 with their three boys, as Milton was assigned to the USS *Black Hawk*. During Wilma's three years in China, she visited Japan and Southeast Asia, traveling on her own. When Milton's assignment was over in 1939, the family exited China over the Burma Road and made their way through India and the Middle East before coming home. Miles returned to China in 1942 as commander of US naval group China, while Wilma worked in nutrition services for the Red Cross in Washington, DC.

In 1950, Miles was designated director of Pan American Affairs and Naval Missions and a senior delegate to the Inter-American Defense Board. He was also a member of the Brazilian-US Defense board and the Mexican American Defense board. Wilma became involved in his work, as it required meeting visiting Latin American admirals and naval attachés and wining and dining them at their home. Milton traveled to Mexico, South America, Central America, and the Spanish Caribbean islands, and as this was official duty, Wilma went along. This was her first introduction to the countries south of the border, and she became enchanted with them, learning their history, and studying Spanish. During her travels, she visited the YWCAs in each country and encouraged their leadership to continue their good work.

On her return home, Wilma wrote, "I wonder how it was possible for us to have been so enthusiastic about so many stops in so many countries. However, it seemed to be no problem at the time. The people, almost without exception, were delightful, and their thoughtfulness almost took our breath. Most of them worked really hard to perfect our schedules and to include whatever would interest us and make us happy." After she recovered from the trip, Wilma was obliged to entertain the naval attachés from each country they visited.

In 1952, the Mileses were invited by the Brazilian navy to cruise up the Amazon to Manaus and then transfer to a Peruvian gunboat for another one-thousand-mile trip to Iquitos, Peru, where there was a naval base. This was only one trip on the Amazon that the Mileses would take over the years. The following year saw them travel to Cuba, the Dominican Republic, Haiti, Trinidad, Venezuela, Ecuador, the Galápagos Islands, Nicaragua, Honduras, El Salvador, Guatemala, Belize, and Mexico.

Given Milton Miles's travels through South America over the years, it was not surprising that in 1954 he was selected as commandant of the Fifteenth Naval District, with headquarters at the Amador naval base on the Pacific side of the country. The Panama that Wilma lived in had been part of Colombia prior to 1903, but the relationship was still fraught with conflict. The Panamanians had unsuccessfully revolted against their rulers ninety-one times in the nineteenth century. It wasn't until the United States signed the Hay–Bunau-Varilla Treaty that gave us the rights to the Panama Canal Company that the United States supported the revolt of 1903, aided by the US Navy. Panama then became an independent nation. According to the treaty, the United States was granted a ten-mile strip in the Canal Zone that was under its sovereign control, paid an annual fee of $250,000 to Panama, and obtained a ninety-nine-year lease on the canal. The United States assumed responsibility for the defense of Panama and, for all intents and purposes, the country was a US protectorate. In 1954, Panama was a constitutional democracy under the leadership of President José Remón Cantera.

For the next two years, the couple traveled throughout Panama. One of the perks of being the commandant was a yacht named *Old Man 3*, which was available for the admiral's use. As the Mileses were inveterate travelers, they quickly took advantage of this privilege to explore the coast of Panama and Colombia. They wanted to visit every area that was under Miles's command. No other admiral had visited local villages, schools, and officials as Admiral Miles did.

During the summer of 1955, Wilma left for Lima, Peru, where she enrolled in a course at the University of San Carlos to improve her Spanish. Once the course was over, she traveled the Inca Road and joined Milton for a trip into the Peruvian jungle. Back in Panama, Admiral Miles was interested in finding alternative routes for a new Panama Canal. There were rumors in Washington that a new canal might be built parallel to the present one. Milton decided to investigate three routes that he had in mind, so Wilma and he made three transcontinental treks with routes through Colombia and Nicaragua over a six-month period.

In 1956, Admiral Miles's assignment in Panama was over, and Wilma and he returned to the United States. Wilma had seen most of Latin America over the years. She was open to new experiences and eager to see the world. In her writings, she described the land, customs, and peoples of Latin America, from the isolated Indian tribes to the cosmopolitan cities. Wilma always prepared herself by reading about the country she was to visit and mastering the Spanish language. She was absolutely fearless, whether she was sailing on the Amazon, trekking through the Colombian jungle, or scaling a Jacob's ladder to board a Cuban ship in stormy seas. And she was as much at ease having tea with President Anastasio Somoza of Nicaragua as she was with meeting the chief of the Kuna Indians. She was always ready to pack her bags and travel throughout Latin America, whether it was by plane, train, bus, ship, or truck. Her travels throughout the region and her impressions give readers a glimpse of Latin America in the 1950s, before economic and political changes occurred.

The following selections are from Wilma's autobiography, *Billy, Navy Wife.*

A NIGHT IN CAYENNE, FRENCH GUIANA

> Some 200 miles farther along our way we landed at the Cayenne Flying Field in French Guiana where we ran out of buildings entirely; there was only a roofed porch. We got to know this field much better than the earlier and more pretentious ones because our plane lost power in one of its engines while we were well up into the sky above the endless, featureless jungle. The pilot turned back and made a perfectly safe one engine landing as dusk was coming on.
>
> What now?
>
> There was no car that could take us to town. Still, that was of small importance because there was no hotel even if we got there. The plane was full of passengers, including a State Department Courier who was locked to the official carrying case of which he was responsible. Mary and George vacated their seats, which were on each side of me, and left me with enough room to stretch out as well as a bottle of mosquito repellant. So I read the

directions, applied the anti-mosquito dope to the most exposed portions of my anatomy, and tried to go to sleep. The mosquitos, however, were like guerrillas, though guerrillas, I understand, do not usually hum. They got in everywhere. After a somewhat less than pleasant night than I might have spent at home, I limped out in the early dawn.

There in the airport shed I found Mary propped on two chairs and George was occupying a two-foot by four-foot table top. The airport manager appeared just then and invited us to join him at breakfast. Where the courier had gone we did not know. But the manager's house, we discovered was the hospital end of a ten year old temporary wartime structure that had once played a part in connection with the also "temporary airstrip". It was still no more than 5:30 A.M., but the manager's wife was busily frying eggs with which to feed our plane crew who had taken turns sleeping in the manager's only spare bed.

After a time a station wagon driven by a young airfield employee arrived from Cayenne, and its driver was promptly told to take us to town. He did so with the best will in the world but we quickly learned why there had been no car available the evening before. That road, both ungraded and unpaved, wound its way through thick, high claustrophobic jungle; it simply wasn't passable at night. We found Cayenne not to be the *beau ideal* of a tourist town. There was one paved street, one restaurant (which was run so frequently by a Chinese), and not much more. It seemed to me that three hardy men, using only one hand each, could have put together a better capital city in only a fraction of the 300 years that had been wasted here.

Government House, which faced a weedy plaza, had a neglected garden among the very old walls of a small fort yet our newly acquitted friend, the station wagon driver, told us that one out of seven of French Guiana's population, even including the upcountry Indians, was employed by the government of the French colony (which is about the size of Iowa). And I, trying to draw sound conclusions from what I was learning, instantly understood that none of these were gardeners.

We viewed Cayenne's new slaughterhouse, which wore the usual crown of black vultures and already bore signs of incipient mildew. With amazement we toured the fort. There were hundreds of piles deeply impaled in the river mouth and a great accumulation of steel girders that were stocked up for some port improvement project. Those piles were standing in water that was hardly three feet deep—a depth that continued as far as we could see-so that nothing larger than native canoes would use that great pier even if it were ever to be completed. Obviously it would take a dredge to bring a deepwater ship even within sight.

With one more day we could have arranged for a launch to take us to Devil's Island, where prisoners were no longer held and which now was strictly a destination for the almost nonexistent tourists. "It's too bad," our young driver friend and guide remarked, "that the Salvation Army ever got Devil's Island closed, because the prison was moved inland to a hotter and less healthy place."

By now we had learned that our plane needed several days to make repairs, but that another plane would be sent in-hopefully before another night. Tucked away, however, at the far end of the airstrip was a U.S. Airforce plane, and Mary drew from its pilot the information that it was to be flown to Belém forthwith. It was apparent that no one in the Air Force was enthusiastic about flying the Admiral, his Aide, or the State Department courier (who all this time had stayed locked to his mail sacks), and, most of all, the Admiral's wife, but they did.

SEEKING A NICARAGUAN CANAL ROUTE

This "expedition" as I have said, was limited to three and the equipment we had was anything but complicated. In addition to the outboard motor and 25 gallons of gasoline, about all we had were three boxes of K-rations (individual food servings), three hammocks, our cameras, a hand-held two-way radio, a fishing rod, a Coleman stove, and three repair kits—one for our inflated boat, one for the outboard motor, and one for ourselves. And once all this was stowed, and secured to our satisfaction, we headed southeast, with the big seaplane astern, the island of Ometepe to port, and the village of San Jorge and our local friends half a mile away to starboard. Oh yes. And on the island of Ometepe, 5200 feet-high volcano named Maderas celebrated our departure (as it marked so many other events in Nicaraguan history) with a display of sparklers and a few puffs of smoke every 20 minutes.

Somewhat to my surprise, and certainly to my relief, I soon learned that our inflated craft was a thoroughly practical boat. Furthermore, I learned that "rubber" boats have few hard edges or sharp angles that impose upon tender portions of one's anatomy. I am not at all certain about what I expected it to be, and I know that we had been warned that Lake Nicaragua was capable of building up some uncomfortably rough seas. But during the next hour or so the lake remained smooth, the weather remained pleasant. Our outboard motor functioned without a hitch once it was started. As luck would have it, too, when we decided, after a couple of hours, to land for the night, we came upon a little island with a beautiful white sand beach where there was enough heavy driftwood to support our hammocks. The little Coleman stove worked perfectly and, when darkness fell, we were glad we had also remembered to bring a gasoline lantern. It was only the supply of K-rations that proved disappointing, for we then and there learned that they were nowhere as palatable as the five-man rations we had eaten several months before. Of the stuff we had now, one tin can contained some sort of stew and another contained biscuits, chocolate, sugar, and coffee, all of which it seemed to me, had a kind of intermingled flavor.

We all slept well that night until 4:00 a.m., the hour we had chosen for striking camp. The water of the lake was smooth as a mirror. Dawn was only faintly in prospect but the east was already beginning to turn pink. Birds were singing in the cool morning stillness as we shoved the little craft into the water. And now we set our course so as to keep an island to port as insurance against the wind which, we had been told, always blew from the north in the morning.

We had been especially warned about the lake. Really high waves could build up in an hour or so if he wind was strong. But the wind, which usually blew from the north in the mornings, changed and blew from the south in the afternoons. We were near the lake's southern end, however, so only north winds were likely to be troublesome. However, wind was not the only potential danger. Ages before, this great lake had been and open to the sea, salty and inhabited by normal marine life. In the course of time, the lake was cut off from the sea, and, with a steadily flowing outlet, had gradually changed from salt to fresh water. Thus, Lake Nicaragua is stocked with freshwater, white sharks. There are also barracuda and sword fish, which suggests that swimmers should take care and small craft, when the waves are high, should be wary as well.

When we started out that morning, the water was beautifully smooth but as the sun rose the wind did too, and by midmorning waves of some size were running. Little by little, as the waves built up, the motion of our craft came to be at least faintly reminiscent of a surfboard doing the mambo but, as time passed, we accustomed ourselves to it and our confidence grew. A storm swept out across the lake but missed us by a mile or two, and an island toward which we were heading continued to be brightly lighted by the sun. As we approached it, however we were surprised to see how high the surf had come to be. For a time we had no inclination to risk it, but presently we found an opening in the surf and passed through into a well-protected inlet. Calm was all around us. Good camping places were there as well. And, with a day and a half behind us, we were already three-quarters on our way to where the San Juan River leaves the lake for its journey to the Caribbean.

It had been 12 hours since breakfast, and we had nothing to eat for lunch but cold hamburgers on the gruesome crackers we had to use in place of bread. It is no wonder, when we had made camp, that our K-rations tasted better than they had the evening before. But we never could eat the chocolate. It was no doubt healthful but was too much heavily fortified with soy beans, vitamins, and paraffin for our taste. The thought did occur to us, though the weather was quite hot and we did not check, that those chocolate "pucketts" would make useful fire starters.

Our breakfast was quick and reasonably hearty, and we were on the water in short order. Ahead of us lay a scattering of little islands and 20 more miles of the lake before we could reach the village of San Carlos at the entrance to the San Juan River.

San Carlos is a Nicaraguan community and the river lies wholly within Nicaragua throughout the upper portion of its course. Some miles downstream, however, it becomes the boundary between Nicaragua and Costa Rica and it continues to act in that capacity all the way to the sea. It was necessary, therefore, for us to have permission to continue on our voyage and Mary had carefully arranged to have the local *Jefe* notified of our coming. Somehow, however, the word had never reached him but we found him promptly, for San Carlos consisted only of one house and a store. The border is often troubled and questionable travelers, no doubt, sometimes appear, so it is not surprising that our *permiso* was not immediately forthcoming. However, the *Jefe*'s front porch was shady and we were glad to be out of the midday sun, so we waited patiently. We even tried to add to our stores by visiting the *Jefe*'s place of business. Unfortunately, however, it had nothing in the way of fresh food except a pineapple and a little bread. These we gladly purchased, and, after some delay, the *permiso* was prepared and signed by the *Jefe*. Then both he and his red-haired wife came down to the river to see us off.

They examined our inflated craft somewhat doubtfully, I thought, and when we finally shoved off they bade us a solemn farewell.

"*Vaya con Dio*s-Go with God," they said, and though I am sure they meant us well, it seemed to me that they expressed themselves a little too fervently. Our black rubber raft had been lying, for an hour or two, in the full glare of the tropical noonday sun and, as we shoved it into the water, we discovered that it was so nearly red-hot that we had to pour water all over it before we dared attempt to sit down on its fat and normally comfortable sides. We presently paddled into a heavily shaded spot beside the bank and, while cooling both ourselves and our boat, we ate the pineapple we had bought. We heard an airplane overhead; perhaps, we thought, it was looking for us. Mary tried to reach the pilot with the little radio we carried. Over and over he called but nobody answered. So we pushed out into midstream, an overhanging tree hid us completely from sight, and when the plane turned and swept overhead again we waved wildly. Obviously, they hadn't heard us and now it was clear that they hadn't seen us either, for they presently disappeared. With the current, on the downstream leg of the trip, we were making excellent headway.

All afternoon we passed fine camping spots but when four-thirty came we couldn't even find one. Such trees as we saw and hoped to use as supports for our hammocks seemed always to be wearing ominous rings of sharp spines that extended all the way up their trunks, and I had long since learned that black palm daggers such as these could readily penetrate either a poncho or our tennis shoes. Finally, dark overtook us as we waded ashore, and somehow strung our hammocks. The day had been a long one and, after our K-ration dinner, I found it easy to go to sleep; we were lulled by the distant and regular cries of howler monkeys. But having gone to sleep, I was so suddenly awakened that I bounced upright. An animal—and I had no idea what kind—was climbing about on my hammock cords. I could hear him, could even feel his motions, but I could not find a flashlight. By the time I found it and I turned it on, the invader had disappeared.

The next day, as we continued downstream, we saw only four huts and of these only one was occupied. But though we were passing through a very lightly populated region, the plane that had been searching for us the day before somehow found us. However, we learned nothing from it, for our radio still could not get through. The only reason we knew that they had us in mind was that they dropped some mail and a Sunday newspaper.

Two of the huts we passed were at empty cattle collecting stations and at the mouth of the entering Santa Cruz River was a sawmill. We stopped, of course, and found that the workmen were waiting for more logs, so we chatted with them about the river. Before long, we were told, we would come to El Castillo where we must check in with *la guardia*. This was news, for we had no word of this particular post, though it was logical that a post would be there, for from El Castillo to the sea the river formed the boundary with Costa Rica. Castillo also was the location of the first, and most severe, rapids in the river and it would be well if we were to ask there just how to run them.

Presently we reached El Castillo and found no village. Instead, there was an actual castle on a hill-a picturesque fort that had been built during the long departed days when pirates sometimes landed at the river's mouth, and came this way in the hope of sacking wealthy Grenada. Even Horatio Nelson, when he was a young officer and long before he became a victorious Admiral and Viscount, once led a shore expedition to this point. The English had captured the fort, too, and had gone up to Lake Nicaragua, but Nelson himself had been sent back ill. We climbed the hill and found that the largely ruined fort had a moat with a drawbridge and also that it overlooked a slight bend in the river. It occupied an excellent defensive position. From the hill, too, we were able to select our proposed course down the rapids—across to the far side past an island before angling back to the boiling middle of the stream.

With our *permiso* in hand, we confidently resumed our way, though our task appeared a bit more difficult when we viewed the noisy, bubbling, yellow-white foam from eye level. Even when we were through the worst of it, our little motor found it difficult to take us to a landing place where we had to show our paper. However, we struggled ashore, and the *guardia* generously provided us with a welcome drink of cold Coca-Cola.

"At M*uchacho* (Bad Boy)," we were told, "be sure to leave the "boiler" and the clump of bushes on your right. Then go as slowly as possible down the middle." We followed instructions and found that shooting rapids was so damp and refreshing that we quite forgot to be hot. However, it would have been difficult to find the good channel through *Muchacho* had it not been for what the guard had told us. Once, in fact, we actually broached and both Mary and I had to paddle madly to straighten us out; C-going's job was to man the motor. I should mention that, as in any naval operation, we had well-defined duties. Mary was captain and navigator and I was chief cook and bottle washer.

Later in the day, when the sun had disappeared in the west, the river was beautiful. Sometimes, too, sudden showers covered the water with countless little splashes that now and then marched toward us like endless regiments of tiny soldiers advancing to attack. Even when we camped it rained. We spread a poncho between some stumps and so protected the stove and our evening meal, but when we crawled into our hammocks for the night, we were wetter than usual.

By now, we badly needed to wash and mend our clothes. In particular, Mary's trousers needed to be repaired. Not only had a seam given way, but also they parted at the crotch. Furthermore, we had foolishly neglected to bring along a mending kit, so I had to use a surgeon's needle and the sutures which were in our first aid kit.

We were looking, now, for a shortcut stream of which we had heard that would lead us with a minimum of travel to the coastal village of San Juan del Norte, but, after another day of downstream travel, dusk caught us just as we came in sight of a clearing. The place, we thought, was perfect as a camping spot, barring the mosquitoes, of course. But then a man appeared, a neighbor, we learned, who was there merely to check on the property of his absent friend. Fortunately, he decided that we were not predatory so he presently left us amid our newfound surroundings.

Under way again the next day, we continued to look for the entrance to the short cut stream we hoped to take, but we missed it and, almost before we knew it we found ourselves in a great lagoon which contained two enormous dredges that had obviously been abandoned long before, for their vast buckets were spilling over with well-grown trees and vines.

Instantly we knew exactly where we were, for on our flight from Panama to Managua, we had scouted our proposed route and had seen these very dredges which had looked like toys from the air. The long straight lagoon in which they lay formed a part of the channel that had been dug at the turn of the century by the Rockefeller group.

So, with this to give us our location, we knew that we had missed the turnoff to San Juan del Norte and instead had come upon the town's old weed-grown landing on the side that faced the sea. Down the coast some 18 miles was the little port of Barro Colorado, in Costa Rica, where a ship was to come to pick us up. And to

Barro Colorado by sea seemed the way to go, unless we were willing to go back some 20 miles upstream against a four-knot current-a task that our motor would find difficult and very time consuming, since it could make only five knots at best.

Mary went off with C-going to look at a channel that led to the sea and came back with the observation that a second river, from the north, joined ours and the combined flow of the waters rushed out smoothly into the ocean. We located an opening into a lagoon that was beautifully filled with antherium, spider lilies, and water hyacinths, all of which had choked the erstwhile port of Greytown. And when our little motor could no longer push through the masses of greenery, we got out and pulled until we finally we were able to tie up to a mass of lily stalks and squish our way to a rotting pier and a decaying warehouse.

Faced by the choice of the 18 mile voyage in the open sea, or two day trip back up the river, we decided on the former. We carefully tied our personal things securely inside our poncho, strung double "lifelines" across out little craft, and tied in the equipment and paddles. As we pushed off Mary reminded us, "remember, the current is too swift for our motor and we can't turn back."

Our first view of the sea was nothing but large, perhaps I should say "huge," waves in our river channel. Apparently the wind had increased from when the men first had looked and we had not noticed the change inland.

Our channel was only about four feet deep. I noted numbers of large gray fish as they glided about, sometimes with their dorsal fins above water.

"Dolphins," explained Mary, but they were sharks and I was not fooled by his calm voice. More rapidly than I would have thought possible, the current swept us out to sea where, almost at once, a wave splashed partly over us and then hoisted our bow to the sky. The motor was completely dunked into the ocean and it died.

C-going climbed up to the bow and "weighed" it down, and both Mary and I grabbed the paddles to keep the boat facing the waves. Then C-going went to work on the motor, which, for a change, started with the very first pull. From this second on, all of us had nothing but praise for that superb reliable outboard motor. And, as we regained headway, the waves became less troublesome. In fact, our craft did very well, and it did even better when, with my rain hat, I bailed most of the water out. The top of our mess kit also made a good water scoop and, with Mary and me both working, we soon had the water down until it was less than ankle deep. By that time, too, we were far enough out to turn south and lay a course that was parallel to the coast. Now the waves seemed, or maybe were, ten feet high and Mary offered the opinion that they would be no less even if we were to go farther offshore.

All we could see now was water except where the surf piled up in great windrows of foam along the beach. Oddly enough, my teeth began to chatter with the cold, so I put on my southwester in the hope of warming up a bit. Our inflated raft was a remarkable seaworthy vessel which climbed the waves nicely, though there was never a still moment.

By now the waves were about 20 feet high, from crest to trough. It was somewhat breathtaking at first but we soon accustomed ourselves to it and the color of the water was lovely—so long as it was willing to stay out of our boat. The current, fortunately, was with us and we calculated that we were probably making all of six knots. Just how the men made their calculation I did not know, but I gladly accepted the answer they got, for I felt confident of being able to remain reasonably active for the three hours that such a rate of speed would suggest for the present leg of our journey.

The outboard motor, I was happy to note, didn't falter for a moment. But a new and very dark cloud was forming ahead of us, bringing streamers of rain that looked, as they approached, almost like waterspouts against the sky. The wind was growing stronger, too, and Mary remarked that this wasn't his idea of a proper way to spend a Sunday afternoon. " A confused sea," Mary called it, and I began to be a bit confused myself when the waves started once more to break over us. As a partial answer to that, we tied a poncho across our raft, making it into a kind of half-covered kayak. But the water still came aboard now and then, so I bailed it off the top of the poncho while Mary bailed from beneath.

The distance from San Juan del Norte to Barro Colorado, as I have said, is about 18 miles, and we had assumed that we could not go that far in less than about three hours. As it turned out, that was about the time we took, but it seemed much longer to me. We kept our eyes open in the hope of seeing Barro Colorado. Presently we could actually make out signs of human habitation ashore. All we knew was that the town was small. We had been told that the harbor was a good one, though, as we stared across the waves, we realized that bit of information was very indefinite. But presently Mary, whose experience in such matters was considerable, came to the conclusion that we were actually approaching the harbor entrance. It is true that we were still well offshore and all I could make out was a lot of foam along the coast, with the town, none too clearly visible beyond it.

For a time, Mary silently studied what he could see. The he said something about "We'll never be able to get in there."

We dared not try to enter; what could we do? So, not daring to risk our raft among the breaking waves, we decided to continue down the coast for another 60 miles or so to Puerto Limon. Maybe we could make it in 10, 12, or 14 hours, and possibly our gasoline would last that long.

It was a discouraging prospect, but there was nothing we could do about it and, for a time, I suppose, I really wasn't looking at anything very clearly. But finally, as we rose on another wave, something caught my eye. It was not in the direction we had been looking, and when we rose on the next wave I looked more closely, and there it was again.

"I see a buoy," I announced, as nonchalantly as I could. But then, with all of us watching, it turned out not to be a buoy after all. It was a ship. "Maybe she's on her way to sea," was Mary's comment. But finally we determined that the ship was actually moored to the buoy.

I suppose that I may been a little giddy with relief, but when we presently chugged up alongside (to the obvious astonishment of a man who was wearing a very holey undershirt) and asked permission to come aboard, he pointed a little farther forward to where a Jacob's ladder hung.

By now a dozen heads were visible over the ship's rail and someone caught the heaving line that Mary threw aboard. Then he gave me the cameras and waited for the proper moment for me to start up the swaying Jacob's ladder. The ship rolled and the Jacob's ladder swayed, but once over the rail and on deck I found not only that I could stand up but also that I had gumption enough to snap pictures of Mary and C-going as they, too, came aboard.

Presently we learned that we were aboard the SS Caribe, out of Havana, a wartime LSM with a superstructure that had been built across its wartime "well deck." The mess space had two tables—one, apparently, for officers, and the other for a dozen or so men. And I was immensely thankful to be aboard the dirtiest ship, with one exception, that I ever saw. The captain of the Caribe was the man with the holey undershirt and, once we were safely aboard, he disappeared. But now he returned, bathed and wearing a clean white shirt over, or in lieu of, that holey undershirt, though he had not shaved.

"The sharks are worse here," the Captain told us, "than anywhere else. Not long ago a small boat overturned and those who were in her were never seen again. It is well that you did not try to make harbor through all that surf. There is only one ship on all this coast—a LSI (Landing Ship Infantry)—that can enter Barro Colorado in dirty weather." And the words had hardly been spoken when that very ship came rolling out of the harbor, streaming a long black plume of Diesel smoke and heading out to sea. And there went the very last chance for the stevedores, or for the three of us, to get ashore until the weather changed.

Food was served, very hot and welcome, and we were offered cots, very dirty canvas ones, for the night. Mary and I could have the wheel house; C-going was given a passageway. And as I headed to the quarters we had been assigned, a shy steward came up with clean white sheet. "It is my own," he whispered, "I washed it myself."

By one o'clock the ship was rolling heavily and Mary was worrying because the heavy mahogany logs were not secured in the hold. I, on the other hand, was worrying about our poor little raft which was bouncing astern with all the photographic supplies aboard. And about two o'clock in came the Captain. "I'm sorry to disturb you," he told us, in flowery Spanish, "but we must get underway. The Chief Engineer had a fall down a manhole and we are taking him to the hospital in Puerto Limon."

I was the first to get dressed and my pants were just about dry. Then we had to haul the raft aboard and, though it came up bow first, everything aboard was well secured and we lost nothing. Even the outboard motor was there, and when the Cuban sailors tuned the craft upside down to empty out the water, they were wonderfully careful of that bit of mechanism. For the trip down the coast, they carefully stowed the motor in a gap among the logs.

Puerto Limon was only about 65 miles down the coast but it was broad daylight when we came to anchor in the harbor. A launch and a stretcher came for the Chief Engineer and then our raft was lowered into the water and hauled forward toward the bow. "Thank you, Captain," Mary told our host as we made ready to depart. "Do come to see us in the Canal Zone so that we may have an opportunity to return your hospitality."

He never came, though we hoped he would as we clambered down to our waiting craft. And as we stepped in and found our seats, C-going pulled the cord and that "superb" outboard motor started.

Ashore, we called the office of the Port Director. It was good to be on dry land again, but we were thirsty, hungry, a bit ragged, and none too clean. Furthermore, we didn't have a *centavo* of Costa Rican money but that made little difference, for a bartender offered to trust us or so he said. And he actually provided us with Coca-Cola before we walked around to the other side of the bay where the towers of the radio station stood. Mary wrote out a message to Radio Balboa, asking that the net-tender that was to pick us up be diverted to Puerto Limon instead of Barro Colorado.

The following morning we were even permitted to exchange some of our dollars so as to pay the barman and, when word came that the net-tender had arrived, I imagine that our story began to look better. We were driven to the harbor stepped into our inflated raft, and chugged out to the ship. The Captain apologized for being 12 hours late for the rendevous. He explained that the seas had been so rough that two sea anchors had been required to keep the ship into the wind and out of danger. That was the same storm through which we had gone to sea in our jolly little raft!

We were pleased with ourselves. Not only had the "expedition" been successfully concluded, but we would be home, and properly clad, before another 24 hours had passed.

Mary had kept an open mind on the idea of a sea-level canal connecting the Atlantic and Pacific. It should be possible to design large bays that would smooth the differences in the tides, about two feet on the Atlantic and 18 feet on the Pacific. However, such a canal in Nicaragua would have to be more than 150 miles long in order to skirt around (and about 100 feet below the normal water level of) Lake Nicaragua. To all of us, a sea-level canal was philosophically better because it would not limit the size of shipping but, at the same time, it seemed that much engineering would be required to overcome major difficulties that as yet were not understood.

Puerto Limón, Costa Rica, Library of Congress

BIBLIOGRAPHY

Agassiz, Louis and Elizabeth. *A Journey in Brazil.* Boston: Ticknor and Fields, 1868.

Bly, Nellie. *Six Months in Mexico.* New York: American Publishing Corp., 1888.

Dahlgren, Madeleine Vinton. *South Sea Sketches. A Narrative.* Boston: James R. Osgood and Co., 1881.

Dickins, Marguerite. *Along Shore with a Man-of-War.* Boston: Arena Publishing Co., 1893.

Dixie, Lady Florence. *Across Patagonia.* New York: R. Worthington, 1881.

Howe, Julia Ward. *A Trip to Cuba.* Boston: Ticknor and Fields, 1860.

Lester, Mary [Maria Soltera,pseud.]. *A Lady's Ride Across Spanish Honduras.* Edinburgh: William Blackwood and Sons, 1884.

Merwin, Loretta L. Wood. *Three Years in Chili.* New York: Follett, Foster, and Co., 1863.

Miles, Wilma J. *Billy, Navy Wife.* Salt Lake City: Publisher Press, 1999.

Pfeiffer, Ida. *A Lady's Second Journey Round the World: From London to the Cape of Good Hope, Borneo, Java, Sumatra, Celebes, Ceram, the Moluccas, etc., California, Panama, Peru, Ecuador, and the United States.* New York: Harper, 1856.

Rollins, Alice Marland Wellington, *From Palm to Glacier, with an Interlude: Brazil, Bermuda and Alaska.* New York: G. P. Putnam's Sons, 1892.

Woods, Josephine Hoeppner. *High Spots in the Andes: Peruvian Letters of a Mining Engineer's Wife.* New York: G. P. Putnam's Sons, 1935.

CPSIA information can be obtained
at www.ICGtesting.com
Printed in the USA
LVHW011500020821
694126LV00013B/1173